THE E BRIDGE

Lessons of Truth on America's Nonprofit Landscape

Joseph F. Phelan

University Press of America, Inc.
Lanham • New York • London

Copyright © 1997 by
University Press of America,® Inc.
4720 Boston Way
Lanham, Maryland 20706

3 Henrietta Street
London, WC2E 8LU England

All rights reserved
Printed in the United States of America
British Cataloging in Publication Information Available

Library of Congress Cataloging-in-Publication Data

Phelan, Joseph F.
The half-mile bridge : lessons of truth on America's nonprofit
landscape / Joseph F. Phelan.
p.   cm.
1. Citizens' Scholarship Foundation of America--History. 2.
Scholarships--United States--History. 3. Benefactors--United States--
Biography. I. Title.
LB2338.P46   1996   378.3'4'06073 --dc20   96-28821 CIP

ISBN 0-7618-0454-4 (cloth: alk. ppr.)
ISBN 0-7618-0455-2 (pbk: alk. ppr.)

∞™ The paper used in this publication meets the minimum
requirements of American National Standard for information
Sciences—Permanence of Paper for Printed Library Materials,
ANSI Z39.48—1984

> To Norm—
> Who was there when all I needed to manage was a varsity team, a gym show, a class dance, or a pony track. Today I know that's where it all began. You are a much valued part of those wonderful, formative years.
>
> Joe Slick
> 10-22-01

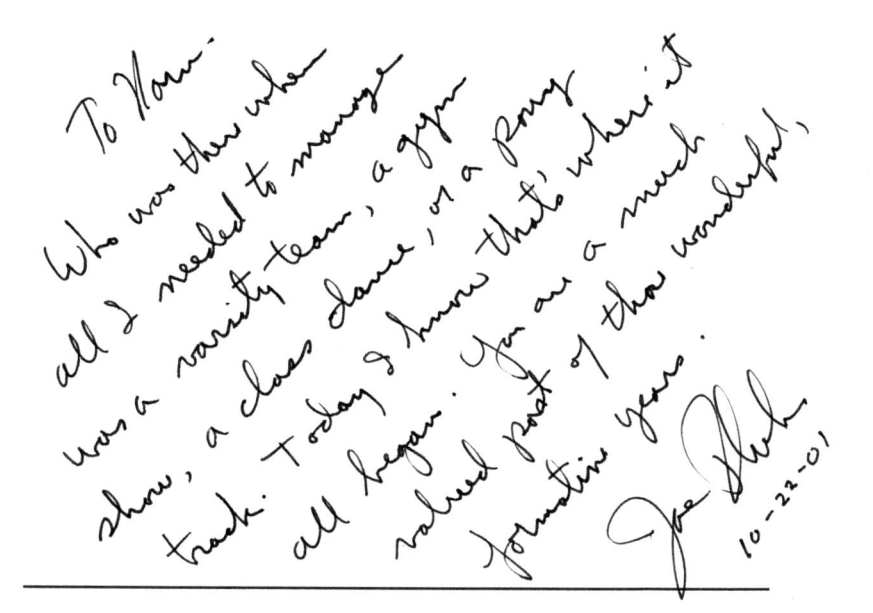

Dedication

The Half-Mile Bridge

is dedicated
to the memory of
Frank E. Morin
and
Howard A. Moreen
who came along
for far more than the ride;
and to
my friend and CSFA benefactor,
Leslie S. Hubbard
of Walpole, New Hampshire,
who to this day continues
to give me more credit and praise
than I perhaps deserve.

Contents

Important Notes	ix
Preface	xiii
Introduction	xxxi

Dr. Irving A. Fradkin, 1957-1962

Chapter One: Irv	3
Chapter Two: When Fate Summons	9

Eugene C. Struckhoff, 1963-1967

Chapter Three: Struck	19
Chapter Four: Two in the Parlors; Forty-three in the Barn	33

William B. Norris, 1968-1971

Chapter Five: Brad	43
Chapter Six: A Lesson from the Holocaust	63
Chapter Seven: Charity Begins Closer to Home	67
Chapter Eight: North to the Poles	77

Edward M. Lee, 1972-1979

Chapter Nine: Ed	91
Chapter Ten: Queens and Corona	109
Chapter Eleven: A Tale of Two Martinis	115
Chapter Twelve: Stand by Me	123
Chapter Thirteen: Skip, Chip and Holly Rust	129
Chapter Fourteen: You Can Call Me Johnson	137
Chapter Fifteen: Good Call but Off the Wall	151

Ralph H. Seifert, 1980-1984

Chapter Sixteen: Cy	159
Chapter Seventeen: An Interlude in Chicago	177
Chapter Eighteen: J. B. Tipton is Alive and Well	183
Chapter Nineteen: Two Bills Come to Call	191
Chapter Twenty: Three Bills Get the Call	199
Chapter Twenty-one: What's Good for General Motors	209
Chapter Twenty-two: Big House on the Prairie	221

Edwin B. Knauft, 1985-1988

Chapter Twenty-three: Burt	245
Chapter Twenty-four: The Lesson of the Half-Mile Bridge	269
Author's Afterword	279
Index	283

Not So Familiar Quotations*

"Tom said to himself that it was not such a hollow world, after all. He had discovered a great law of human action, without knowing it--namely, that in order to make a man or a boy covet a thing, it is only necessary to make the thing difficult to attain..."

--Samuel Langhorne Clemens, *The Adventures of Tom Sawyer,* 1876

"The plan itself is very simple and its success is in proportion to the value a city places on its desire to help its children aspire to higher education."

--Dr. Irving A. Fradkin, on "The Fall River Plan," May 15, 1961

"The success to date of Citizens' Scholarship Foundation of America is not to be measured in terms of the accomplishments of an individual. Nor should it be so measured in the future."

--Joseph F. Phelan, on his retirement from CSFA, June 30, 1986

*With a single possible exception.

Important Notes

In May of 1992 I was approached by the leadership of Citizens' Scholarship Foundation of America and asked to chronicle my twenty years (1967-1986) with the national scholarship organization. This project was billed as "the official history" of CSFA. I readily agreed to undertake it, but at the same time I realized that my initial employment with CSFA in January of 1967 followed by nearly a decade the inception of the program in Fall River Massachusetts. Therefore the envisioned "history" would be regrettably incomplete if nearly a third of the chronology was missing.

In 1994, when I was well into the writing of the book, one of CSFA's former trustees suggested that the eight or so years since my departure in July of 1986 were also important to the "history" and that some means should be found to provide a historical record that would be as up to date as possible at the time of the book's release. *The Half-Mile Bridge: Lessons of Truth on America's Nonprofit Landscape* accommodates both my realization relative to the first ten years and the request of the former trustee relative to the most recent nine. But whereas placing the precedent decade before the main body of the text proved easy and logical enough, adding the most recent years at the far end presented me with a paramount difficulty.

From the very beginning the story of the half-mile bridge was intended to be the book's concluding chapter. It marks the closing of my formal leadership position with CSFA and relates as well what I believe to be the greatest lesson of that experience. My dilemma was resolved when another former trustee suggested I place the most recent material in the front of the book, perhaps as a preface. I elected to do so with, I believe, very good results.

The core of the book covers the terms of the first five CSFA board chairs, beginning with Eugene C. Struckhoff in 1963 and ending with Edwin B. Knauft in 1986. Each chapter identified with a name--Struck, Brad, Ed, Cy, and Burt--introduces a section of the book and provides a summary of the progress of CSFA during each respective term. In theory, at least, a reader could elect to read only those five chapters in an effort to gain a quick, but reasonably complete, historical perspective of Citizens' Scholarship Foundation of America. To do so might well be a disservice to both the reader and the organization.

The Half-Mile Bridge is not so much the history of an organization as it is a chronicle of the wonderful, and principally volunteer, personalities that made it happen. Additional anecdotal chapters in each of the five sections either expand on an event mentioned first in the summary chapter or describe an event that happened during that particular term, even if the chair was not directly involved.

The reader needs to accept, too, that much of the documentation, though historically accurate, is not lineal. As examples, I met Brad Norris, Ralph Seifert, and Ed Lee, during the term-as-chair of Gene Struckhoff. I met Burt Knauft during the term-as-chair of Ed Lee. Therefore, as I describe for each the genesis of my relationship and the longer-term impact each has had on CSFA, the book may appear to revert to a period of time already covered. The same situation holds true of the anecdotal chapters. An event that had its origins during the term of one chair may well have spilled over into the term of another. Every effort has been made, however, to keep all events in historical perspective.

Beyond this bit of guidance, a few other explanations are in order. First, those people intimately familiar with CSFA know that in the early years (1957-1970) the members of the national board were called directors as opposed to trustees. For the sake of continuity, the term trustee is used throughout the book. Second, community affiliates of CSFA are identified herein as either Citizens' Scholarship Foundation® of (city, town, or school district) or (city, town, or school district) Dollars for Scholars®. Local boards are almost always made up of "directors." Third, the distinction between "fiscal" years and "calendar" years throughout the book is not particularly important unless specifically mentioned as one or the other.

Beyond these few considerations I sincerely believe that *The Half-Mile Bridge* is an accurate accounting of the growth and development of Dr. Irving A. Fradkin's original "Fall River Scholarship Plan." Any errors, discrepancies or omissions may be attributed to a seemingly endless review of an estimated twenty-foot pile of documents and, despite the fact that he lived through most of it, also to possible flaws in the memory of the author.

Joseph F. Phelan, December 31, 1995

Preface

The Minnesota River is a contrary phenomenon. It owes its origin to Big Stone Lake at the midpoint of Minnesota's western border with South Dakota and establishes an ordinary passage southeast, drawing its volume from lakes and streams in south central Minnesota. But then the river, as if rejecting the notion of entering Iowa, abruptly alters its direction. The river snakes itself north through Blue Earth County, bisecting Mankato and North Mankato, twists its shore at a point described in terse Scandinavian terms as "Bend in the River," and enters St. Peter--"the almost capital of Minnesota"--within sight of a Hardee's fast-food restaurant on the right-hand side of the southern end of Minnesota Avenue.

The avenue, St. Peter's main street, bisects a collection of Midwest-typical, two-story, brick store fronts, over a quarter-mile segment of Highway 169. The highway itself is 350 miles long and is the old central artery that, sixty or so miles north of St. Peter, continues on to tie Minneapolis

The Half-Mile Bridge

and St. Paul to Grand Rapids, Hibbing, and Ely in the north. Sixty miles south of St. Peter the highway takes dead aim at Fort Dodge as it intersects the Iowa border. For a time the Minnesota River on its northern journey toward the Twin Cities parallels Highway 169. And in so doing the river finds its way to the headwaters of the Mississippi River at St. Paul--the for-real capital of Minnesota--thereby making its contribution to the mighty river that at once divides and unites the states sprawling east and west from its respective shores.

St. Peter meanwhile, declares itself the "Home of Five Governors" and the modern-day home of sixty-eight hundred living souls when the twenty-three hundred or so students of Gustavus Adolphus College are away for the summer or are otherwise on holiday. St. Peter is but a narrow cityscape on the western shore of a river that provides irrigation--and at times of flooding, irritation--within the great corn and soybean expanse of the nation's midland. The main street is wide indeed, and a left turn across from the Hardee's Restaurant on South Minnesota Avenue onto Jefferson Street leads within 500 feet to a cross intersection at Third Street. A left turn on Third finds the blacktop running south through a shaded, single-story neighborhood, on a track roughly parallel to Minnesota Avenue, though not quite in sight of it. At a measure of four or five city blocks Third Street hooks right and west and contributes its short remainder to the foothold of the highest elevation in town.

Third Street ends its abbreviated uphill journey just past the bowling alley at Washington Street. Across this two-way stop, Third continues as Riverview Road, and begins a northwesterly climb through a fifty-unit, moderately upscale area defined in earlier architectural times as a housing development. The one and two-story, attractive if

Preface

eclectic, homes on winding Riverview average two thousand square feet of living space, the presumed ideal size for a family with 1.5 children, 1.5 automobiles, and .75 snowmobiles.

On the crest of the hill at 1505 Riverview sits the largest structure of all, an impressive two-story Northeast-meets-Midwest architectural wonder of twelve thousand square feet. Its upper level, with its not-quite-Wedgwood blue siding, white trim, and small-paned windows and doors, appears from a lower elevation vantage point to be a many-gabled, neo-Nantucket summer "cottage," resting on an eleven-foot foundation of shades-of-ocher, rough-hewn blocks of Kasota limestone. The 111-foot horizontal intersect of wood-meets-stone is for the most part defined and united by a white, narrow, banistered deckway that originates just to the right of the west-side ell and terminates at the intersecting wall of the building's east-side ell. The deckway is supported by five white wooden pillars set fifteen feet apart. Two frame, indirectly, a Palladian window that rises eighteen feet from the near ground to the near roof peak of a gable just right of center of the building's expanse.

Over the peaked roof of the building and just to the right, appear the top ten or so feet of three sturdy aluminum flag poles, each bearing a standard that straightens and whips in the near constant prairie wind, itself a balm in the sauna-like summers; a blight in the crystalline winters. The Stars and Stripes; the Minnesota state flag; and a third, white rectangular banner with a contrasting green border and centered insignia--briefly visible as a mortarboard resting on an open book--flutter and snap in unison. The three flagpoles are placed to the left of double, solid oak paneled doors, or main entrance of the building. From this front-on, still higher perspective, the building expanse

The Half-Mile Bridge

appears to be of only a single story. The steep incline of the hill obviates, within the fifty-foot width of the structure, the need or space for the limestone foundation. Here the building's front windows overlook twenty level acres of a former soybean field that separates this property from the high end of Jefferson Avenue and the southernmost entrance of Gustavus Adolphus College.

High upon this same hill, the students, faculty, and staff of Gustavus Adolphus share a lofty daytime vista with the occupants of 1505 Riverview Road, though the better view of the Minnesota River valley is afforded the latter, and maybe more appropriately, because 1505 is the home of another contrary phenomenon on the American landscape. Here Citizens' Scholarship Foundation of America, together with its non-mnemonic acronym CSFA, and its more popularly known--if not always associated with--"Dollars for Scholars" trademark, today rather quietly represents annually $41.5 million in privately sponsored student aid. CSFA in 1995 is in all likelihood the largest private student aid organization in the world, and if not--for a few scholarship-related organizations decline for whatever reason to disclose dollar volume--CSFA will certainly be so by the year 2000.

Within the clapboard siding and limestone walls of 1505 Riverview, twenty-one scholarship program managers, assisted by a cadre of seasoned and seasonal "Score Corps" personnel, select 19,900 recipients from among a universe of nearly seventy thousand applicants to share $33.6 million. Without the building, and miles beyond those offices and walls, seven CSFA regional directors assist, cajole, applaud, and reward 750 cities, towns, and school districts throughout the United States that have embraced the "Dollars for Scholars" volunteer spirit and in so doing release from the "home folks" $8 million more to the

Preface

benefit of 14,500 college-bound and technical school-bound resident students.

All of this activity is under the direction of Dr. William C. Nelsen, the unassuming president of CSFA. Bill during his term as president has built mightily on the efforts of those who came before him and has increased the scholarship impact of CSFA more than threefold over that of CSFA's first twenty-five years. When commenting on this progress, Bill in his typical fashion says: "Yes, CSFA has experienced tremendous growth in the last nine years, but what we--and I do mean board members, other volunteers, and staff alike--have accomplished since 1986 has been built on the strong foundation of those who came before us."

In 1986, when Bill Nelsen at age forty-four left his position as president of Augustana College in South Dakota to assume the presidency of this quiet if not obscure scholarship foundation, he inherited a rather loosely affiliated and fairly static family of 268 volunteer-operated community Dollars for Scholars chapters active in thirty-two states. The legacy also included 185 internally managed company and foundation-sponsored student aid programs. The clients of CSFA's Scholarship Management Services program retain CSFA on a fee-for-service basis, first to design tailored and often innovative scholarship programs and then to direct the scholarships to dependents of employees or to other students of sponsor interest.

CSFA's operating budget in 1986 was just over $1.2 million; its income exceeded expense by $105,000; and its fund balance, including funds held for future scholarship distributions, was in excess of $631,000. Scholarships originating with its community Dollars for Scholars chapters, together with CSFA's internally managed company and foundation programs, totaled $11 million.

Oversight for these dollars and the programs that nurtured them was the responsibility of a seventeen-member, volunteer board of governing trustees, including four current or former officers of *Fortune 500* companies; four representatives of smaller companies or entrepreneurial local businesses; four current or former representatives of CSFA's community Dollars for Scholars chapters; two vice presidents of nationally recognized nonprofit organizations; one small-town attorney; the founder of CSFA; and CSFA's then president. Bill contemplates the Minnesota River valley through the double French doors of his attractive office as he reflects on this group.

> The board I inherited was really extraordinary on two counts. First because many of the women and men who were serving had histories of twenty years or more with the organization. And second, what seemed to be lacking in personal wealth, prestige, and power was more than compensated for by a collective, directed energy. I stress "directed," because this board was well informed, committed to CSFA's stipulated mission, and very active. In fact, in recognizing the best future interests of the organization, the board had recently established term limits for all trustees.
>
> My own leadership's best interests were also served, because I realized that over a relatively short period of time I would be able to recruit new board members, people who could help CSFA to develop and pursue an agenda for the future. That eventuality came to pass. When I looked around the board table at the September 1994 CSFA annual meeting almost everyone seated had been elected during my first eight years in office.

Of the few exceptions, one is especially noteworthy. Edward M. Lee, a semi-retired attorney from Westfield, Massachusetts, had in the 1970s served eight years as

Preface

CSFA's chairman. He was not at the table as a reward for longevity, but rather as a representative of an unusual group. He represented CSFA's Honor Roll Trustees, a small cadre of past chairs and other trustees who over many, many years had provided exemplary service to the organization. Election to the honor roll represents the highest honor bestowed by CSFA. Of greater importance is the fact that this group represents collectively over two hundred years experience with the organization. The majority of its fourteen members remain active and committed as resource people in CSFA's volunteer system, but at the same time all clearly recognize and accept that their governance role with CSFA is behind them. Each chair *pro tem* of the honor roll brings to the board table a historical perspective that can impact on decisions made during the term of any chief executive. "I believe," Bill says, "this particular structure is unique to CSFA. It shouldn't be, because it represents a wonderful way to keep outstanding people involved in the life of an organization."

Bill moves to the small Scandinavian-design table that serves as his desk. He opens a large, three-ring binder that summarizes the scholarship activity of now more than 500 sponsored scholarship programs. Many listed companies, such as Chrysler Corporation and General Electric Company, are household names. A few, such as Otter Tail Power Company and Precision Castparts Corporation, are not. Bill leafs through the binder.

> At the time of my arrival CSFA was efficiently structured internally as well. This building's design really supported the foundation's operations, although no one could foresee at the time it was built, that we would so quickly outgrow it. The entire lower level, some six thousand square feet, is devoted to the management of corporate and foundation

scholarship programs, but even the fact that we added another sixteen hundred square feet of workspace downstairs could not help preserve other areas on the upper level.

This happy problem of accelerated growth engulfed the board room and library in the east ell of the building and the wonderful town house formerly identified as "The Guest Quarters" in the west ell. But even though we have filled this building to capacity, expanded our "headquarters" operations to other facilities both here in town and in Minneapolis, and opened seven new regional offices, most of the operational procedures that were in place in the mid-eighties remain in place today. Most of what we have done managerially, especially I'm pleased to say, in the areas of scholarship services and annual fiscal operations, are matters of scale. The refinements we continue to make in our operations are designed to align efficiency with volume. We now involve everyone on staff in our change-making process with very good results.

Bill then thumbs through a file and holds up a copy of an article entitled, "Incentive-Based Management for Nonprofit Organizations," one that he authored for *Nonprofit Management and Leadership* in 1991.

One other exciting example of something I found when I arrived is the employee incentive program. My predecessor somewhat facetiously referred to it as "the nonprofit profit-sharing program." That program, too, has undergone refinements, but it still has the same fundamental purpose: It shares the success of this organization with the employees who work hard to bring it about.

Bill lowers his trim, six-foot frame onto one of two facing taupe-fabric couches, and locks his fingers behind his follicley-challenged head.

Preface

The real importance of what I found here in 1986 goes well beyond the pleasure inherent to assuming the leadership of an efficient and productive organization. I have never seen myself as a gate keeper. Early on I suspected, perhaps as early as the interview process, that something of great importance was lurking just below the surface of the hum of all the scholarship activity.

Maybe I was influenced by the conviction of CSFA's founder that the money represented by the thousands of scholarships was not the most important impact of the organization's work and service. Irving Fradkin insisted from the very beginning that Dollars for Scholars dollars only provided a means for people to reach out to help others; to declare visibly the crucial importance of education for their community and our nation.

In 1986 most of the attention of Citizens' Scholarship Foundation of America was focused on the amazing development of the Scholarship Management Services program. And with good reason. Following nearly fifteen years of hand-to-mouth existence, CSFA had found its financial cornerstone. This program generated an income stream that not only underpinned financial stability, but also permitted CSFA to rejuvenate the expansion of its charitable purpose, its community-based Dollars for Scholars program.

I, of course, arrived seriously committed to the continuing growth of Scholarship Management Services. At the same time the great potential of Dollars for Scholars quickly caught my attention. My heart as well as my head reacted with compassion to the great stories of people who had dedicated the wonderful commodity known as volunteer leadership to raising scholarship dollars for local kids. In my own time here I have learned of a construction company owner in Chittenango, New York, who helped to start a Dollars for Scholars program there in the mid-eighties. Every year he organizes the local phone-a-thon, arranges a fund-raising dinner, builds a concession stand for a local festival, and persuades other community leaders to attend regional Dollars for Scholars workshops. Why? "Because," he says, "kids are our future."

In Parkers Prairie, here in Minnesota, a retired hardware store owner returned to his home town to enlist the aid of his old friends for starting a Dollars for Scholars chapter. He and his compatriots then created the "P-547 Club," named for the identifying number of the local school district. They challenged residents to contribute $547. A whole bunch did. In four years the chapter raised over four hundred thousand dollars.

And we are not talking here of just the rural landscape. Two years ago residents of several housing projects in Atlanta raised over fifty thousand dollars to help "project kids" who had been stereotyped as "kids who shouldn't be expected to go on to college."

Dollars for Scholars is where I saw and continue to see the real potential for the involvement of hundreds of thousands of people in the mission and future of Citizens' Scholarship Foundation of America. Here is where I believe my earlier experiences with the Danforth Foundation and my involvement early on with the civil rights movement could help me to form a vision for the future of CSFA and perhaps lead us to the funding required to bring it about. Here is a place for me to put to work my deep personal faith and strong convictions. Am I excited about this vision? You bet!

Bill reaches over to his desk and picks up another document, spiral-bound and nearly a half-inch thick. For the moment he deliberately covers the title with his right hand as he places the document in his lap.

Great visions are not formulated in either a day or in isolation. It's one thing, and I might add, a very good thing, to have a board formulate a long-range plan. It's quite another to involve that board and a hundred or so

Preface

other volunteers in the creation of a vision, and then to have the board and the staff translate the vision to an action plan.

When I arrived on the scene, CSFA was ready for a vision. I give great credit for that readiness to the board chairman who was seated when I arrived. Bert Knauft was then executive vice president of the Washington-based Independent Sector. Before that he had been an executive in the corporate giving program of The Aetna. He devoted his four-year chairmanship--two before me and two with me--to training the Board of Trustees. He very effectively streamlined the overall governance of CSFA, a remarkable job. Burt was followed in 1988 by Lloyd Brandt, another product of corporate philanthropy with First Bank System in Minneapolis. Lloyd prided himself in long-range planning. He was clear in his own mind of the important distinction between long-term goals and annual strategic plans. But of greatest importance to me was his empathy for Dollars for Scholars.

From a practical point of view, Lloyd as CSFA's sixth chairman, believed Dollars for Scholars created a point of entry for school district residents to become reinvolved with the local high school. He further believes that every school administrator and teacher should embrace the notion of Dollars for Scholars and should work to make it successful. Why? "Because," Lloyd says, "any activity that creates cooperative good will between the school and the public serves the best interests of both. This interaction invariably leads to understanding. And," he concludes: "Nowhere is that understanding more productive than at bond issue time."

Lloyd harbors a more theoretical conviction as well. He is convinced that CSFA's almost limitless potential to serve directly corporations and foundations, does not overshadow its even greater potential for community scholarship programs. "Irv Fradkin's initial idea," he says, "has always driven the organization; has always excited

xxiii

the volunteers at every level. We always come back to it." Lloyd sees Dollars for Scholars as CSFA's nonprofit franchise.

Lloyd Brandt's acumen and Bill's philosophy would prove to be a potent amalgam. In the course of Lloyd's chairmanship (1989-1993) the number of CSFA Dollars for Scholars affiliates grew from 268 to 627. Scholarship moneys raised in Dollars for Scholars communities increased from under $2 million per year to over $6 million. Bill speaks to the fueling of this growth.

> Much of this Dollars for Scholars activity was underwritten by residual income originating with CSFA's company and foundation scholarship programs. During Lloyd's four-year term the number of our internally managed accounts rose from 250 with distributions of just a shade under $10 million, to just over 400 with distributions approaching $20 million. This rather remarkable growth was a combination of momentum and a very talented, long-term, design and marketing team led by two staff vice presidents, Stuart Johnson and Marlys Johnson. But the residual income from CSFA's Scholarship Management Services could not keep pace with the costs associated with the accelerated expansion of the Dollars for Scholars program.
>
> I decided to call on my prior experience in fund raising. I began approaching foundations that had been helpful to me or to CSFA in the past, and met with some early success. The Lilly Endowment, a number of regional foundations, an anonymous donor, and one of CSFA's former trustees, collectively committed more than $2 million for Dollars for Scholars expansion. We then went about setting up a number of regional offices necessary for systematic Dollars for Scholars chapter development.
>
> The renewed appeal of Dollars for Scholars with major funding sources encouraged us by 1991 to establish and

Preface

staff CSFA's first development office. "Development" is higher education's euphemism for fund raising. We as an organization believed CSFA had the case, the appeal, and the potential to undertake a national campaign. We also had great campaign leadership in the person of Ralph Seifert, another of CSFA's former, dynamic chairmen.

So, during Lloyd's four years we reconfirmed the viability of the national Dollars for Scholars program. We doubled the number of sponsors within CSFA's Scholarship Management Services. We formalized a development operation and raised $2 million. And we completed the planning process for a national fund-raising campaign. That process involved the perspectives and advice of literally hundreds of volunteers from the community level to the corporate world. The product of all of this activity and the thousands of hours required for it is this little booklet.

Bill then holds up for view a plain, lilac-colored, writing-pad size booklet entitled simply *Vision 2000*. The numbers within are heady. *Vision 2000* forecasts that CSFA's operating budget in the year 2000 will approach $10 million, up from $4 million in 1994. The vision anticipates CSFA will realize approximately $55 million through its national campaign, with a major share of that sum dedicated to expanding the Dollars for Scholars program to communities in all fifty states. It forecasts total scholarship distributions at the turn of the century in excess of $75 million; originating with over one thousand corporate and foundation scholarship accounts and over fourteen hundred community Dollars for Scholars programs.

Bill is animated now. He sits forward on his couch cushion, arms crossed, elbows on his knees.

> This vision is not so much about money as it is about people--a citizens' movement in education. Our success with *Vision 2000* will mean that millions of Americans will be directly involved with the future of the next generation. Involvement will lead to "voice," and voice, I believe, will help lead to meaningful improvement in educational achievement.
>
> This vision is about people's expectations and aspirations. Why do I believe we have a chance to be part of the solution? I'll tell you why. All over this country people of good faith and good intentions are coming up with plans and schemes to change the course and quality of education. Proposals include longer school days, longer school years, changes in curriculum, changes in teaching methods, merit pay, larger schools, smaller schools, schools within schools, choice of schools, you name it. But a growing body of knowledge suggests that achievement is essentially the product of expectations. I am convinced that the highest expectations may be set and realized only at the closest proximity with students: the family and the community.

Bill stands, moves to his wall cabinets, and removes a book from a mahogany shelf. "This book, *Educational Renaissance*," he says, "reminds us that Japanese children excel, because their parents expect them to excel." He selects a second manuscript.

> Look at this. The late James Coleman at the University of Chicago conducted this study of public and parochial schools throughout the United States. He found that student achievement was highest where the surrounding communities or parishes set higher expectations for the schools and the students, and also provided encouragement and support.
>
> And what about aspirations? John Gardner says: "The growth of a person is a dialogue between the individual

Preface

and his environment." I believe it. We have a film, a video, here at CSFA entitled *When I Grow Up, I Wanna Be...* It is the story of a little girl who is very much in touch with her environment. She ultimately decides she wants to be President. Realistic? Maybe. Maybe not. But I believe aspirations are fundamental to personal growth and again are nurtured by our closest environments. Along the way somebody convinces us that we can be something. That somebody, a parent, a coach, a teacher, pastor, priest, or rabbi, or perhaps a friend, encourages our development and also helps us to overcome distractions.

In my day the distractions were pretty ordinary--girlfriends, boyfriends, clothes, fads, competing activities. Today distractions are much more powerful--drugs, alcohol, violence, deteriorating schools, and most serious of all, low expectations for many young people by the people closest to them. I believe CSFA can help to change all that. I contend that the missing ingredient in nearly all proposed reform movements is citizen action. I am convinced that nothing is more effective than a community organized to visibly encourage and reward students for their past achievements and to provide tangible encouragement for their future aspirations. That's what Dollars for Scholars is all about, and that's the heart and soul of *Vision 2000*. It's not just about money.

CSFA's *Vision 2000* has a reasonable chance of becoming a reality. The fact that it represents the thinking and "collective, directed energy" of Bill's board and his staff and several hundred volunteers holds promise. The fact that board members and staff and other close friends of CSFA have already provided $13 million toward the campaign's eight-year financial goal is encouraging. And the enthusiasm and outlook of CSFA's seventh chairman are key. John A. Wedum is also president of Wedum Associates and president of the Minnesota-based Wedum

The Half-Mile Bridge

Foundation. His association with CSFA dates back to 1985, the year before Bill's arrival, when his foundation was successfully encouraged by CSFA to provide incentive matching grants to several Minnesota communities organizing local Dollars for Scholars chapters.

In the years that followed, his foundation found other ways to assist CSFA, including the purchase of the final puzzle piece of CSFA's twenty-five acre quadrangle atop the hill in St. Peter. John joined the CSFA board in 1989 and became its chair in 1992. Bill is enthusiastic about his newest leadership ally.

> Lloyd Brandt speaks for all of us when he says that John is the ideal person to have in place on the front end of this national citizens' movement. Lloyd sees John as an entrepreneur. One that knows that big organizations are generally bereft of excitement, seldom imaginative, and are almost never entrepreneurial. If our *Vision 2000* is to be transformed into collective, positive, power and influence, then participating people will need to be "empowered." That power, John Wedum believes, cannot simply emanate from a dot on the map called St. Peter, Minnesota. John is dedicated to seeing that *Vision 2000* will be ten thousand lights on the landscape.

Bill Nelsen returns to his sofa and once again assumes his more relaxed pose.

> You know, come to think of it, this idea of a "vision" really is a good one. You remember back in the early 1960s the television personality, the late Sam Levenson, called Irving Fradkin "an optometrist with vision." That was a time when a man with no money and no influence and no power, put together, on the strength of his own enthusiasm, Citizens' Scholarship Foundation of America. Many people discouraged him. Some told him it simply

Preface

couldn't be done. All he had was conviction, a few willing friends, and of course, a great idea. I often think of his determination and the determination of so many others over the years in the CSFA "family." And some days as I walk up to my office from my home just a few blocks down the hill, I stand both amazed and very grateful at how it all came about.

June 30, 1995

Introduction

In 1876 or thereabouts Mark Twain's young Ben Rogers picked up a proffered paint brush and applied whitewash to Aunt Polly's fence. In that instant the "Tom Sawyer Theory of Management" was born. The theory assumes that willing and enthusiastic people graciously accept responsibility for a demanding task and then come to believe in their hearts that they are truly happy undertaking it.

The second recorded application of that theory would surface more than seventy years later, when in 1949 a boy of ten in the quiet community of Hudson, New Hampshire, faced a dilemma. He was asked by his next-door neighbor, a somewhat portly and balding, cigar-wielding politico, for assistance with an upcoming election. This assistance, with remuneration attached, required the distribution of five hundred leaflets to a like number of households throughout the community. The reward for the task was five dollars, a very heady sum at a time when ten dollars a day was considered a reasonable working wage.

The Half-Mile Bridge

The young man in question unfortunately had no bicycle and neither his pre-adolescent stamina nor his high-top PF Flyers were up to the task. He clearly had a problem. He arrived at a solution. He carried the bundle of flyers to Charlie's Variety Store, the drop-off point for the *Nashua Telegraph*, the area's only daily newspaper. He knew that the five paper boys had bicycles, and he offered them fifty cents each to deliver one hundred leaflets along with the daily paper. They were happy to do so, as this stipend effectively increased each carrier's one-day earnings by 50 percent. The deal quickly consummated, the young man from number four School Street walked home with a clear profit of $2.50 in hand.

The Tom Sawyer management model would not surface in this boy's life again for another seventeen years. But during the interval fate and fortune, luck and circumstance, would prepare him for its re-emergence. At the age of fifteen as a sophomore at Hudson's Alvirne High School, he secured his first summer employment at Benson's Wild Animal Farm, a precursor theme park that brought tens of thousands of people up or down Route 111 to Hudson Center. Now long closed, Benson's was in 1955 a major site for family delights: horse and tiger acts; snake and monkey houses; camel and elephant rides; polar bear and platypus pens; giraffes and zebras; cotton candy; train rides and a merry-go-round. Hot summer breezes, rich with smells of hot dogs and popcorn, mixed mildly at times with the acrid odors of decimated fish in the turtle ponds and the droppings of the park's menagerie.

Central among the park's attractions was the pony track, an eighth-of-a-mile, dusty oval mostly open to the summer sun. Lines of patrons, sometimes on a Sunday fifty deep, would wait impatiently to place a three or four-year-old on the back of Cora or Snowball or any of the other dozen

Introduction

ponies. First-time, teenage male employees at Benson's were usually assigned to the track where they could expect to spend one or more arid summers leading ponies, one in either hand, around and around the oval as many as forty times a day. The young man's older brother, David, had done so for three consecutive summers, beginning at a wage of 65 cents an hour in 1952. He was overdue for some kind of promotion, and was scheduled for 80 cents an hour in the summer of 1955. But much to his relief and that of his size thirteen feet, he found another summer job. His younger brother, Joe, was hired as his replacement, and he fully expected to take his place dutifully among the walking winded. He would, however, be spared this honest rite of occupational passage.

Record keeping in the front office of Benson's was somewhat uneven, so when Joe Phelan arrived for his first day of work, no one in the payroll office noticed that he was not David. In consequence he started at 70 cents an hour, was increased to 80 cents after two weeks on the job, incredibly given Sundays off--the busiest day of the week-- and was awarded general supervision of the pony track.

For whatever reason Joe's first boss outside of the home, Al Smith, allowed the situation to stand. Perhaps in his more than sixty years he had not quite seen everything. Perhaps the circumstances simply reinforced the credo Al had posted on the wall of the pony barn tack room. It read: "There must be a harder way." But in any event this kind and amiable "year-rounder" evidently decided to make a manager of Joe. He in fact clearly and effectively demonstrated to Joe the value of occasional unilateral decision-making when on one July morning Jack Frost, a dedicated and anxious stud pony, broke loose in the barn full of restrained mares. "You really can overdo a good thing," Al advised.

The Half-Mile Bridge

In his subsequent summer-work seasons life, luck, and upward mobility continued for Joe. In the summer of 1957 at age eighteen he was hired as a driver by the Procurement Lab at MIT in Cambridge, Massachusetts, to deliver and retrieve top-secret missile guidance system parts from an array of subcontractors throughout New England. In 1958, his first college summer break, he rocketed from short order cook at the Meadows Restaurant in Hudson to co-manager of the same owner's Big Burger, sixty miles to the north on Lake Winnipesaukee. In the summer of 1959 he rose in stature in the space of six weeks from an entry-level carton smasher to front-office helper at the Doehla Greeting Cards Company in Nashua, New Hampshire. And, then, two short years later when at age twenty-two he began his career in earnest as a high-school teacher of English, he was almost immediately named department chair. He was, among a faculty of twelve, the only full-time English teacher.

To be sure during his five plus years of teaching he was relatively successful in persuading his students to complete writing assignments and to participate in the analysis of poetry. Some even believed they enjoyed it. But in reality the "Tom Sawyer Theory of Management" did not surface again in its purest form until 1967 when at the age of twenty-seven Joe began his twenty-year career with Citizens' Scholarship Foundation of America. During those two decades hundreds of volunteers and scores of staff, in the spirit of Master Rogers, Billy Fisher, and Johnny Miller, would pick up the CSFA paint brush and collectively create a montage of the early history of an organization that would emerge from obscurity to become the largest single source of scholarships in the world. And of greater importance, almost to a person each believed the experience to be exhilarating, enjoyable and personally rewarding.

Introduction

Here, then, in *The Half-Mile Bridge* are the stories of Citizens' Scholarship Foundation of America. Here are its people, both affiliated and transient who carried a concept from trial to triumph in the space of thirty-four years. One tale is of Nelson Smart, a funeral director in Skowhegan, Maine, who rallied his community in 1967 to provide tens of thousands of dollars for young people in his school administrative district. Another is about Mrs. Jimmie Williams who in 1972 inveigled the congregation of a small church in the Corona-East Elmhurst section of Queens, New York, to come to the aid of the parish's minority students. Another is of David McLaughlin who, as president of the Toro Company in 1976, made a polite request that in its granting secured the future of CSFA perhaps for all time. And another is of Gisle and Eva Johnson, man and wife who, childless, frugal, and successful in Owatonna, Minnesota, in 1989 bequeathed $1.5 million to help young people in their city.

The Half-Mile Bridge shrouds in anonymity a modern day John Beresford Tipton who distributed the wealth of unnamed donors in a successful effort to spiral, thirtyfold, the amount and number of CSFA stimulated scholarships throughout New York State. And it describes agreements and contracts with the likes of Burger King, Bank of America, The Bristol-Myers Fund, NYNEX, Levi Strauss, and General Motors Corporation, among hundreds of others.

The Half-Mile Bridge is still more. Its stories reveal lessons of truth on the nonprofit landscape. The lessons were learned at times by design, at times by chance or accident, sometimes by default, sometimes through gestalt, and at times through trial and error. And along the way your narrator, Joe Phelan, expects you to conclude that he is *not* the Horatio Alger of the not-for-profit world. He is, in fact, the man who went to meet Kathy Iococca in a Lincoln Town Car. He is also the man who asked for Sweet and Low with his coffee when first visiting Searle Pharmaceutical, the inventors of Nutrasweet. He is the man who, as a dinner guest of the trustees of the Cogswell Trust in Manchester, New Hampshire, dumped six ounces of tomato juice on the merge point of his gray flannel trousers, and while cleaning up the mess by employing every napkin within arms' reach, never paused in his pitch and presentation.

His complete stories of the people of Citizens' Scholarship Foundation of America are too many to tell within the confines of a single, brief history. As is true, too, of accounts of other notable campaigns, his generals and colonels receive the bulk of attention. The lieutenants and noncoms remain relatively in the shadows. But he does believe that this sampling of events and the stories of "people who did the work and enjoyed it," sufficiently portrays the spirit and character of the organization in its early years. So as you wander with him through a portion of the lives of the doers and real heroes, keep in mind that you are traveling with the man who in 1967, on the occasion of first meeting Charlotte Fradkin, the wife of CSFA's founder, Dr. Irving A. Fradkin, punctuated his glib conversation by nearly destroying his only good suit.

Part I

Dr. Irving A. Fradkin

1957-1962

Irv
When Fate Summons

Chapter One

Irv

An optometrist with vision," the late comedian Sam Levenson called him. "The Paul Revere of Education," proclaimed the July 7, 1961, issue of *Time Magazine*, complete with a picture of this slight, bespectacled man of forty-one years, his thinning scalp concealed by a three-corner colonial hat. "The Pride of Fall River, The Scholarship City," announced the daily local *Herald* news sheet in 1961 and perhaps a thousand times since. Here is the way this Massachusetts visionary, Dr. Irving A. Fradkin, tells his story.

> Nineteen fifty-seven was one of a number of very difficult years for the Fall River economy. As a practicing optometrist, I had ample opportunity to see the eyes and faces of families whose breadwinning jobs were moving south with the vanishing textile industry. As a result I thought a lot about the plight of my adopted city, and I came to believe that the only salvation for the next generation was education. As the son of Russian

immigrant parents I was especially blessed to have had an opportunity to attend the New England College of Optometry. I was, I suppose, proof of sorts that education is the key to each succeeding generation's success in a democracy.

I recognized even back then in the days before the outpourings of massive federal and state aid programs, that education beyond high school was simply out of the question for most of the graduates of Durfee High School and five local parochial high schools. Scholarships were few in number, and those that did exist usually were given to a few students at the very top of the class.

One evening I asked Charlotte, my bride of eleven years, if she thought that the residents of Fall River would be willing to give one dollar or more each to a general scholarship fund. She thought the idea was certainly affordable. With her encouragement and blessing, I decided to run for the local school committee on a platform that included a city-wide scholarship plan.

The election did not go my way, and for a short time I abandoned any idea of involvement in the difficulties of our local students. But many students were also my patients, and enough of them voiced their disappointment over my unsuccessful foray into politics, that I came to believe the vote count was not the down-and-out count. I was encouraged by the feelings of the students and by the willingness of a few close friends to help out. I organized a meeting in my office where I again raised the question of a citizens' movement for higher education. The answer was a cautious but reasonably enthusiastic 'yes,' and on February 20, 1958, the Fall River Citizens' Scholarship Plan was born.

Well, this story is not the complete story, nor is it exactly the way Irv Fradkin would tell it. Irving's story is recorded in great detail in his autobiography, released by

Branden Publishing Company of Boston in 1993. But minimally Irving would want you to know that he and "Charl" had some difficult times on the way up, and that at one early point in his marriage he scolded her dearly for wasting precious pennies on a jar of cherries. He would want you to know that his decision to turn over the management of his real estate holdings to a third party, so that he could help other cities and towns establish scholarship programs, left him with no holdings at all. And he would share with you tales of a dozen or so other foibles that classify him as a normal human being.

Irving holds, he says, the modern-day record for a honeymoon, the latest estimate at forty-eight uninterrupted years. He would make you aware that at his own expense he has traveled the equivalent of eight times around the globe, more like Johnny Appleseed and less like Paul Revere, in spreading word of his citizens' scholarship movement. "Slowed only," he would tell you, "by five hip replacements and one heart attack."

You would be reminded that his voluntary commitment to his missionary zeal was a compounded burden. Beyond the out-of-pocket costs, every day away from his office helping some community to "get organized" resulted in a corresponding loss of income. He would assure you that the Fall River Plan was a "hand up," not a "handout," as he intended, even expected, that every student who benefited from the program would someday in some way "repay" the community.

Uniformly loved by every Rotary Club, Lion's Club, Junior Women's Club, and BPW that heard him out, Irving was able in the early going to help organize eleven community scholarship programs modeled on his Fall River Plan. In the year when his chapters came together in his city to incorporate Citizens' Scholarship Foundation of

America, the representatives were undaunted by the absence of a budget, a source of funds, or a plan of any kind. Eleven charter incorporators, community volunteers all, signed the necessary papers leading to the May 15, 1961, incorporation of CSFA. Irving was named the first president and served in that volunteer capacity for the next nineteen years.

Irving was not short on chutzpah. While others in his profession were spending Wednesday afternoons on golf courses, he was on the phone calling elected federal and state officials to tell them of his own American Dream. He received in turn modest contributions from the likes of Eleanor Roosevelt and warm letters of encouragement from President Eisenhower and Senator John F. Kennedy. He sought and got himself on radio and television talk shows from Boston to New York. He set up an office at 100 Purchase Street in his city and then traveled to Manhattan to meet with Roy Larson, chairman of the board of the Ford Foundation. He came away with $12,000, a sum sufficient in the early sixties to staff the office in Fall River.

The word was out on the American landscape. In 1962 Irving received three anonymous gifts in the mail. The postmarks on each package appeared to have been deliberately smudged. The return address in Phoenix turned out to be a vacant lot. The first package held $1,400 in cash; the next, $1,600; the third, $2,000. These gifts in the aggregate could not support an ongoing national program, but each provided encouragement. So, too, did the interest of others. Sam Levenson, who had traveled to Fall River to "kick off" the scholarship program, captured seven minutes with Dave Garroway on NBC's "Today Show" and spoke eloquently of the optometrist's dream. The broadcast resulted in five thousand inquiries on the Dollars for Scholars program.

"We didn't even have the capacity to respond," Irving remembers. "We were able to get *Better Homes and Gardens* to help us with promotional materials, but the postage alone was beyond our means."

In late 1961 Fall River was visited by an initially skeptical representative from the *Reader's Digest*. "Robert O'Brien didn't come to see me," Irving says. "He came to talk with just about everyone else." But before he left, he came to my office to tell me the *Reader's Digest* would probably do a story on my Fall River Plan." The *Digest* ultimately did two.

Irving is the first to admit that his organizational skills were lacking. He spent those early years talking with virtually anyone who would listen. If the listener had any aura of interest, wealth, or prestige, Irving's battle cry was "You wanna be on my board?" An inadvertent nod of the head or stifled sneeze was sufficient to find someone enrolled. But the law of averages favored Irving, and as the ears were bent, so would grow the tree.

Chapter Two

When Fate Summons

At about the time Irving Fradkin was first thinking about running for the Fall River, Massachusetts, school committee, some 130 miles to the northeast in Hudson, New Hampshire, the Alvirne High School Class of 1957 was rehearsing "The Halls of Ivy" in anticipation of its impending June 14 graduation. At about the time Irving was gathering together his eleven Dollars for Scholars chapters for the purpose of incorporating Citizens' Scholarship Foundation of America, the University of New Hampshire Class of 1961 was finishing up its last-ever final exams. I was a member of both classes, a non-scholarship student I might admit, and although my academic careers were undistinguished at both institutions, my life's professional path was, I believed, set straight before me.

I had known since my sophomore year in high school that I wanted to teach. I had known from my sophomore year at the university that I wanted to teach high-school English. And more than a month before I addressed my graduating classmates on the university's Cowell Field in Durham, I had a teaching contract in the picturesque Lakes Region town of Bristol, New Hampshire. That contract would be renewed annually until I elected in the fall of 1965 to accept a graduate assistantship at Morehead State University in Kentucky.

My Masters Degree program at Morehead State provided the first, if at the time unrecognized, hint that my professional path would divide in the yellow wood. At Morehead I was a curiosity. One student even asked me if New Hampshire was part of Rhode Island. But something I did there proclaimed me, comparatively speaking, a resident genius. Given a choice of either a teaching assistantship correcting a faculty member's student papers, or a proposal-writing assignment, I chose the latter. Up until 1966 and despite several attempts, Morehead State had never successfully competed for a National Defense Education Act (NDEA) federal grant. In the fall of 1965 the chairman of the English Department, Dr. George Boswell, asked me to author a proposal for an NDEA summer institute for teachers of English from Ohio, Indiana, and Kentucky.

The proposal was one of eight submitted by Morehead that year to the U.S. Office of Education. It was the only one authored by a student and the only one funded. As the wellspring for $48,500, I became and remained a high-honors graduate student. Upon reflection I now realize I was then, long before Kentucky's commitment to educational reform, simply buoyant in a sea of mediocrity. Morehead was a school where, despite the outstanding qualities of the English department faculty, one twin-tower dormitory was named for the president's wife--first name, mind you. And where one president was rumored to have distinguished himself nationally when he interrupted a basketball game to argue a call on the court with a game official. So despite the fact that ahead of my graduation in August of 1966 I was offered a fund-raising position in the development office at Morehead State, I respectfully declined, happily anticipating a return to teaching.

Recently a colleague asked me if I had in any way foreseen the professional experiences that would follow my graduate education. I replied: "Absolutely not." My three goals in August of 1966 were the same as those of the high-school senior in 1957: one, teach; two, have a yearbook dedicated to me; and three, earn $10,000 a year, because I didn't know anyone who did.

Achieving the first two proved easier than expected. The third was a bit more elusive, but is nevertheless part of the fabric of my experience with Citizens' Scholarship Foundation of America. In fairness to the colleague who bothered to ask, the twenty-year experience with CSFA, the enduring lessons learned from it, the disappointments encountered, and the successes enjoyed, are in fact a retrospective as opposed to some grand design. The experience was a tapestry patterned by triumphs that, over time, more than tempered the early travails.

My introduction to Citizens' Scholarship Foundation of America was to be sandwiched between my undergraduate years and graduate studies. In September of 1961 I nervously took my place on the teacher's side of the desk in a Bristol, New Hampshire, classroom. Bristol was my town of choice because I was newly married, and my wife was still an undergraduate at Plymouth State Teachers College, some twelve miles to the north. Bristol Memorial High School enjoyed a fine reputation then, both academically and athletically. Much of the credit for this reputation was vested in the personality and demeanor of the school's principal, Albert D. Genetti, a no-nonsense administrator:

"I'm Mr. Genetti; you're Mr. Phelan; she's Mrs. Ruell; no teacher has a first name in the classroom or in the halls."

Al Genetti was and remains the standard by which I still judge all public school administrators. He was not universally loved, but he was universally admired and respected by every one of the 250 or so students and the twelve faculty members in the combined junior-senior high school. He was clearly the icon of authority, and his teachers were free to teach. During that first year of teaching I sent just one student to the office. No one wanted to go.

Al Genetti is important to my story because the year 1962 marked the close of his fifteen-year career in Bristol and the beginning of the end of my love affair with public school teaching. I did not see the looming separation at the time, but Mr. Genetti was followed during the ensuing four years by principals who, in the eyes of a faculty that had known better, ranged from awful to average. At a time when both drugs and alcohol began permeating the classrooms, strong leadership and resolute courage were among the most required, but most seemingly absent qualities. We as teachers not only did not know how to handle these new problems; we were also uncertain as to what they were. While we were not blind to the sense of deterioration among some of our students, we believed our superiors, in the face of greater knowledge, were perhaps looking the other way. In the midst of these unwelcome changes two noteworthy things happened. One, the Class of 1963 dedicated its yearbook to me. Two, nearly two years later I was asked to do something for the community.

One of the peculiarities of teaching in a small New Hampshire town in the early 1960s was that teachers were always regarded as transients. That is, despite a teacher's popularity with students, or parents, or the school board, the likelihood of inclusion in the town's social circles or service clubs was remote. Teachers tended to befriend teachers and to spend Friday evenings playing cards and consuming the beverage of choice, purchased out of town with the collection taken up on Friday afternoon.

A personal experience in the course of a town meeting in 1964 illustrates the level of disenfranchisement The town moderator was fielding questions on a warrant item concerning the possible purchase of a new and very heavy fire truck. As a duly registered voter I raised my hand and asked my question about the likelihood that the secondary road surfaces could withstand the weight of the proposed equipment. While I was awaiting a response from Nate Morrison, the town road agent, I heard a male voice behind me ask, "Who's he?" Another male voice replied: "Teaches over t' the high school." The first voice then said: "A teacher? What the hell's he know 'bout fire trucks?"

In the face of this social separation, I was both surprised and pleased when on a February morning in 1965 I received a telephone call from David Williams, president of the town's largest employer, International Packings Corporation. Mr. Williams asked if I would join him and about a dozen other townspeople for lunch at the Grace Louise Diner, a local restaurant often referred to unfairly by my students as the "Greasy Louse." He said he wanted to share with all of us news of a new scholarship program that might be introduced in the seven towns of the Newfound Region.

There I found myself for the first time in the combined august company of Mr. Williams; Larry Denton, the bank president; Larry and Margery Fields, the publishers of the weekly newspaper, *The Bristol Enterprise*; Mel Hicks, local funeral director and president of Rotary; and a number of other area dignitaries. "The Dollars for Scholars program,"

Mr. Williams told us, "is really quite simple. If you people agree to help, we as a steering committee, will recruit a few others, organize a Dollars for Scholars chapter, and set out to raise one dollar for every resident in the Newfound Region. If we are successful, we will have about five thousand dollars for scholarships for the graduating class of 1965.

We discussed the program within the confines of the lunch hour, and at a few minutes before one o'clock we voted to organize a chapter. We also adopted the $5,000 goal. My assigned and accepted task was to involve my students in raising 10 percent of that amount. According to the guidelines that came along from the "national" organization, the best way to involve students in Dollars for Scholars was to hold a school-wide assembly, explain the program, and ask for volunteers. I decided on a different approach.

As soon as I returned to the high school, I asked Martha Parsons, the senior class president, to gather all class officers for a meeting with me in the school library at three o'clock. When we were all assembled I said, "I have a problem. I need to raise $500 for scholarships before June graduation. I need help." Within a short time we agreed that, one, we would accept money only for services performed; and two, we would need about fifty students to get the job done.

On the Saturdays just ahead of Easter Sunday and Mother's Day we washed and waxed cars for $5 apiece. We held a community work day. We wrote to all of the nonresident people who owned summer cottages on nearby Newfound Lake and offered to clean the cottages--the keys were always left with the local realtor--for $20 each. By mid-May I was able to report back to the Dollars for Scholars committee that the students had raised $860 toward the agreed-upon goal. My new friend Dave Williams said "great, because we have $5,000 to go with it." To place that sum in perspective, in that year my wife's tuition at Plymouth State College was $90 a semester. Tuition at my undergraduate alma mater was $480 a year; and Dartmouth of the Ivies would let parents get by with only $2,725 for tuition, room, and board for a full academic year.

Graduation evening in June of 1965 proved to be very special. I do not recall the name of the guest speaker, nor do I recall the evening's theme, for which I, as chairman of the English Department, was directly responsible. It no doubt had something to do with stopping by woods, or swinging on birches, or taking those less-traveled paths. What I do remember is the spontaneous class reaction to one announcement. When little Eddie Phelps, an average, industrious student who had been accepted in a two-year agricultural program at the University of New Hampshire's Thompson School, received an $800 Dollars for Scholars award, the senior class rose as one and cheered.

Was this the magical moment that would change my life forever? Well, yes and no. Yes, because without it this story could never be told. But no, because I certainly didn't recognize it as such. I was busy with my applications for graduate school. And following that interlude in Kentucky, I would return to Bristol not only as an upgraded classroom teacher, but also as assistant principal. The pay differential was $500 and the total salary was $5,800, a figure more than halfway to my third and most elusive goal.

Up until a more recent time when I became friendly with a few deans of students at the college level, I believed that an assistant principalship was the most horrible job in the world. As chief school disciplinarian, a position not even required during my first year with Al Genetti, I concluded that I had three major responsibilities. First, compensate for a principal who was afraid of students. Second, compensate for teachers who could not control their classrooms. And third, police the dress code in an effort to determine that the boys kept their shirts tucked in, and that the "mini" in the girls' miniskirts did not violate generally accepted standards of morality or decorum. By mid-October, my enthusiasm for public education was behind me. Whereas in my earlier four years almost no infirmity could keep me from my classroom, the fall of 1966 found me hoping each morning for any discomfort that could lay claim to my accumulated sick leave.

Later in the month my wife, who was somewhat dismayed by my unhappy situation, called to my attention an advertisement in the state-wide teachers' newsletter, *The New Hampshire Educator*. The ad read: "Wanted: Northern New England Regional Director for the national Dollars for Scholars program. Purpose: organize volunteer-based community scholarship programs in, Maine, Vermont and New Hampshire. Apply: Citizens' Scholarship Foundation of America, 43 Leon Street, Boston, Massachusetts, 02115, or call (617) 445-1790." That moment was clearly the one that would change my life and consume at least 20 percent of it.

Part II

Eugene C. Struckhoff

1963-1967

Struck
Two in the Parlors, Forty-three in the Barn

Chapter Three

Struck

The name Eugene C. Struckhoff is today synonymous with the design, development and growth of an American phenomenon known as "community foundations." In the 1970s, his decade as vice president and then president of the Council on Foundations, he literally authored the book on community foundations. He served then as now as the foremost authority and most qualified mentor for the volunteer leadership of major cities, counties, and at times, even states, who wished to stimulate new philanthropy for the arts, education, ecology, historic preservation, social services, and public welfare.

In its basic essence a community foundation seeks to attract gifts and grants from the widest possible base as a precursor to providing gifts, loans, and challenge grants to a wide array of charitable organizations and causes within a defined geographical area. "Struck," as many people affectionately know him, is a world-class proponent of citizen philanthropy, and that particular prediliction attracted him to Irving Fradkin's Fall River Scholarship Plan.

Struck's involvement with Citizens' Scholarship Foundation of America predates my own. In fact I was no doubt correcting my first ever set of mid-year exams at Bristol Memorial High School in the winter of 1962, when some thirty miles to the south in New Hampshire's capital city of Concord, a prominent attorney in a rather prestigious law firm was pondering the merits of the Fall River Plan and ruminating on how it might find a wider application in his home state.

Irving Fradkin had unknowingly brought his scholarship program to Struck's attention. Shortly after the incorporation of CSFA in 1961, Irving found a new friend in one Paul Newsome, the head of the Boston-based advertising firm, Newsome and Newsome. Paul suggested that one of the firm's clients, and specifically the regional production facility of Carling Brewing Company, might be persuaded to provide a little underpinning for the new organization. On the strength of that suggestion he introduced Irving to the Carling regional vice president, Roger Williams.

Roger remembers the occasion well.

> Dr. Fradkin is a wonderful man, but when I met him in 1961 he was naive as hell. He was putting so much time into his scholarship program that he was in danger of losing his optometry practice. I had a little community service fund at the Natick plant, and from it I gave Irving enough money, fifteen hundred dollars in the first year, I think, to allow him to hire a part-time secretary in Fall River. I increased the sum over the next few years to the point where he could have a full-time secretary who worked exclusively on Dollars for Scholars. I continued this support until 1965, the year I left Carling.

This Carling connection proved to be very important to the future of CSFA. Later in 1961 Roger Williams hosted a dinner for community leaders in eastern Massachusetts. Among those seated around the tables at the 1812 House in Framingham was Ralph Seifert, who in the late 1940s was one of his fraternity brothers at Brown University. Cy Seifert would stay as a volunteer with the Dollars for Scholars program at local, state, regional, and national levels for the next thirty-five years.

Roger also recalls a more direct connection to Carling Brewing Company.

> One of the corporate vice presidents out of Cleveland, Brad Norris, was in Boston in late 1962. He and a guy from New Hampshire, another attorney not connected with Carling, were involved with the Unitarian Universalist Church, and were in town on church business. I invited Brad and Gene Struckhoff to dinner at Durgin Park, and in the course of our dinner conversation, I told them about Irving and the Dollars for Scholars program. At the time both seemed pretty interested.

My first encounter with Attorney Struckhoff occurred early in November of 1966 during my participation in a second round of interviews for the first Northern New England regional directorship of Citizens' Scholarship Foundation of America. At that time in his capacity as a partner in the Orr and Reno law firm, he was serving also as secretary of the Spaulding-Potter Charitable Trusts, the then largest single source of philanthropic dollars in the Granite State. Income and resulting distributions from the $8 million fund had over the years effectively touched the lives of thousands of New Hampshire residents.

The terms establishing the trusts also provided for its dissolution. Those terms required that all principal had to be distributed to worthwhile charitable endeavors by June 30, 1972. Secretary Struckhoff worried that the vacuum created by the dissolution of the trusts would prove detrimental to current and future charitable good works within his state. Ten years ahead of the dissolution date Struck began planning for the future of philanthropy in and for New Hampshire. Part of his planning process was to accept an early role with Citizens' Scholarship Foundation of America, and it was in this capacity that I was summoned before him at 93 North Main Street that November morning.

Attorney Struckhoff's physical demeanor was not particularly imposing. His neatly-trimmed, wavy sand-colored hair framed a somewhat cherubic face atop a reasonably trim, forty-six-year-old 175 pound frame. His brusque and direct manner, however, proved certainly intimidating for his twenty-six-year-old guest. Coatless, he sat back in his leather chair with one foot wedged against the top of his desk and chewed absently on a clove-flavored toothpick, the first I had ever seen.

"Well," he said, without preamble, "we've narrowed the field of thirty candidates to two, and you're one of them. We've decided that because you're a high-school teacher, you're probably not afraid to talk to people, and I guess you can write okay. If you're the guy, when can you start?"

"January, " I replied.

"What if I said we need you on board by November fifteenth?"

"I guess," I said, "you'll have to give the job to the other guy. I'm under contract with my school district. I need to give the superintendent and principal some reasonable amount of time to find my replacement."

"Okay," he said, "I'll get back to you." End of interview.

I later learned that my refusal to abridge my teaching contract without reasonable notice was the compelling factor in my favor when I was ultimately selected to become CSFA's first-ever regional director.

Struck may have agreed with me philosophically that January 3, 1967, was a reasonable starting date, but his patience did not extend to recognizing that day as my first day of training. One December evening he loaded me in his car and carried me some one hundred miles to Portland, Maine. Within the first few miles I came to know this Colby College valedictorian, consummate organizer and planner, well-respected attorney, and this gentleman with the heart of gold encased in an iron chest. He would in short order become my mentor, and the person who would shape, for all time, my personal and professional philosophy, ethics, and approaches to the challenges of the nonprofit world.

We were on our way that evening to meet with Richard Woodbury, managing editor of the *Portland Press Herald and Evening Express*. Mr. Woodbury also chaired the State of Maine Citizens' Scholarship Foundation, a loosely organized federation of eight existing Dollars for Scholars chapters, predominately in the Portland area. In the course of the two-hour drive Struck explained to me his interest in the Dollars for Scholars program. He shared with me his concern for the future of privately sponsored student aid programs, especially those originating with the Spaulding-Potter Charitable Trusts. He said that in early 1962 he began his search for a program that would in New Hampshire more than compensate for the loss of the trusts' aid-to-education funds.

Within a few months following his conversation with Roger Williams at Durgin Park, Struck got wind of a Dollars for Scholars program already underway in the

Connecticut River valley town of Claremont, New Hampshire. There residents were contributing money to help Stevens High School graduates go on to college.

Struck was intrigued with the concept of "leveraging" charitable dollars. He wondered if his Spaulding-Potter trustees might be interested in providing funding and impetus for a wider citizen-based scholarship movement in New Hampshire. If so, he reasoned, every dollar the trusts invested might well return multiple dollars from the citizenry base. To satisfy his curiosity he spent some time with Irving Fradkin. Within the confines of two hours, Struck reached three conclusions. First, that the Dollars for Scholars program was viable for New Hampshire. Second, that the Spaulding-Potter Trusts should be encouraged to "seed fund" such an effort. And third, that Dr. Fradkin's scholarship program was, in its present form and structure, woefully inadequate for any task at hand. As a citizens' movement the national organization did not, to Struck's way of thinking, conform to its rather lofty title. Citizens' Scholarship Foundation of America was still a rather informal, not particularly well-defined, affiliation of representatives from now twenty-four Dollars for Scholars chapters. As such, its bylaws were in need of refinements; its mission in need of articulation; and its Board of Trustees--made up primarily of "letterhead" friends of Irving Fradkin--was in need of persons of "some stature" who were also willing to work.

These existing frailties did not dilute Struck's enthusiasm for the Dollars for Scholars idea. He decided that he could provide what was lacking or needed fixing. With the blessing and gratitude of Irving Fradkin and his charter-member affiliates, Struck gave form and substance to this fledgling scholarship organization. He rewrote the bylaws and recruited to work with him the likes of Charles

Radman, CEO of a national market chain; his friend and colleague from Cleveland, William B. "Brad" Norris, vice president and legal counsel for Carling Brewing Company; Dr. Asa Knowles, president of Northeastern University, and Dr. Thaddeus Seymour, dean of Dartmouth College. In January of 1963 Struck became the first elected chairman of the board of Citizens' Scholarship Foundation of America.

Satisfied that CSFA was in good enough condition to accept and properly administer charitable grants, Struck successfully encouraged the trustees of the Spaulding-Potter Charitable Trusts to commit $79,000 over three years for the creation of Dollars for Scholars chapters throughout New Hampshire. The greater share of that sum was earmarked as challenge grants to cities, towns, and school districts. The earliest chapters to form would receive three dollars for every dollar raised at the community level. Later ones would receive two dollars and the last few, in year three, would receive one dollar for every dollar raised. The incentive grants would be discontinued at the end of the three-year period on the assumption that the chapters would have sufficient momentum to compensate for the loss of external funds.

Beyond the borders of New Hampshire, Struck persuaded his CSFA board in 1964 to move the national office from Fall River to Boston. CSFA's first executive director, Fred Margolis, a Fall River native hired by Dr. Fradkin on the strength of the $12,000 Ford Foundation grant, chose not to make the move. Once CSFA had settled into its three rooms on Leon Street, adjacent to the campus of Northeastern University, the board hired Daniel A. Walker, a Yale graduate who had been active with the formation of Dollars for Scholars chapters in Rhode Island.

Dan Walker was still serving in that capacity when I first met him during the interviews of November, 1966.

As Attorney Struckhoff and I entered the Maine Turnpike in Kittery en route to Exit 8 in Portland, he mused over his debut in big-time fund raising. He had decided early on that a staffed national CSFA office was requisite to the successful conduct of statewide Dollars for Scholars initiatives in New England or elsewhere. Even in the absence of a clear strategy for long-term survival, Struck set about the task of finding seed money for the nonprofit corporation. He had, he said, embarked earlier on a few unsuccessful appeals to major foundations, but in 1963 he was provided an introduction to a $21 million private foundation on Wall Street. With great optimism and limited testimonials and exhibits he traveled to New York for the much-anticipated appointment. Struck remembers the event with great clarity.

> I had an hour, and I told Irving's story with animated enthusiasm. I spoke to the vision of thousands of Dollars for Scholars chapters one day providing millions and millions of grass-roots dollars for local students. I confidently predicted that every dollar raised to support a national CSFA office would return twenty or more dollars in actual scholarships at the local level.
>
> The president of the foundation loved the story. He couldn't say enough good things about it. But he did, at the end of the hour, have one disappointing thing to say, and that was "our foundation won't fund your program."
>
> I was dismayed and devastated, and obviously crestfallen. So as a consolation of sorts, the foundation president suggested another foundation in Indiana as a possible source of funds and offered to provide me with an introduction. Somewhat disheartened but nevertheless grateful for the lead, I returned to New Hampshire and

wrote an elaborate proposal. I dropped it in the mail. About three months later I was tempted to telephone the foundation; but while I was getting up my courage, my mail brought me a warm letter from John Lynn of The Lilly Endowment, along with our first Lilly grant of $67,000, a sum sufficient to underpin for a time, at least, a national CSFA office.

With the seed funding in place, Struck turned his attention to developing a systematic strategy for the expansion of Dollars for Scholars throughout the country. For four very good reasons he decided to use New Hampshire as the Dollars for Scholars laboratory. First, the size of the state is manageable. The widest distance between Maine to the east and Vermont to the west can be traveled by car in under three hours. The longer distance between Massachusetts and Canada can be traversed in less than four and a half. Second, New Hampshire is politically conservative, and its residents, fearful of state or federal intervention in their day-to-day lives, were more likely to embrace community-based, self-help initiatives. Third, Struck believed the trustees of the Spaulding-Potter Charitable Trusts would see the merit in providing seed money for a statewide Dollars for Scholars project. And fourth, Struck's law office in Concord would facilitate his active participation as a volunteer in the project and permit him to keep a close eye on its progress.

The three-year New Hampshire project, under the able, if necessarily part-time direction of former state's attorney general, Gordon Tiffany, proved to be a remarkable success. By the close of 1965, forty Dollars for Scholars chapters were serving nearly 150 cities and towns. This success inspired the Kettering Foundation in Ohio and The Lilly Endowment once again in Indiana to underwrite similar projects in those states. Those initiatives, augmented with spontaneous inquiries from other states-- stimulated mostly by favorable publicity in *Time, Life, The Saturday Review of Literature* and a follow-on article in the *Reader's Digest* in 1965-- increased the number of Dollars for Scholars affiliates to 188 by December of 1966. Such was the status of Citizens' Scholarship Foundation of America, under Gene Struckhoff's leadership, as we turned into the parking lot of Valle's Steak House in Westbrook, Maine, on December 17. During that evening, where history left off, education and enlightenment began. Over dinner Struck, Dick Woodbury and I spoke of plans for the State of Maine. Encouraged by results in New Hampshire and Ohio, the Agnes M. Lindsay Trust of Boston had provided $38,500 in support of a statewide Dollars for Scholars initiative in Northern New England with a primary focus on Maine and a secondary interest in Vermont. The term of the project was eighteen months; the objective was for me to form thirty chapters in that year and a half. Prior to dessert, I did not have a clue as to how that objective would be addressed and met. One hour following the final coffee I had the strategy, if not the confidence required, to bring the project to fruition. With the table bare Struck spread out before us a map of Maine. The geography is greater than one might imagine, some three hundred and fifty miles from Kittery at the southern extreme to Madawaska on the Canadian border. The distance between Kezar Falls on the western boundary and Eastport, the easternmost extremity of the continental United States, is about the same.

Maine has nearly two hundred cities, towns and territories served by ninety-five school districts. The potential for thirty Dollars for Scholars chapters clearly existed, but where would I begin? "Well," Struck said "here's a way you might do it." Struck first drew a bold line further defining the Maine Turnpike that runs north 100 miles from Kittery to Augusta. He then extended the line another 200 miles along Interstate 95 from Augusta to Houlton. And for good measure continued his line north along US Route 1 another fifty or so miles from Houlton to the Canadian border. He then used the same marker to highlight communities some fifty to seventy miles apart that included one or more college campuses as part of the infrastructure. Included among these towns and cities were Waterville, home of his alma mater, Colby College; Orono, home of the University of Maine; Farmington, home of Farmington Teachers College; and Presque Isle in the far north, home of Presque Isle State College.

Struck then placed the base of the table's candle holder on the map and using the college communities as center points, he scribed a three-inch circle around each. He looked up.

> What you need to do is develop interest in Dollars for Scholars in at least ten towns within each circle. Within those towns or school administrative districts recruit ten people to attend an area Dollars for Scholars workshop. Then persuade the presidents of the respective colleges to host the workshops and maybe pay for a dinner to which the committed volunteers are invited. I'll ask Colby to do it for you; you will then be able to persuade the other colleges.
>
> At each dinner encourage the college president to speak with conviction about the need for community scholarship initiatives. Then, Dick Woodbury here, or one of our CSFA board members, will extol the virtues of Dollars for Scholars. At this juncture community volunteers from one of Maine's existing eight chapters will talk of their success and encourage the represented school districts to go ahead

> with the program. Allow time for questions, but keep in mind that the most important part of the evening is yet to follow. Before anyone leaves, try to have at least two people in the audience announce their plans to move ahead, 'salting the mine' if you will. Other people will follow their lead.
>
> Complete this activity in circle one before you move to circle two. Keep in mind that the only successful action or activity is the one that leads to another action or activity. The event is never the key event unless and until a chapter is formed and raises money. Work as much as you can in contiguous circles. That approach saves both time and money.

As much as this sounds like Polonius admonishing Laertes, the advice was great. He went on.

> What should happen is that as you work with the committed areas and new steering committees in circle one, you will be stimulating new interest in circle two. Within a short time chapters will be formed and active in circle one, while steering committees vote to organize in circle two, while you develop new interest in circle three. Make sense?

It did.

> You will need some advance publicity to help establish your credibility. Dick Woodbury represents the *Portland Press Herald*, the *Kennebec Journal*, and the *Bangor Daily News*. Those newspapers encompass nearly all of the daily news coverage in the most populous areas of the state. As you move along your way, Dick will place favorable articles and editorials in the respective newspapers. He will also introduce you to key people within the Gannett newspapers and in Maine's radio and television stations. Get before the cameras and get on

the popular "luncheon chat" local radio talk shows. Dick also has a handle on the best, most articulate volunteers in the existing Maine Dollars for Scholars chapters. He will recruit them for your use at the college presidents' dinners and for testimony with newly formed steering committees. Schedule at least four appointments for yourself each working day and evening, including luncheon and dinner programs with civic and social organizations, daytime media contacts, and evening chapter formation activities.

Your weekly reports to Dan Walker and me will describe the nature and level of activity within each circle. I know you will make enough calls, create enough excitement, and use your dollars and people wisely. If you do, you will get the chapters.

Thus ended my introductory course on grass-roots organizational dynamics. The strategies were clear, and my confidence level slightly elevated. Because of Struck I felt better prepared for the task ahead. At the same time I was vastly unprepared for the uncertainty and trepidation that confronted me two weeks later when I stepped off my front stairs in Alexandria, New Hampshire, and pointed my new 1967 Pontiac Tempest toward Skowhegan, Maine.

Chapter Four

Two in the Parlors;
Forty-three in the Barn

Anyone who has ever set out to make the first door-to-door sale of an encyclopedia, vacuum cleaner, baby furniture, or a life insurance policy, knows just how I felt at six-thirty in the ebony morning of January 3, 1967. Armed with a few rather rudimentary brochures and a single name, Jean Corrigan, provided to me by Gene Struckhoff, I began my two hundred mile journey to Skowhegan, Maine. I had chosen Skowhegan for two reasons. First because its proximity to Waterville and Colby College placed it within the rim of one of Struck's three-inch circles. And second, because the name I carried with me was my sole lead among the then 1.2 million inhabitants of my neighboring state.

Maine, when one comes to know it, is a wonderful place. I would come to know it very well during the following eighteen months, for during that period I would travel by car some 65,000 miles within its borders. In many cases I would actually find myself where the road ends. Many such roads ended on the three hundred-mile rocky coast where fishermen eked out a living on mackerel, cod, and haddock, sea worms, clams, and lobsters. Others ended where the great and powerful paper companies in the north central part of the state determined passage should cease, be it on remote logging roads or at cul-de-sacs defining and limiting the expansion of neighborhoods in each company town. Still others terminated in vast blueberry fields north of Maine's central coast. And the most remarkable roads of all were those to be found north of the immortalized Hainesville Woods, where, in an almost separate nation called Aroostook County on Maine's northernmost border, people prosper on potatoes and sugar beets; the success of each year's crops and corresponding market prices signaled by the numbers of new automobiles on dealer lots.

That winter morning, however, as I meandered northeast through central New Hampshire--State Route 104 out of Bristol; east to Route 25 in Meredith; northeast to Route 16 in West Ossipee; due north to a hard right-hand turn on U.S. Route 2 in Gorham; then east-northeast into Maine--my mind was only on Skowhegan. The beauty of the sky edging from ebony to indigo to brilliant blue, and the contrast of winter snow, ice on granite hills, and the seemingly endless expanse of white birch trees, was totally lost on me. I was the reluctant missionary traveling to a foreign land and quite convinced that my intended destination was a place I would not care to be. My negative predisposition was reinforced as I traveled through Rumford, Maine, where even on this sharp winter day the condensed sulfur fumes from the local paper mill caused me to wish that breathing were optional. This day was one of the coldest in my memory. When I finally found an outdoor phone booth at 10:30 in downtown Skowhegan, the bank thermometer read three below zero.

I placed my first CSFA business call to Mrs. Corrigan, president of the Business and Professional Women's Club. When she answered on the third ring, I said: "Hello, this is Joe Phelan. I'm with Citizens' Scholarship Foundation of America." She paused and replied:

"Cystic Fibrosis; I already gave to Cystic Fibrosis." The day became colder still.

We did after a minute or so of clarification manage to move toward a more productive phone call. She allowed as how the BPW would not have a particular interest in my program, but she suggested I call Nelson Smart, owner of Smart's Funeral Home and president of the local Rotary Club. She gave me the number. With little choice--I had nowhere else to go--and far less optimism, I dutifully called Mr. Smart. To my relief he was home at the home. He invited me over, and ahead of the noon hour we sat in an otherwise unoccupied parlor and talked about Dollars for Scholars.

Nelson Smart was a handsome man of forty-six years, standing six feet tall, his facial features finely defined against his graying temples. Nelson was an empathetic man who readily saw the potential of Dollars for Scholars for his city and its adjacent community of Norridgewock. He also provided me with the first truism in my experience with community-based volunteers. He said near the close of that first conversation, "It's a great idea, but I'm just too busy to take it on." I learned from this instance and from countless others to follow that when I heard that disclaimer, or a similar statement, I usually had identified my eventual chapter president.

Nelson did agree that January day to work with the local Rotary Club program chairman to schedule me as a guest speaker at a not-too-distant Rotary luncheon. He provided me with the names of other Rotarians in nearby communities, thereby augmenting my leads list. He also suggested that when I returned to Skowhegan to speak to the Rotary, I should plan to be a guest of the Smarts.

The winter of 1966-1967 had been particularly harsh on the residents of west central Maine and particularly good for local funeral directors. So when I accepted Nelson's offer of hospitality, I fully expected other, quasi-paying guests would be at rest in his house. The February evening prior to my luncheon presentation gave me ample opportunity over dinner with the Smarts to learn something more about the funeral business. I casually asked if any customers were in repose on the first floor. Nelson as casually responded that, "yes, two folks are in the parlors and forty-three more are at rest temporarily in the receiving vault in the barn." Certainly I should not have been unnerved. I know harmless when I see it. But later that evening when I a bit too forcefully closed my bedroom door behind me, and the once fully-drawn window shade raced to the top of its casing, rattling on its pins and springs, I knew my night's rest would be an uneasy one.

Nevertheless, I was awake and ready on Rotary day at the O Sole Mio Restaurant to tell the story of Dollars for Scholars. My own experience as a volunteer in Bristol, New Hampshire, proved extremely valuable on that occasion, for I quickly learned that anecdotes are far more powerful and compelling than simple exposition. I also learned something that almost belabors the obvious: "If you need help, ask for it." I did. I asked the Rotarians to help me to organize a Dollars for Scholars chapter and to provide leadership for it for a period of three years. I asked the members to create a steering committee that would include community representation beyond Rotary's circle. I asked the club to make the first financial commitment to the local program. The Rotarians so moved, voted, and carried all three requests. And in the bargain I got Nelson Smart.

Throughout February and March, Nelson and I worked with the local steering committee, he in the capacity as chair. The committee adopted with minor changes the CSFA-provided chapter agreements and bylaws, and then set about planning a community-wide Citizens' Scholarship Foundation organizational meeting to be held at North Elementary School in early May. The committee also agreed early on to have solid representation at the Colby College dinner event already on the calendar for March 21. By mid-March, 110 people representing more than twenty communities had responded favorably to the Colby President's invitation.

In the summer of 1994 when I had an opportunity to visit with the retired funeral director in Skowhegan, Nelson reflected on the ride home from that Waterville dinner.

> With me in the car was our high-school guidance counselor. His name I remember was Robert Fiddler. He had a seminary background, Jesuit, I think. Bob was the kind of person who didn't say much, but when he spoke people paid attention. As we neared the city he said, "Nelson, we need this program for the kids in Skowhegan." I reminded him that the tasks of organizing and promoting the program were daunting and would require a tremendous amount of time. He responded: "Nelson, we can always find time for the things we want to do." I knew at that moment we would definitely move ahead.

Skowhegan Rotary did it right. Nelson and friends decided to make the organizational meeting a media event and specifically requested that Dr. Irving Fradkin be on hand for the evening. This development, along with my own professional concern for the quality of the event, required me to spend still more advance time in Skowhegan. On one such occasion in mid-April I called Nelson to ask if I might visit with him to review the entire plan and logistics for Dr. Fradkin's visit. He agreed to do so but warned me that "he was very busy." And we would have to "talk and work at the same time." I didn't quite understand what he meant until I arrived. He and I then spent a warm spring day interring without ceremony a number of folks from his receiving vault. The frost was out of the ground; and the vault's former occupants were going into it.

The May 2, 1967, event was an unqualified success. Some four hundred people came to hear Dr. Fradkin and to vote unanimously to form a local Dollars for Scholars chapter to serve School Administrative District 54. The media coverage was extraordinary for such a remote location. Thanks to Dick Woodbury and his friends, television coverage came from as far away as Bangor some fifty miles distant. This event was my first with Dr. Fradkin and I was determined to use him advantageously. My determination was well satisfied until the very end of the evening. By the time the interviews with the press were over and good wishes wished all around, the hour was approaching midnight. In my earlier zeal to make the good doctor's evening memorable, I overlooked one essential detail--the fuel gauge in my Tempest. On the way back to the local motel we ran out of gas and ended up in the wee morning hours tossing pebbles against the second-story windows of a local mom-and-pop store to rouse the owner and get access to one of the two gas pumps.

The evening was, then, all the more memorable for the doctor and me. And during the years following that May event, I would, when my pathway permitted, stop and visit with Nelson. What he and his friends had made happen would result over time in $70,000 in new scholarships for 410 students of SAD #54. And I'm pleased to say that during the eighteen months inclusive of January of 1967 through June of 1968, the Struckhoff circles in the state of Maine hummed with organizational activities, so much so that part-time people had to be hired and many volunteers recruited from existing chapters to keep up with the presentations, persuasions, and affiliations. Dollars for Scholars had arrived in Maine.

Part III

William B. Norris

1968-1971

Brad
A Lesson from the Holocaust
Charity Begins Closer to Home
North to the Poles

Chapter Five

Brad

Safe to say that while I was traipsing through the state of Maine, establishing nearly permanent residences at the Holiday Inn in Westbrook, the Jefferson Motel in Waterville and the Paul Bunyan Motor Lodge in Bangor, I paid very little attention to the events in CSFA's Boston-based home office. CSFA's second executive director, Dan Walker, who was technically, I suppose the third, for one retired military man lasted one day, kept me reasonably informed and supplied, and from time to time would put me together with my fellow J. Appleseeds in Ohio and Indiana. In the Buckeye State, Bob Longsworth, a retired school superintendent, was having good fortune that was comparable to my own. Not so in Indiana, where a series of state directors failed to demonstrate either talent or progress. But CSFA was moving ahead in late 1967 and early 1968 with the number of Dollars for Scholars chapters of record approaching 250 and local awards approaching $1.5 million.

The national CSFA office facilities were not to be envied. Northeastern University had provided, at President Asa Knowles's request, three adjacent and connecting rooms in an old pharmaceutical factory at 43 Leon Street. The building was scheduled for eventual demolition to make room for either a new football field or the long-embattled, cross-city connector of Interstate Highway 95. Neither was ever realized.

The national office work force consisted of Mr. Walker and two secretaries, Inez "Sita" Levy and Kay Gressel. None of the three dared to wear light-colored clothing, because no amount of cleaning could remove decades of dirt and soot from the sills, floors, and walls. But beyond the dark patina of the high-grime offices and the high-crime neighborhood, CSFA was enjoying reasonably good times. When Gene Struckhoff resigned his chairmanship after four years, he had, in his usual visionary fashion, provided for his replacement. In the early 1960s Struck's Orr and Reno law firm represented in New Hampshire, Carling Brewing Company then of Cleveland, Ohio. Carling was in the process of successfully defending an antitrust case in the federal district court in Concord. William B. "Brad" Norris, Carling's vice president-legal and secretary, had come east to retain Mr. Struckhoff's firm in connection with the dispute. Struck had, in fact, met Brad Norris earlier through their common interest in the Unitarian Universalist Church.

Struck was impressed with Brad, who like Nelson Smart was graying, tall, handsome, and in this case, prototypical of corporate lawyer demeanor. In the course of their professional relationship Struck reminded Brad of a Roger Williams-hosted dinner in Boston where they both heard for the first time the story of the Fall River optometrist's community scholarship program. He then recruited Attorney Norris to join the new CSFA Board of Trustees.

Brad proved to be an enthusiastic board member. Early in 1967 on one occasion of great importance to me, he, on very short notice, flew in from Cleveland to Bangor, Maine, to speak at one of my Maine project collegiate dinners. He had also given time to the successful negotiations with the Kettering Foundation, and at one point convinced his employer to provide CSFA with literally tons of promotional items without reference either to the sponsor or its product. Brad also encouraged his company in 1961 to provide the first ever, one thousand dollar corporate annual sustaining grant to the CSFA national office. Over the ensuing years Carling's total support would exceed $25,000.

Given that CSFA's thirty-four member board at that time was still heavy on name recognition but light on participation, Brad Norris stood out among the gallant few who gave serious time, counsel, and service to CSFA. In April of 1967 he was by all counts--appearance, dedication, and persuasive powers--a logical choice for the second chairman of the board.

His persuasive powers were particularly impressive. He talked me into doing something I had no intention of doing. My regional director contract with CSFA was scheduled to expire on June 30, 1968. By the first of March I was naturally pursuing and considering other opportunities. During the evening of Friday, March 15, following my return from a Maine community some 400 miles distant, the telephone rang in our Alexandria, New Hampshire, apartment. The caller was Dan Walker. Dan advised me that he had just announced his resignation as CSFA's executive director in order that he might take a position in Yale University's development office. Dan asked if I might be interested in his job. I answered flatly "no thank you" and wished him well.

Within the hour the telephone rang again. The caller this time was Brad Norris. He was, he said, in Boston as a member of the Continental Board of the Unitarian Universalist Association. He asked if I would be willing to drive down to Boston, a distance of well over 100 miles, to talk with him about the executive directorship.

"Tonight?" I asked.

"Well, yes," he replied, because he would be scheduled in meetings on church business all day Saturday.

"Brad," I said, "I have just driven four hundred miles; I'm tired; and I'm not at all interested in the job."

"Well," he said, "we ought to at least talk about it. How about some other time this weekend?"

"Brad," I said, "I've been away all week; I need my weekend, and I'm not interested in the job. A trip to Boston would be a waste of my time and yours."

"Well," he continued, "how about if I stay over until Monday, so that you can at least talk to me on a business day?"

I was, of course, very much aware of the great demands on Mr. Norris's time, and for him to spend another unscheduled day away from Cleveland was a sacrifice indeed. "Okay," I said, and we agreed to meet at the Harvard Club at 10:00 a.m. on Monday. The meeting did not go for me as I had planned.

"Why don't you want this job?" he asked.

"Because I have a firm offer of a job in Maine that pays $3,000 more than I'm now making."

"We'll raise that offer by $1,500," he countered.

"I hate Boston. I would rather drive one hundred miles every day in Maine, than one mile a day in Boston." I knew from experience that either trip could take about the same amount of time.

"You won't need to be here every day. Plan your time so that you average only two or three days in the city a week."

"I like living in New Hampshire. My home in Alexandria is too much of a commute to Boston."

"Find a place closer to Massachusetts. We'll pay your moving and resettlement costs."

"I've worn out two cars on this job already. I can't afford to wear out another one."

"We'll lease you a company vehicle."

"Oh," I said.

I remained for the moment unconvinced. Then Brad played his final card. "Well," he said with some resignation, "if you won't take it, I guess we'll have to offer it to your counterpart in Indiana."

"You wouldn't!" I retorted. "That would never work."

"What choice do we have?" Brad asked contritely. "Bob Longsworth certainly won't leave Ohio."

I left Boston after lunch as CSFA's third or fourth executive director, and with a feeling in my stomach much akin to the one I experienced fifteen months earlier on the morning I first turned my Tempest toward Skowhegan, Maine.

Because my "promotion" was to be effective on July 1, 1968, I had time to finish up my assignments in northern New England. Chief among them was a commitment I made to CSFA to raise funds in the region sufficient to sustain operations there for another three or four years. The target sum was $100,000. Both the Spaulding-Potter Trusts in New Hampshire and the Agnes M. Lindsay Trust in Boston were sufficiently impressed with our progress to date to together provide $90,000 toward the objective. Smaller gifts, however, ranging from $500 to $5,000 were sought from companies and individuals throughout Maine, New Hampshire, and Vermont. Harry A. Rosenberg of Claremont, New Hampshire, one of CSFA's newer trustees, helped me to create a "request" formula for companies of various sizes, and he would often accompany me on the calls. Our appeals were surprisingly well received, and by the end of June our New England office account stood at one hundred and fourteen thousand dollars.

This success proved to be very important to me. It marked my professional debut as a fund raiser, a vocation I had earlier spurned in Morehead, Kentucky. I have said oftentimes since that I never trained to be one; I just woke up one morning and was one. And of greater, yet unforeseen, importance I was shortly to learn as I assumed the executive directorship of Citizens' Scholarship Foundation of America that despite the national office's apparent good fiscal health, debilitating financial illness was just over the clouded horizon.

During the Struckhoff years CSFA enjoyed five sources of support. The first was annual dues income from the two hundred or so CSFA Dollars for Scholars chapter affiliates. And while not all chapters paid on time, or at times at all, CSFA could budget annually about $10,000 from this source. An additional $2,000 or so resulted from sales of the promotional items--bumper stickers, posters, coin holders, and the like--provided gratis by Carling Brewing Company. The third source was modest "sustaining" grants from national corporations.

Such unrestricted gifts, averaging about $1,250 each, originated in 1968 with Carling Brewing Company, S&H Foundation, Sinclair Oil Corporation, General Electric Foundation, American Can Company, Time, Inc., and a smattering of others. Collectively, these sustaining grants provided just under $10,000 in support of national operations.

CSFA, as is true of many nonprofit organizations, also benefited from a fourth source of support, "unrealized expenses," including voluntary legal and accounting services provided by certain board members, together with Northeastern University's *de facto* rent subsidy, and a steep discount from CSFA's auditor, Arthur Andersen and Company.

Fully one third, however, of each $30-$40,000 annual national office budget was funded through the fifth source: indirect cost recovery and administrative "take downs" from private foundation-funded state and regional Dollars for Scholars development projects. In 1967, the final Dan Walker year, overhead recovery was scheduled with project grants in place provided by The Lilly Endowment, the Kettering Foundation, the Spaulding-Potter Charitable Trusts, and the Agnes M. Lindsay Fund. What I did not know in the spring of 1968, as I reviewed the audited financial statements for 1967, was that two of the statewide projects--Ohio and Indiana--would terminate on schedule in 1968. Neither did I know that no proposals of any real promise were then under consideration for Dollars for Scholars projects in any other region or state. Nor did I know that the Kettering Foundation had never been formally approached on the question of an "administrative allowance," or that the authorized overhead recovery provision in the original Lindsay grant for Maine was moot, because the CSFA board was so taken with the momentum of the project that *it* had authorized deficit spending for the project in the amount of $9,000. I, in fact, in my own naiveté, did not know enough to know that I should know.

These circumstances were compounded by the fact that no provision had been either suggested or made by the

"You're allergic to your job," he said.

"That's terrible," I reacted.

"No it's not," he assured me, "it's very encouraging. Think about it. Other people who suffer with this kind of stress end up with ulcers, severe depression, or even heart trouble. We can easily control your problem with over-the-counter drugs."

Was that news good news? Well that news was the best news I had that spring. I learned that a cure for the woes of Citizens' Scholarship Foundation of America was a probable cure for the ills of its executive director. The search for an antidote would require seven years, hundreds of antihistamine tablets, and several thousand facial tissues.

Brad Norris was not, of course, oblivious to or detached from the prevailing situation. He would once a month or so fly in from Cleveland to New York City principally on Carling business, and he would set aside a day or two with the blessings of his employer, to make fund-raising calls with me in Manhattan. He knew, as did I, that the corporate call is at best a difficult undertaking. Perhaps the competitive level of fund raising today has made the process even more challenging, but it was certainly difficult enough in the late 1960s and early 1970s. Armed with information available from the Council for Financial Aid to Education and the then New York-based Council on Foundations, I would, well in advance of our New York rendezvous, draft what I hoped were attention-getting letters addressed to two dozen or so of New York City's corporate "philanthropoids" (a term coined, I believe, by J. Moreau Brown then of General Electric Foundation). Following a respectable interval of ten days or so, I would call the office of each corporate contributions officer and request an appointment. With any luck fifteen or twenty telephone calls would result in three or four appointments.

At first I found this ratio disappointing and discouraging, but I later learned from Helen Brown, who served for many years as executive director of CBS Foundation, that she received upwards of five hundred letters a week, and everybody wanted an appointment.

The most difficult trick for me was to cluster appointments. The objective, utilizing the old Struckhoff standard, was four in one day. Clustered appointments would minimize expenses and limit my time in New York, a city at that time I detested even more than I abhorred Boston. But even with appointments granted, Citizens' Scholarship Foundation of America was a tough sell in New York in 1969. No one questioned the value of the Dollars for Scholars program and its positive impact on predominantly white, middle class, rural and suburban communities. Everyone was impressed with the fact that every dollar spent organizing or supporting local, volunteer-centered Dollars for Scholars chapters would stimulate twenty dollars or more in actual scholarship dollars for local residents. But in 1969 and 1970 many of America's cities were literally on fire. Midtown Manhattan's *Fortune 500* corporations were trying to quell the conflagrations with buckets of cash poured on neighborhoods north of 116th Street. Our neighbor-to-neighbor, help-build-a-barn type program seemed quite remote compared to the consequences of the smoke visible from the upper stories of every corporate building on Sixth Avenue.

We were not without some success. Ten calls would usually produce one grant of between $1,500 and $2,500 with an implied promise of support for three or more years. "Getting on the list" was all important, Moreau Brown had advised us. "Someone might forget to take you off." And while my dominant impression of those times in New York consists of wet feet in dirty slush and snow on cold and windy February days, and $22 nights at the then dreary Edison Hotel in the noisy West Side theater district, CSFA did find new friends and backers with the likes of Continental Can Company, Avon Products Foundation, IBM, Martin Marietta, Uniroyal, and American Airlines. The resulting income was not nearly enough in the aggregate to balance the deficit budget, but when each check arrived, CSFA's two employees were certain to be paid, and Mr. Black received a bit more than he had the month before.

The Edison Hotel brings to mind a story worth sharing: "The Day I Met Charlotte Fradkin." Brad Norris was not the only member of the CSFA board willing to make calls with me in New York. Among the three or four trustees who were predisposed to such activity was the most inspired of all, CSFA president and founder, Dr. Irving A. Fradkin. I had, of course, in 1967 and 1968 spent many hours with Dr. Fradkin both in Maine and within the confines of CSFA board and Executive Committee meetings. I was in 1969 still somewhat in awe of a man who had been written up, not once, but *twice* in the *Reader's Digest.* We agreed to meet for lunch one April noon at the Edison Hotel.

If I came to enjoy anything at all in New York, it was dining in the now defunct Cattle Baron Restaurant just off the hotel's lobby. In great contrast to the majority of Manhattan dining establishments, this restaurant actually welcomed solitary, itinerant business people and would from time to time delight the lonely diner with a complimentary appetizer or an after-dinner drink.

Irving in the face of his own frugality may well have introduced me to the hotel and its dining room, for he, no doubt, had suggested the meeting place. The plan was for me to have lunch with Dr. Fradkin and Charlotte before he and I called on two or three companies in the afternoon. I was dressed to impress favorably both the corporate folks and the Mrs. Doctor Fradkin. I wore my first and only $135 Hart, Schaffner, and Marx suit. With introductions behind us, we were seated at our table, Irving on my right; Charlotte to my left. She, in some contrast to her husband, is soft-spoken and demure; and the total petite package under the light brown curls and incandescent blue eyes, weighed, I would guess, just a fraction over or under one hundred pounds. After we placed our orders, I shifted my head, arms, and upper torso to the left in order to engage Charlotte in conversation. This minor gymnastic raised my left elbow plus-or-minus six inches above the table surface. In this posture leaning to port I did not see the waiter to starboard arrive with the entrees. Nor did I see him place my selection just to the right of my right elbow. So, when I shifted back to perhaps say something eloquent to Irving, the elbow to luncheon plate trajectory became fixed and I buried my right elbow to a height of approximately three inches in a generous serving of lasagna.

Tomato proves a stubborn stain, all the more difficult I would suggest if the stain is massive and on one's only suit. But in my favor was the fact that the suit in question was predominantly brown, so tomato and ricotta on the right sleeve proved not terribly distracting. During the afternoon I learned how to sit with my arms folded in such a way that my left hand concealed my right elbow.

For anyone, save the uninitiated from New Hampshire, the debacle should have ended with the final appointment of the afternoon. But Irving had planned a night out in New York. He told me at lunch that we would go to "someplace really nice" for dinner and that he had "twofers" for the theater later in the evening. The "someplace nice" turned out to be the dining room at the Sheraton West-Side Hotel, where Irving had discount coupons for dinner. I from the country was impressed. Red velvet draped the walls and marvelously set off the several suits of armor stationed around the room. In honoring the spirit of the evening I placed no restraint on my gustatory experience and culinary knowledge. I ordered roast beef.

Everything associated with the meal was served with a flair, including the sour cream for the baked potato. This condiment was presented by the waiter in a silver tureen and served with a long-handled silver ladle. The ceremony of the sour cream required him to fill the ladle to overflowing, and then with a flourish some several inches above my plate, to plop the contents in the center of the split, steaming and waiting potato. He did so, and I was appropriately awed. I was also a bit puzzled, because the volume of the ladle did not readily compute with the amount of the white substance on the potato. Where had the rest of it gone? The question was shortly answered by a wet sensation on my right knee. I looked down to find a trail of sour cream originating there and terminating in my right shoe.

I did not join Irving and Charlotte for the theater that evening. I returned to the Edison Hotel and worked at my second suit-salvage session of the day. These two events further reinforced my negative attitude--no matter how fleeting--toward life and times in New York City.

In the meantime Brad Norris was doing a little business on his own in downtown Boston. We came to realize early on that either Boston learned from Texas, or Texas learned from Boston, the art of provincial philanthropy. Few if any of the foundations or corporations within Boston's city limits felt any obligation to distribute charitable dollars to organizations that benefited the deserving beyond the

Route 128 beltline. But members of that Brahmin community were more than happy to provide referrals to other possible sources of support, say perhaps in Cleveland.

In something of a reverse twist, Brad from Cleveland was in Boston seeking some local support for CSFA's national office. That office, by the way, was no longer on Northeastern's campus. I convinced the board's Executive Committee in May of 1969 to permit me to move the office ten miles west to Waltham, and unfortunately, two blocks west of Route 128. Brad had been understandably reticent in agreeing to the move because he felt our Boston address was important to our fund-raising efforts. He was somewhat assuaged when the Waltham postal authorities permitted us to use the 195 West Street mailing address, followed by Boston, MA, followed by a Waltham zip code, 02154. CSFA occupied four rooms on the second floor of a white-frame building that bordered a nature preserve. Because our "national" work force was down to two people, Sita Levy and myself, we were able to sublet one room to a manufacturer's rep and thereby offset in part our $190 a month rent.

The move to Waltham did not signal any improvement in CSFA's fiscal condition. Within the confines of the new offices I learned for the first time that a "fund balance" is not necessarily money. That revelation was disarming because some few months later, as I studied the Arthur Andersen report for 1969, I could not comprehend how my fund balance could be positive and my bank balance negative. Then someone, no doubt Bea Morse, our once-a-month compassionate bookkeeper, explained to me that the "fund balance" was all of our physical assets, including the Dollars for Scholars trademark, carried at its 1968 purchase price of $3,000. Because our office furniture--World Wars I and II relics all--was carried at allowable, but probably somewhat inflated value, the balance sheet looked deceptively encouraging with literally no money in the till.

CSFA's Board of Trustees in the fall of 1969, was in somewhat better shape with thirty-seven members of record. The true working crew numbered about half of the twelve members of the Executive Committee. Other than Brad Norris, five were community volunteers still serving their local Dollars for Scholars programs. We made some progress in adding more readily recognized names to the board. Among the additions were J. Moreau Brown, associate secretary of the General Electric Foundation; James M. Cass, education editor of *The Saturday Review of Literature;* Robert S. Hatfield, senior executive vice president of Continental Can Company; Clarence E. Lovejoy, editor of *Lovejoy's College Guide*; Rexford G. Moon, Jr. of the Academy for Educational Development; Roger Mudd of CBS News, and Dr. Vernon Alden, chairman of the Boston Company. Vern Alden was one of the "you-can-call-on-me-once-in-a-while," variety of trustee, and Brad Norris in 1969 had decided to do so. Brad was seeking Dr. Alden's counsel on the survival of Citizens' Scholarship Foundation of America. Vern had earlier put CSFA on to a Boston-based trust that by virtue of its early 1900s governing documents could not make grants in excess of $200. The trust managers were stymied at the prospect of having to make twenty or more separate awards until CSFA suggested the grants be apportioned among the then forty or so Dollars for Scholars chapters in Massachusetts.

On this particular day Vern was advising Brad of two situations in separate cities. He said he knew a certain Jim Lipscomb back in (you guessed it) Cleveland, Ohio, who was president of the George Gund Foundation, and who might, if properly motivated, encourage his foundation to provide support for CSFA. He said he also knew a young guy in Washington by the name of Bob Gale, who with a few other fellow Peace Corps retirees, all in their late twenties, had started Gale Associates, a new fund-raising counseling firm. "Perhaps," Vern suggested, "CSFA should try to tie Gund to Gale and launch a national campaign." Brad took the suggestion to heart, returned to Cleveland, convinced the Gund Foundation to "guarantee" up to $25,000 in campaign costs, and CSFA retained Gale Associates for that purpose.

Now, in the absence of a clear survival plan, CSFA almost appeared to have one. By today's textbook capital campaign standards the approach appeared reasonably erudite. Brad Norris arranged for a loan of $25,000 from the First National Bank of Cleveland, Ohio. The loan was secured by the "Gund Guarantee." I and a few core trustees kept after the New York corporations. Thad Seymour and I also returned to Indianapolis to visit with John Lynn at The Lilly Endowment to encourage him to cover the $20,000 shortfall in the fiscal 1970 national operating budget. Local Dollars for Scholars chapters were encouraged to provide modest, one-time grants to the national office. And we had Gale Associates in place to pursue the long-term survival of CSFA.

The "plan" almost worked. Corporate grants increased slightly. The Lilly Endowment sent the twenty thousand dollars. A few Dollars for Scholars chapters of long standing sent in modest gifts. But survival campaigns are almost always doomed to fail. I recall a meeting with a company officer in New York where after Brad Norris and I told the wonderful Irving A. Fradkin story, I said, "if companies like yours don't help us, we won't survive."

"Show us you can survive," the officer replied, smiling, "and we might help you."

At the time that mandate had overtones of a cruel paradox, but in later years I came to accept the notion that corporate philanthropy generally prefers to ride with winners. No appeal with any substance or chance for success can be predicated on a negative. Neither is *status quo* a growth industry.

The Gund-guaranteed $25,000 campaign war chest was quickly consumed, and at the time the campaign was out of steam and out of money and unofficially over, CSFA looked essentially the same as it had at the outset. Gale Associates, too, barely survived the experience, and shortly thereafter was not to survive at all. Both outcomes were not for lack of trying, and some good came out of the combined effort. One such outcome in public relations was the publication of "The Other 90%," the first professionally developed report on CSFA and its Dollars for Scholars program. Even by today's "high-tech" publications standards "The Other 90%" is a quality piece. The design and layout were provided at no cost by Harold Cabot and Company of Boston, not so coincidentally a public relations firm that did business with Carling Brewing Company. The title originated with an inside-front-cover article on Irving Fradkin that appeared in the December 1965 issue of the *Reader's Digest*. The article was a rare follow-on to "The Fall River Plan" story in 1962. "The Other 90%," a sixteen-page, black-and-white, eight-inch by eleven-inch publication, would serve as CSFA's only available promotional centerpiece for nearly ten more years.

A second favorable outcome was a renewed and closer connection with an important news personality who, up until the campaign, was merely a name on the trustees' listing. Gale Associates had assigned Michael Valentine to the CSFA account. Michael was a curly-haired, athletically-structured, highly-motivated, self-confident person. One evening on a Northeast Airlines flight from Washington, DC, to Boston, Michael recognized a passenger in the First Class section. Michael left his seat in coach, went forward and sat down beside Roger Mudd. Roger remembered very little about CSFA. He had agreed some years earlier to lend his name to the organization as a special favor to his friend Thaddeus Seymour of Dartmouth College. Thad had been one of CSFA's early champions and an ally of Gene Struckhoff in New Hampshire.

Michael gave Roger a quick reorientation on CSFA and asked if he would be willing to help in some small way with the campaign. Roger said maybe, and tentatively agreed to meet with Brad Norris and me in Washington ahead of any final decision on his part. Brad and I remember the evening well. We met Roger Mudd in the lobby of the Washington Sheraton Hotel and found our way downstairs to the Kon Tiki Restaurant. As we entered the dining room Brad recalls the following scenario: "The maitre d' in an effort to make big points with a luminary he obviously recognized, unctuously exclaimed, 'Why good evening, Mr. Kalb.' Among the three of us, Roger was the most amused."

Roger agreed to give CSFA what time he could. He agreed to being named national chairman of the campaign. He further agreed to appear on CSFA's behalf at two luncheons one each in Boston and New York. In each instance we were moderately successful in gaining corporation and foundation representation. He also appealed to his own employer's corporate charitable foundation and successfully encouraged what proved to be over the next ten years, a $50,000 relationship with CBS Foundation. But that $5,000 annual CBS grant represented 50 percent of the net campaign results, and when Brad

Norris resigned his chairmanship in the fall of 1971, no one could say with any assurance that CSFA would survive the term of his successor.

Looking back at CSFA's first capital campaign, Brad today relates with humor his follow-up meeting with Jim Lipscomb at the Gund Foundation.

> When I sat down with Jim in Cleveland, I told him I had both good news and bad news. The bad news, I explained, is reflected in the final report on the campaign. The receipts did not even cover the campaign's expenses. But the good news is that the payment of the Gund Foundation guarantee qualified Gund for a singular honor. Gale Associates had advised CSFA to establish donor categories, and I was pleased to advise Jim Lipscomb that the $25,000 surrender payment qualified the Gund Foundation to be at the time the only "Lifetime Member of CSFA."

In retrospect Brad did more during his term than either he or any of us realized. In addition to his determined pursuit of financial support, he secured for CSFA and on a no-cost basis, the services of the Washington-based law firm Cushman, Darby and Cushman, perhaps the most prestigious patent and trademark firm in the country. This firm, and the relationship with it, in the person of Attorney James M. Dooley, has lasted until this day. Mr. Dooley represented one of those "unrealized expense" items in that he voluntarily registered CSFA's three trademarks and helped CSFA to successfully battle occasional trademark infringements, especially the unauthorized use of the more popular trademark, "Dollars for Scholars."

Brad added to my personal professional managerial skills as well. He informed me early on that I was free to bring any problem to his attention, but at the same time I was required also to bring "at least one possible solution." "We may or may not adopt that solution," he said, "but the best executives always think beyond the problem." He also taught me the technique of "permission by exception." In one instance where no clear provision had been made relative to an overhead charge on the administration of a project grant, Brad advised me to write to the foundation in question and use the language of exception: "Unless I hear from you to the contrary, I will assume CSFA is authorized to assess an administrative charge of 10 percent against the grant." No response was all the response required. The auditors were, of course, a bit apprehensive, but at a time of desperation I felt absolved, and I have ever since.

Chapter Six

A Lesson from the Holocaust

Of all the people I came to know during my early years with Citizens' Scholarship Foundation of America, the one for whom I developed the greatest affection was Harry A. Rosenberg of Claremont, New Hampshire. Harry was the short, balding, rather swarthy, gruff and stocky, president of K-Ross Building Supply. His company was located in Lebanon, New Hampshire, another mill town near the Vermont border, halfway between the Massachusetts state line and Canada.

Harry actually bridges my experiences as northern New England director and executive director of CSFA. He, even before my directorship, had been active with the promotion of Dollars for Scholars in New Hampshire and had served as the first president of the Claremont Dollars for Scholars chapter. Harry today speaks fondly of this city of 12,000 just inland of the Connecticut River valley.

Claremont has always been a poor town; very poor in 1962 and perhaps by comparison, poorer still today. But one real source of pride in the early '60s was the success of its Dollars for Scholars program, maybe the first north of Massachusetts. The chapter galvanized the community. In fact on one weekend each year the priests, ministers, and rabbis would urge their respective congregations to give generously to the local scholarship program. We were so successful that our chapter was used as testimony in the proposal for the "New Hampshire Dollars for Scholars Project" submitted to the Spaulding-Potter Charitable Trusts.

When I first met Harry in 1967 he, in his mid-forties, was serving as volunteer chairman of Citizens' Scholarship Foundation of New Hampshire. This statewide organization had been very active in promoting Dollars for Scholars during the time of the Spaulding-Potter grant. Then, during my regional tenure of 1967-1968 when my responsibilities in New Hampshire were mostly of the chapter maintenance and cheerleader variety, Harry was willing and even anxious to help me with evening chapter start-up activities in Maine and Vermont. And I knew by then that in approaching a new community, my having along an experienced, committed, and knowledgeable volunteer provided a mighty asset for getting things done. No one in the new community was going to be asked to do half as much as Harry was already doing. Harry was my model volunteer, and in that capacity he accompanied me on many long evenings by car to remote locations in Northern New England. On the way to and from those destinations, I learned a great deal about Harry and a good deal about life.

Harry told me that in 1937, his parents, in fearful anticipation of the horrors to come, sent him at the age of fifteen from Germany to the United States of America. He had been directed specifically to Claremont in west central New Hampshire because the climate there was "most like that left behind in Cologne." His first job as a young man in this country was selling wristwatches and household goods to men who worked in the remote logging camps. "The men," he said "were able to buy the watches on time, so after I sold one, I would have to return every week after payday to collect another fifty cents from the lumberjacks."

Harry's second job was selling dresses door-to-door in the city of Claremont and in surrounding towns. "I learned by selling dresses," he said "that sales is all in the law of averages. Make enough calls, you'll get enough business." He may well have had other jobs during and immediately following the war years, but within that mix he did two things that impress me to this day.

The first involved a lovely, young Dutch woman named Liesel. In her childhood in Europe Liesel Kaufmann had known Harry Rosenberg. Harry was, in fact, the only person she knew who had emigrated to the United States. She had spent her late teen years in an attic in the Hague and had "come out at age twenty wearing the same clothes she had on when she went in four years before." She somehow located Harry and wrote to him seeking his sponsorship. He agreed and then married Liesel two weeks after she arrived in New Hampshire.

The second noteworthy event transpired in 1959 when Harry purchased a small structural steel company that had come on the market in Lebanon, New Hampshire. When he shared that story with me I said "Harry, you sold watches and dresses, what in the world did you know about structural steel?" Harry laughed.

> I didn't know a damn thing about structural steel or any kind of steel, but I knew one thing, and it has never failed

me. The only thing a salesman has to sell is service, nothing else. Somebody else has the same goods as the first guy, and maybe cheaper. When I began in the steel business, if I said the steel would be on the job site Monday at seven in the morning, it was always there. People will pay for reliable service. If anyone was dissatisfied with my product, I hurried to replace it, and I threw in a few extras and discounted the cost. I never tried to be the lowest bidder, just the smartest and most reliable. It almost always worked.

I asked Harry if he inherited the company name along with the purchase of the building and inventory. "No," he said and smiled. "K-Ross is made up of parts of Liesel's and my last names. For some reason in New Hampshire in 1939, I thought it was a better choice than "Rosenberg's" Building Supply.

I later learned from others that Harry gave of his own resources one thousand dollars a year to each of the Dollars for Scholars chapters in Claremont and Lebanon. On the strength of his total commitment, in late 1967 I suggested Harry for CSFA's Board of Trustees. Shortly after his election in November, he was named treasurer of the national organization. Harry was the person who in CSFA's bleakest hours would send a personal check to cover the payroll. I once asked him why he was so committed personally and financially to CSFA and Dollars for Scholars. He said simply, "I never want to happen in this country what happened in Nazi Germany. Dollars for Scholars makes a community look at all of its people and care for the welfare of everyone. Education is part of the answer, but caring is more important. Caring is what makes this country free."

Chapter Seven

Charity Begins Closer to Home

Little lights can cast long shadows. And at times the shadows obscure the promise of the light. So it was with Citizens' Scholarship Foundation of America in 1970. Without question the national foundation was at its crossroads with no direction clear. The national office had all it could do to produce and distribute four newsletters a year to its 238, and declining, community scholarship programs. In the absence of any state or regional funding beyond the dwindling resources in Northern New England, the number of new community Dollars for Scholars chapters could not outpace, on an annual basis, those fragile chapters lost through attrition. And even when the national office became aware of an existing or impending difficulty with one of its affiliates, unless that chapter was within short driving distance of southern New Hampshire or Waltham, Massachusetts, no remedial assistance could be provided.

On May 20, 1970, Brad Norris called a special meeting of CSFA's twelve-member Executive Committee at the Waltham office to consider if CSFA should cease to exist as a national nonprofit corporation. Brad had, a few days ahead of the meeting, directed a letter to all forty or so members of the Board of Trustees. In it Brad addressed the irony of the value of the organization as compared to its fiscal plight.

> The CSFA budget ending June 30, 1970, called for approximately $49,000, but economies have been necessary, and we will end the year spending approximately $41,000 in total. It may well be that additional contributions may come in between now and June 30, but at the present time it appears that our total income for this twelve month period will be approximately $28,000. You can see that at the present time it looks as though we will be closing this current year with a $13,000 deficit and realistic planning forces us to consider a $16,000 deficit for the coming twelve months. It is anomalous that at a time when many of our chapters are stronger than ever, and CSFA is generally regarded as one of the most exciting agencies on the American scene, that we find ourselves in financial difficulties forcing us to go on a hand-to-mouth existence... We must put this financial house in order so as to insure the potential that exists in this idea, originally born by the farsighted Irving Fradkin.

Brad's letter went on to spell out the need for short-term support originating hopefully from the board itself, and the need for a longer-term "endowment fund drive" that would permit CSFA to secure its operating budget "out of income each year."

The Executive Committee, with barely a quorum present, deliberated the condition of the "agency" and the contents of Brad's letter and took a curious course of action: it voted raises for its three employees, including the current New England regional director. The committee also encouraged Brad to continue his negotiations with the George Gund Foundation in Cleveland in an effort to secure a $25,000 guarantee of expenses for an envisioned endowment campaign.

The year-end figures at June 30, 1970, softened Brad's dire prediction, but not by much. Income of just over $34,000 was six thousand dollars better than expected. But expenses approaching $44,000 were also some three thousand dollars over his projection. The result was a deficit of just under $10,000, which as a portion of the operating budget equaled 23 percent. This deficit followed hard on a 1969 shortfall of just over $12,000. All reserves were depleted. Outstanding bank loans totaled $5,000. The organization's fund balance--made up chiefly of furniture and equipment, promotional supplies, trademark value, and fixtures--showed an accumulated negative balance of $3,153. CSFA was most certainly broke, but, though no one knew it at the time, not irretrievably broken.

At some point between the May 1970 meeting and those discouraging, end-of-fiscal-year statements, the telephone rang. The caller, thankfully, was not one of CSFA's creditors seeking a portion of the $9,000 in accounts payable; nor was it the "angel of endowment," who never appears when the need is greatest, but shows up rather when times are great. The caller was another angel of sorts, the angel of inspiration. I picked up the telephone.

"Citizens' Scholarship Foundation," I said cautiously, expecting a demand for payment. "Good morning. This is Joe Phelan."

"Hi," came the ebullient reply. "This is Jean Hennessey of the New Hampshire Charitable Fund. How are you?"

"Fine," I equivocated.

"Great," she exclaimed, "you and I just have to get together. This tax reform stuff is really going to be terrific for both of us. Don't you think?"

Well I did think, but not much about tax reform. My knowledge at the time of the federal Tax Reform Act of 1969 was confined to my ongoing efforts to prove to my contributors' satisfaction that CSFA was not a "private foundation" as described in Section 509(a) of the Internal Revenue Service Code. No final guidelines were available at the time, and I was, in fact, uncertain if Section 509(a) described a private foundation or the exception.

"Uh, yes," I said, and we set a date.

In the spring of 1970 the New Hampshire Charitable Fund was housed in a small, colonial-red home on School Street in Concord, New Hampshire. Jean, the Charitable Fund's second executive director, succeeded one Eugene C. Struckhoff. Struck had built this state-wide community foundation in 1972 on the strength of a $2 million grant from the dissolving Spaulding-Potter Charitable Trusts.

Jean L. Hennessey radiates enthusiasm. To be in her presence is to be caught up with her fervor, imagination, and sense of humor. A woman of somewhat "mature proportion," as described in today's fashion catalogs, Jean often pauses in her animation, removes her eyeglasses, and brushes a lock of brown hair away from her forehead. As we visited in her office that morning, she said: "I think that lots of small, and maybe not so small, foundations and trusts will no longer want to stay in business."

Jean explained to me that while the federal tax reform act intended to restrict and monitor the charitable activities of a small number of presumed miscreant major private foundations, the rules and regulations blanketed nearly all private foundations and would make life very difficult for a number of well-intentioned people. She also explained that in New Hampshire a goodly number of moderate-size and smaller foundations and trusts awarded scholarships as a principal activity. She then noted that both the New Hampshire Charitable Fund and Citizens' Scholarship Foundation of America were exempt from the provisions of the federal legislation, and maybe under some cooperative arrangement the two could provide relief for the as yet unwitting victims of tax reform.

Jean was right, of course, and our discussion that spring morning would eventually lead to the creation of the New Hampshire Charitable Fund Student Aid Program. This program, with assets today of over $12 million, is the largest single source of private student aid in New Hampshire.

The program began modestly enough. Jean and I approached the three trustees of the Concord-based John H. Pearson Trust, an entity that for more than fifty years had been awarding "honor loans" to New Hampshire residents.

"The list reads like *Who's Who* in New Hampshire," Jean said, "but the trustees have never had the capability of encouraging repayments. If we can assume management of the trust, we'll also get a pretty potent potential donor list." Jean explained to the Pearson trustees that the New Hampshire Charitable Fund planned to become a central repository for hundreds of scholarship and student loan funds. NHCF would, where practical, acquire the assets of participating private foundations and trusts, invest those assets, and then make funds available for annual distribution.

On cue from Jean, I explained that Citizens' Scholarship Foundation of America, would distribute, accept, and process applications originating with New Hampshire students. The process would be identical to the awards system utilized by our Dollars for Scholars chapters. The actual selection of recipients would be made by a volunteer advisory committee made up of New Hampshire citizens mutually agreed upon by NHCF and CSFA.

The Pearson trustees readily agreed to participate, and as a consequence we had our first $20,000 available for distribution in 1971. Jean and I then traveled together throughout the state holding evening forums for bank trust officers and other trustees of privately held funds. We also promoted the availability of the awards with high-school guidance officers, college financial aid officers, and the leadership of the twenty or so surviving New Hampshire-based Dollars for Scholars chapters.

In the early going our success in publicizing the availability of funds far outpaced our success in garnering more. As a result both Jean and I became concerned that the ratio of applications to awards would be disparate. And in view of the fact that we had to charge students a modest application processing fee--$2.50 for residents of Dollars for Scholars communities, and $3.50 for others--we were sensitive to the potential for criticism if we processed hundreds of applications but made only a handful of awards. One response to such criticism, Jean and I decided, would be to provide each applicant with some useful information on the availability of student aid beyond those funds administered by the Charitable Fund.

As is true of many other states, New Hampshire has available a directory of charitable trusts, together with other published information on local, county, and state-wide sources of student aid. CSFA, by virtue of the business it was in, was aware of many of the significant, national student aid initiatives, both public and private. Jean and I wondered if some method might exist to selectively provide this information to applicants for the

Pearson Trust and a handful of other funds. We were thinking even then about the potential of the computer to match eligible students with the requirements and restrictions of student aid funds.

I carried this notion to a very savvy man, Edward M. Shapiro, the president of New Hampshire College. The college is a private, proprietary, business-oriented school located in Manchester. Ed, in turn, called in a member of his faculty whose specialty was management information systems. William A. Hunzeker, or "William the Hun" in the eyes of his protegés, was fascinated with the proposition and offered to recruit his best students to work on the project. He volunteered his time, and said that my costs would be limited to small stipends for the students, data entry expenses, materials, and computer time.

I returned to Concord and talked again with Jean on the question of developing this student aid referral service without placing the burden of the costs on New Hampshire students. Because of the prevailing tenuous condition of CSFA's financial picture, I also insisted that any time I or my small staff put into the project would have to be on a paid-for basis. We agreed that the probable cost of developing the service would be in the range of $10,000 to $15,000. Jean agreed to approach the distributing directors of the Charitable Fund for a portion of those costs if I could find one or more co-funders. I was later successful in securing a $10,000 grant from United States Steel Foundation in Pittsburgh, and within a few months The New Hampshire Scholarship Locater Service was born.

Consistent with the development of most new computer software, the earliest versions were not without serious flaws. But because the developmental costs were not being borne by the Charitable Fund's student aid applicants, we had sufficient confidence in the information produced to provide it gratis to New Hampshire students. Later versions produced by the students at New Hampshire College became surprisingly accurate and reliable. We were dealing with only a few hundred aid sources with eligibilities limited to a handful of criteria--residence, high school attended, church affiliations, and the like. In using such criteria, we were able to provide a student, on average, with information on seven to ten other sources of aid that an applicant might choose to pursue.

While CSFA was focusing on the refinement of the Scholarship Locator Service software and data, Jean Hennessey was pursuing the dollar-volume growth of her student aid program. Jean, among all her other attributes, is a tenacious visionary. Beyond her idea that New Hampshire students would eventually be able to apply for multiple scholarships, grants, and loans through use of a single application and one set of references, Jean was among the first in New Hampshire or elsewhere to give special attention to the adult learner and the re-entering student. As early as 1971 she successfully sought funds that could be used by single parents pursuing short-term, certificate education programs, or longer-term, course-at-a-time baccalaureate programs. She established an emergency loan fund to respond to students of any age who encountered unexpected disasters--loss of a home by fire or flood, a death in the family, or abandonment by a spouse.

But Jean also realized in 1971 that her state and the nation would require new generations of philanthropists, not necessarily of the mogul variety, but rather people who would be willing or even anxious to give something back. She, like Irving Fradkin, believed that a scholarship recipient today was a potential donor tomorrow. "Those who are helped, will help," she said. "These people are the future of the New Hampshire Charitable Fund." I believe the years between 2001 and 2030 will prove her right.

Jean and I both recall with joy the heady experience of building the student aid program. We recall with laughter a letter from one of our selected recipients. The young lady in question was not given a scholarship but was offered a very-low-interest loan. She declined the offer by stating, "If God had wanted me to get loans rather than scholarships, He would not have made me this smart." Jean also recalls, with pleasure I'm certain, the persuasion she was to use toward the close of 1971 that would ultimately convince the trustees of CSFA to move Citizens' Scholarship Foundation of America in its entirety to New Hampshire. Jean wanted CSFA both as a tenant and a limited partner of the Charitable Fund. Her offers of a rent subsidy and a fees-for-services arrangement proved compelling to a CSFA Executive Committee that a few months earlier had unequivocally concluded that much more than a Boston mailing address was required for survival. But neither Jean nor I, nor any member of either governing board, foresaw in 1971 the incredible influence both the student aid program and the Scholarship Locater Service would have on the future of Citizens' Scholarship Foundation of America.

Chapter Eight

North to the Poles

On a map of Maine, published by the American Automobile Association, a legend reads: "Scenic highways designated with black dots on this map have been selected by AAA Road Reporters for their unusual interest." While this statement holds some ambiguity as to whether the roads are indeed scenic, or rather that the road reporters have unusual interests, as Road Reporters might well have, one thing is certain: neither the Maine Turnpike nor Interstate 95 carries any such designation. In fact, were I to have the privilege of placing a sign over the toll booths in York, just nine miles north of Maine's border with Portsmouth, New Hampshire, it would read: "Welcome to the Maine Turnpike: Please Spend Your Day on Monotony Way."

The turnpike and the interstate are one for a time, as the sometimes six lane, sometimes four lane highway cuts some three hundred miles from Kittery in the south to Houlton in the almost north. The only possible stimulation for the road traveler is an exercise of imagination, when, at some unmarked and indistinguishable point north of Portland, on a murky day or night, you may find yourself confused and disoriented after an off-turnpike relief stop in the uncharted and potentially harmful region identified by a Mr. Stephen King of Bangor as Jerusalem's Lot, Castle Rock, and Derry. But beyond that zone and the capital city of Augusta, located fifty-five miles north of Portland, the weary traveler can easily become mesmerized by Maine's ofttimes sparsely traveled highway and endless, rolling wooded landscape.

Another eighty-three miles finds the traveler in Orono, home of the University of Maine. From this point on in the late 1960s and throughout the 1970s, one hundred or more miles of the interstate were reduced, between construction intervals, to two-way lanes--a fact easily forgotten by the driver accustomed to cruising along in the passing lane of a four-lane highway. The sudden appearance of another vehicle, often a logging truck, in the oncoming lane was both confusing and confounding, at times with spectacular results. But up until 1981 when the last few miles just south of Houlton expanded to four lanes, a driver's attention and concentration were an absolute need but were nearly impossible to maintain.

Interstate 95, however, leads to one place of very unusual interest and discovery. The highway terminus is in Aroostook County, the largest defined land area in the State of Maine. The county encompasses the entire northern arc of the state, and its crescent border with Canada extends 250 miles. Aroostook County seems almost a country unto itself. Its people feel, with a sense of independent pleasure, somewhat isolated from the down-country Mainestream. The county's economy is vested in its plentiful forests, and in its sugar beet and potato fields. Its living schedule is agrarian. Spring is a time of frantic planting; summer a time of weeding, watering, and attending. The demands of the harvest up until the mid-1980s required students be released from school three weeks every fall to bring in the giant Aroostook potatoes. When the crop is safely in the huge barns ahead of the frost, the social season begins and continues throughout the winter.

The people of Aroostook County are, in contrast to some recent popular fiction, welcoming, caring, and independent. So despite the miles that separated this land mass from the rest of New England, Aroostook, or "The County" as the natives prefer, was viewed in 1967 and in years beyond as ground also fertile for Dollars for Scholars chapter development. This assessment proved to be accurate, and at one time no fewer than eight school districts in this rather sparsely populated territory were raising dollars for the futures of the county's young people.

During my year-and-one-half term as Northern New England regional director of CSFA, I had my share of pleasant times in northernmost Maine, including the winter when the snow banks on roads north of Caribou reached almost to the cross arms on the utility poles. But following my ascension to the executive directorship in 1968, I assigned Aroostook County to one of my three former Maine project field people. Following the completion of the project, Carl F. Brown of Portland was appointed New England regional director of CSFA. Carl was forty or so when I first met him in 1967. Tall, with thinning black hair, and for some good and positive reason, a man of perpetually rosy complexion, Carl was a vision as he packed his 200-pound frame into his tiny, black Volkswagen "bug." He always insisted that he had one black wool suit and one black car, and whenever I saw him, winter or summer, he was sporting both. The suit, surprisingly, was to remain in better repair than the Volkswagen that carried him from time to time the one hundred miles north beyond the interstate highway terminus at Houlton, Maine, into the heart of the county.

Carl was a wonderful worker. More given to task completion than to creative thinking, he would call me every Sunday evening to get his assignments. And he would then invariably carry them out. I often said that if I had decided to tell Carl on Sunday to see the governor of Maine on Monday, somehow he would have succeeded. His tenacity was only interrupted by his frequent encounters with a seasonal influenza or any other mildly debilitating condition that came along. He would every week, as required, dutifully submit his impressive progress reports. Once or twice a month, especially in the winter, his reports would make mention of an illness covering a span of two or three days. A brief entry would read: "In bed with a cold."

All reports on our progress in Maine in 1968 and 1969 were widely distributed within CSFA. Dollars for Scholars in Maine was still the hottest item on CSFA's agenda, and the trustees were fascinated with our progress both in the more populated areas and in the hinterlands. Carl's reports were oftentimes commented upon. So while I was not particularly surprised to receive from one of the trustees a returned set of Carl's reports with marginal notations, I was amused to see that Ralph Seifert had circled all of Carl's health-related entries and then added the bold question: "In bed with a cold *what*?"

Once every six weeks or so Carl and I would get together to evaluate things on a more personal basis. We would sometimes meet in Portland and sometimes in my home in New Hampshire. One Monday morning as he drove into my driveway, I noticed even before he rolled to a stop that his Volkswagen was beaten and battered. The car was a mass of dents, the windshield cracked, and a headlight broken. My first thought was that poor Carl had fallen asleep out on that great interstate highway and had rolled his car into the woods or a potato field. However, he appeared unscathed and in remarkably good spirits. "What happened?" I asked.

"Sugar beets," he responded.

"In a field?" I asked.

"Nope, on the road," he replied.

"*In* the road?" I questioned.

"Nope, *on* the road, " he repeated. "The tailgate on a dump truck came down." Carl had been bombarded by more than a ton of three-pound sugar beets.

While the sugar beet episode did not fracture either Carl or his enthusiasm for Dollars for Scholars, he would by the close of 1969 tire of the endless driving in northern New England. Carl left CSFA in early 1970 for other unknown-to-me pursuits. But in the summer of 1994, as I was driving south from Southport, Maine, I caught a news item on a Portland radio station. A certain Carl Brown of Portland had at age seventy successfully sued his employer on the question of age discrimination. This plaintiff had been awarded damages and had been reinstated in his position as a custodian. I wondered about this Carl Brown. The age was about right, and if it was the Carl I had known, his case was indeed probably just. He was, as noted, an incredible worker.

Carl, however, was not the only industrious CSFA regional director to experience the eccentricities and electricity of Aroostook County. Roger Leo Berlinguette, a true native of Manchester, New Hampshire, and CSFA's fourth New England regional director, would have a unique adventure of his own. Roger had taught school with me in

1964 and 1965 in Bristol, New Hampshire. His specialty was French, but he was also a member of my fragmented English department. We became good friends almost immediately upon his arrival, and because of that friendship, I almost overlooked him as a potential employee of CSFA. I harbored the seemingly logical philosophy that the surest way to destroy a friendship was to make a friend an employee. For that reason, when the regional position opened up in 1970 following Carl's departure, and Roger expressed an interest in it, our friendship became his liability and he was denied the job. When the position opened up again one year later, and again Roger expressed an interest, I called Chairman Norris and related my dilemma. Brad said his way of thinking was contrary to my own. Hiring a friend, he assured me, was a much smarter move than hiring a stranger. "Whom do you know better," he asked, "someone you've known for ten minutes or someone you have admired, respected, trusted, and whose company you have enjoyed for years?" When I then mentioned the risk of the loss of the friendship, Brad said simply: "Do what's best for the organization." I hired Roger.

The decision was best for CSFA. Roger, trim of frame with thinning hair, brought with him high energy, imagination, and the rarest of all commodities, common sense. He also brought another sense, that of humor--a quality that sustained us in the most trying times. One of eight children of French Canadian parents, he would at once express pride and amazement at his heritage. "In my neighborhood when I was growing up," he said, " you were expected to have accomplished three things by age sixteen. You were expected to quit school, go to work in the mill, and you were expected to get your first set of false teeth." On another occasion a few years later when we were able to add people to Roger's staff, he said: "Thank God. Now I'm a supervisor. My father could never understand what I did for a living as a 'regional director.' After he and my mother left vaudeville, almost all of his working years were in the Amoskeag Mills. He never heard of a regional director, but he knows what a *supervisor* is. Now when he asks me for the hundredth time what I do for a living, I can say: 'Dad, I'm a supervisor.' He'll say: 'That's good. My son is a supervisor.' Now he can tell all his friends at Dee Ann's Bar: 'You know what? My son Roger is a *supervisor*.' They'll all understand."

During CSFA's pre-computer years of the early 1970s Roger Berlinguette developed on five-by-eight note cards the methodology and procedures that today, in and among the microchips, help determine how recipients will be selected for CSFA-managed scholarship programs. As one of his many responsibilities, he oversaw the administration of CSFA's role with Jean Hennessey's New Hampshire Charitable Fund Student Aid Program. One day, while he was in the throes of reviewing applications for that program, he came into my office and said: "Here's one for you. A family with six kids on Manchester's West Side: Yvette, Babette, Nanette, Suzette, Bridgette, and...Roland." He dearly loved his heritage, and he expressed his affection at a time when soft ethnic humor was not regarded as malicious, degrading, or incorrect.

But as was true of regional directors before him and those now in greater abundance to follow, much of Roger's time was spent out on the road working with Dollars for Scholars chapters. CSFA had learned almost from the beginning that community volunteer fund-raising initiatives are fragile entities. The oftentimes inspired and spirited initial local leadership is sometimes followed by leadership by default--"I'll do it if no one else will." Default leadership is defective leadership. The weakest of leaders are often the last to acknowledge the need for help, or to seek it. The poorest of leaders are most likely to hold in disdain any prospect of "interference" from any "outside" source, and at times prefer dissolution to admission. And sometimes, even with the best of local leadership in place, the good folks giving of their time and other resources require and deserve the reinforcing praise, restimulating reassurance, and rejuvenating evangelism that sustains volunteers' endorphins at fission levels.

So Roger traveled throughout New England ministering to one hundred or more Dollars for Scholars chapters, including the eight in Aroostook County, Maine, some 400 miles from Roger's front door. While his visits to "The County" were infrequent, his experiences were nevertheless memorable. One in particular he delights in sharing.

> It must have been in the late fall of 1973. The potatoes were in the barns. You couldn't see anyone up there until they were. But my heritage was a definite asset in an area where every tenth man was nicknamed "Frenchy," so I had a relatively easy time in setting up appointments with the chapters. One evening I was in Caribou, about sixty miles south of where Route 1 enters the Canadian Province of New Brunswick. The chapter president, whose name I can't recall, worked for Maine Public Service Company. The utilities in Maine had been particularly helpful in introducing me and Dollars for Scholars to various cities and towns. We were chatting a few minutes before the local chapter meeting. He asked me if I was getting out to see any of the area sights. I said I really didn't know what to look for. He asked if I had ever visited a potato farm. I hadn't, and I said so. He said: "If you're interested, I'll call a friend of mine tonight and see if we can go out to his place tomorrow morning. I think you'll be impressed."

Well considering the entertainment options, it sounded like a pretty good deal, and we agreed to meet at seven the next morning. He picked me up with the morning frost still glistening on his white company van, and we headed out into the rolling countryside. At one juncture where we were running parallel to a huge potato field he said: "You know, we have something of a mystery right about here. A couple of months ago we were putting in new utility poles along this road. When we came up two weeks later to run wires, two of the poles were gone. They're no good for fire wood. I can't imagine what anyone would want with them."

We continued on for about another mile before we arrived at his friend's farm. I *was* impressed. The potato barn was huge, designed, I had been told in advance, to keep hundreds of tons of potatoes fresh for many months. My new friend's friend was waiting for us alongside his payloader. Following introductions and pleasantries, I was offered a tour of the buildings--the bagging plant, the equipment sheds, and the massive barn. The entire process from seed to sales was explained to me. As the tour was coming to its natural close, the farmer turned to my friend and said: "Heard you had an electric project comin' this way."

"Right," said my friend, sliding easily into the casual rural vernacular: "Word is you had a project, too."

"Yessir,' said the farmer," I added space to the storage barn."

I wasn't really tuned into this conversation, because I was really overwhelmed by the tons and tons of bagged produce. I was also a bit confused by an odor in the barn that was competing with the distinctive aromas of cool earth and new potatoes. I looked overhead and found the source. Creosote. Lots of creosote. If the weather had been warm, we might've been under a black, indoor rain. "Hey," I said to my power-company friend, "there's your telephone poles."

Things were pretty quiet for a minute. Then my friend said: "Geez, Bub, whyd'ya steal those poles?"

"Didn't steal 'em," he replied, "found 'em growin' on my land. Figured they must be mine, so I took 'em down for the barn. Make good ridge poles, don't ya think?" My friend looked at me wearily and sighed. "I guess I never saw this. Time to go."

We loaded my complimentary fifty pounds of giant Aroostook potatoes into the power company van, and headed back toward Caribou. "Well," my friend said, "that amounts to the most excitement I've had this year, even if I can't tell anybody about it." I looked at him.

"Well, I was wondering myself what you people do between the picking and the planting. The winters must seem awfully long."

"Not really, he said grinning. "Most of the time we just sit around and scratch...anywhere we think we might eventually itch."

Roger stayed with CSFA until 1977, the year CSFA's third chairman, Ed Lee, declared that all staff officers would commit substantial time to marketing CSFA's new scholarship management services throughout their regions. Roger by this time had three very active, very young sons at home. Their combined energies were depleting the stamina of Roger's wife Hilda. He could not be on the road any longer. He did not want to leave CSFA. Hilda, who had also been intermittently on staff, did not want him to leave. I did not want him to leave. The specter of the risk in hiring friends returned. I brought the situation to the attention of CSFA's eight-member Executive Committee. One member of the committee, Leslie S. Hubbard of Walpole, New Hampshire, saw that the outcome was clear. "Sometimes," he said, "when you think you are doing someone the greatest injustice, you are actually doing them the greatest favor. I think this is one of those times." I did not think so at the time and neither did Roger. Our friendship tie was tested. The rope frayed but thankfully held. Today, following seventeen years of dedication and service, he is the academic dean at the New Hampshire Technical College at Manchester. "Dean of Days," he calls it. The sons are now all grown and on their own. Roger and Hilda are thinking of eventually retiring, perhaps Down East to Castine. Roger speaks fondly of CSFA. He speaks reverently of his adventures in Maine.

Part IV

Edward M. Lee

1972-1979

Ed
Queens and Corona
A Tale of Two Martinis
Stand by Me
Skip, Chip and Holly Rust
You Can Call Me Johnson
Good Call but Off the Wall

Chapter Nine

Ed

My earliest recollection of Edward M. Lee is that of a man who arrived at Citizens' Scholarship Foundation of America in 1967 at just about the same time I did. The difference was that this lawyer, then forty-three years of age, arrived at a CSFA board meeting in a 1962 MGB convertible. Ed, with his solid athletic frame, his light-brown wavy hair, his clean-cut Irish features, and his tastefully tailored suit, was an appropriate match for his red British-Leland sports car.

Ed had earned his stripes, both as a navy commander in World War II and as a veteran of Irving Fradkin's community Dollars for Scholars program. In 1961 Ed's Rotary Club in Westfield, Massachusetts, invited Dr. Fradkin to speak on the "Fall River Plan." Following the formal presentation, Dr. Fradkin asked that a volunteer from Rotary attend a statewide workshop on the formation of new Dollars for Scholars chapters. The president of the club pointed a finger at one Rotarian and said, "Ed, you're the volunteer." And so he would be for the next thirty-four years.

Ed served in succession as fund-raising chairman and as president of the newly organized Westfield Citizens' Scholarship Foundation. He then joined the all-volunteer, statewide Massachusetts Citizens' Scholarship Foundation board in 1965 and became president of that board in 1966. In 1967 he was named to the Board of Trustees of Citizens' Scholarship Foundation of America. He became chairman of the board in November of 1971 and served eight years, a record that may never be eclipsed.

Ed recalls with grim humor the day in 1967 when he was up for election to the national CSFA board.

> They invited me to a meeting in New York City. We met, I remember, at the Hotel Roosevelt near Grand Central Station. I was there representing the Massachusetts state CSFA board. Once the meeting got underway, the nominating committee recommended a few people for membership. My name was on the list. While I sat there, the people around the table debated whether or not I would add anything of substance to the board. The proceedings were more like a fraternity initiation than a board election. Finally, maybe to save me further embarrassment, I was elected to the board. That's an experience not easily forgotten.

Over the next several years the question of "substance" would be answered to everyone's satisfaction. Ed was from the beginning a model trustee. He gave the same energy and commitment to his volunteer role as he gave to his successful law practice. He was among the first trustees to make a serious personal financial commitment to CSFA. At one point in 1970 he helped CSFA to secure a desperately needed $2,000 loan from a western Massachusetts bank and then retired the loan with his own resources. His generosity does not presuppose that he had a great deal of personal discretionary income. During one period in his life with CSFA, three of his six children were enrolled respectively at Wheaton, Smith, and Mills colleges. And because of his success as a small-city attorney, he was ineligible for any federal or state financial assistance.

My second impression of Ed Lee was one of a man with infinite patience. Ed was among the few trustees who, even prior to his chairmanship, actually enjoyed calling on Manhattan based companies in our quest for sustaining grants. During one of our earliest trips together, his patience would be tested.

Ed had markedly improved my appointment scheduling by providing this excellent advice. "Joe," he counseled, "whenever you call any of those very busy people to ask for an appointment, always provide two time frames, such as Monday afternoon or Tuesday morning. By providing a choice, you may avoid a 'no.' Always give a choice between something and something. Never between something and nothing." So on this particular occasion Ed and I looked forward to a full afternoon of calls in the city.

I caught up with Ed at lunch time in New York following a morning of other CSFA-related business in nearby central Connecticut. Because of an understandable personal preference to take the train into the city, I had elected to leave my car in a parking garage in Waterbury. Following our afternoon of corporate calls Ed offered to go a bit out of his way on his drive back to Massachusetts. He wished to save me a hassle and CSFA my train fare. He had an eight o'clock social engagement in Westfield, but he estimated he could still afford the detour through Waterbury. He might have been able to, but for two considerations. The first was that I had left the parking-garage ticket for safe keeping in the glove compartment of my car. The second was that Waterbury has any number of parking garages within walking distance of the train station. We arrived in Waterbury at about 6:30 p.m. and located the car just ahead of nine o'clock. He never in the course of the search verbalized what he had to be thinking. Perhaps this experience was the first test of a bond that has endured as friendship for twenty-eight years.

My third impression of Ed Lee was formulated upon my first visit to his Westfield law office, appropriately located at 70 Court Street. Among the array of interesting wall decorations were a score or more of framed bank checks. The checks represented payments from local clubs and charities that had engaged Lee & Pollard at one time or another. But unlike the "first dollar earned" often seen on the mirrors of barber shops and over the counters of local diners, the presence of these checks meant that Ed had never deposited the drafts. His service to the local nonprofits was generously given, and of equal importance, the beneficiary organizations knew the value of it.

My next one hundred or so impressions of Ed Lee were formulated during his eight-year chairmanship. No other person has so affected my outlook on life or my approach to challenges and adversity. Ed's job as successor to Brad Norris seemed fairly simple in syntax but very complex in execution: Save Citizens' Scholarship Foundation of America.

Brad had for both business and personal reasons announced his impending resignation on September 16, 1971. Because at that point, the terms of chairs were pretty much open-ended, the unexpected announcement left no heir apparent for the struggling nonprofit's leadership. In fact, another CSFA trustee, Les Hubbard, graciously agreed to serve as interim chairman until a successor could be found. The job of finding a successor was mine alone. For nearly a month I pondered the future of CSFA and speculated on who might be courageous enough, or foolish enough, to address that future. I decided on Ed Lee, and in October I drove the 132 miles from my home in Auburn, New Hampshire, to Westfield, Massachusetts, to ask for his additional commitment.

I sat rather nervously in Ed and Pat Lee's formal living room at number 4 Lathrop Avenue. During the pre-dinner social hour I asked Ed if he would consider the chairmanship of CSFA. I remember little about the details of the conversation that followed, except that it ended with his agreeing to serve. Typical to his character, his only reluctance in standing for election had nothing to do with the organization's financial woes. He called to my attention that a certain Ralph H. Seifert of Mansfield, Massachusetts, had service to CSFA at local, state, and national levels predating his own. He worried that "Cy" Seifert might feel "stepped over." I again said the choice was mine to make, and he was my choice. He then consented.

At the time of Ed's election, November 21, 1971, CSFA's "hand-to-mouth" existence was still the order of the day. He announced to the board that he would take as his mandate the decision reached by the Executive Committee in May of 1970 at the meeting called by Chairman Norris to determine whether or not CSFA should remain in business. The committee members present, including Messrs. Norris, Fradkin, Lee, Hubbard, Seifert, Rosenberg and David L. Steele of Lancaster, Pennsylvania, determined that it should survive, but declared that for an indefinite period total emphasis would be placed on survival. No new or expanded services would be accorded the 240 or so existing Dollars for Scholars chapters, nor would new chapters be formed or attended to, unless under the aegis of the currently funded development projects in New England and Indiana. "The survival of CSFA," said Chairman Lee, "is dependent on the dogged pursuit of corporate sustaining grants in New England, New York, and elsewhere."

In support of this pursuit, Ed Lee and I were quick to develop a routine we would use when making a first-time call on a corporate executive. Ed's role was to tell Irving Fradkin's story and then relate how Attorney Lee became involved in the Dollars for Scholars program. Ed always enjoyed stressing the implicit sacrifice made by dedicated volunteers. He liked to point out that both he as a lawyer and Irving as an optometrist were self-employed, and time away from the office was income lost and forgiven. "Dr. Fradkin," he would say, "not only devotes his Wednesdays to helping cities and towns all over New England form Dollars for Scholars chapters, he also dedicates several evenings a week to working with community volunteers. If necessary, and it often is, Irving gives up other weekdays to drive a hundred miles or more to address a service club or to appear on a radio talk show or local television program. Whenever he's away from his office he isn't bringing home the bacon. His dedication can't be measured simply by his commitment of time or expenses."

Following one very long day in New York when I had heard this presentation no fewer than four times, I lifted my glass to Ed and said: "Ed, I have to tell you that no matter what else Irving Fradkin does on any given day, he doesn't bring home *bacon*." He thought a moment, smiled and agreed. The allusion was forever dropped from his script.

With or without bacon, the frequent calls in New York and adjacent environs were showing improved results. In November of 1972, Ed issued his call to the trustees to attend the annual meeting in New York City.

> I am now completing my first year as chairman of the board of Citizens' Scholarship Foundation of America. It was my privilege to build on the excellent efforts of Gene Struckhoff and Brad Norris before me. And as you are aware, some of those earlier years presented difficult and demanding challenges to my predecessors. During the past year CSFA has undergone an encouraging transformation. The industry of trustees and staff during that year has brought our agency to the point we aimed for in 1970. We have today secured the basic operating budget of our national scholarship program. As of June 30, this year, CSFA finished the fiscal year with nearly $1,000 in income over expenses. This is not much, to be sure, but it speaks well for the future.

The achievement of 1972 did not, as Ed and I well knew, suggest that the future of CSFA was secure. The $1,000 surplus did not erase the accumulated deficits of prior years. The board was also aware that corporate grants would not sustain CSFA indefinitely. The newness and novelty of Irving Fradkin's story would eventually wear away. So, too, the board knew that much of the success of the year just ended was the product of renewed support in the amount of $135,000 from The Lilly Endowment, shared by both the Indiana Dollars for Scholars project and for CSFA's national office. A portion of the Lilly grant had underwritten nearly half of the year's operating budget. But impetus is indeed impetus, and one year later, end-of-June figures showed an $8,043 surplus above an operating budget of just under $50,000. The number of corporate grants had grown from a handful to twenty.

The search began in earnest in 1974 for something more; something perhaps as elusive as the Holy Grail: CSFA's self-sufficiency. The board estimated that CSFA had at best two or three years to find the key or keys to its long-term future. What no one realized in 1974 was that the keys were already on the ring. We had not yet unlocked the proper door, and in fact, for a time along the way the organization would find itself in the wrong corridor.

The CSFA trustees were fascinated by the application of technology within the New Hampshire Scholarship Locater Service. The fact that the distributions from the New Hampshire Charitable Fund's student aid program had grown from $20,000 to more than $75,000 a year, did not seem half as impressive as the computer-driven, tailored aid-match service. The trustees were quite taken with the sample scholarship and loan listings generated on green-bar computer paper. "What if," the board reasoned, "the locater service was expanded throughout New England and marketed on a fee-for-service basis? Might this service be part of the answer to CSFA's pursuit of financial well being?" The answer proved to be something of a paradox.

So taken were the trustees with the scholarship locater service, that four among them, Ed Lee, Irving Fradkin, Ralph Seifert, and Leslie Hubbard, made available to CSFA $10,000 each of their personal resources for the expanded development of the service. Each hoped one day to be repaid; none was guaranteed repayment. CSFA then retained a small public relations firm in Massachusetts, and hired college students during the summer of 1974 to comb the remaining New England states in an effort to identify and catalog the majority of sources of privately sponsored student aid in the entire region. New Hampshire College, the developer of the original scholarship-match software, refined the programs and coded and loaded the aid data. The public relations people developed an attractive "fulfillment package," and in early 1975 "The Dollars for Scholars Fund Finder" was born.

The Fund Finder was an attractive if imperfect service. Its imperfections were the product of the natural volatility of scholarship information. From year to year sponsors come into and go out of business. Heads of scholarship committees change. Numbers of awards change; levels of awards change; eligibility rules change. Data today on file for thousands of sources of aid soon becomes compromised by continual change. Yet, the Fund Finder printout and its accompanying advice-to-students booklet was clearly the best product of its kind in a growing, competitive marketplace. Unfortunately, "best of its kind" was not saying enough, loudly enough.

Many a charlatan was active in the field. Parents and students were continually seeing advertisements from other firms proclaiming, for example, that "$13.5 million in scholarship assistance goes unclaimed every year!" Families were assured that aspiring sons and daughters were definitely "eligible to receive some of this money!" The ads appearing nationwide admonished: "Don't be left out!" For user fees as high as $85, students were promised "a listing of five or more sources for which you are eligible. Guaranteed!" Desperate parents, looking ahead even then to ever increasing higher-education costs, often took the bait. The result was usually a mediocre listing of well known federal and state aid programs, plus a smattering of widely publicized, privately sponsored programs such as the National Merit Scholarship program and the Harry S. Truman Scholarship program. The $13.5 million, if it existed at all, was in all likelihood under-utilized, federally subsidized, student loan funds.

CSFA's Fund Finder, with its $10 user fee, was not in 1975 the only legitimate entry into the student-to-aid matching business, but it was one clearly devoid of marketing skills and promotional revenues. This program with a conscience did not have the capacity to establish itself in the marketplace. It did, however, catch the attention of another very legitimate organization located in New York City: The College Entrance Examination Board, or as better known, the College Board. CEEB had been considering for some time an entry into the aid-information dissemination business. The College Board had reviewed and tested several products already on the market and judged the Fund Finder to be the best, if not quite up to College Board standards. This judgment led to somewhat protracted negotiations between the College Board, New Hampshire College, and Citizens' Scholarship Foundation of America. The negotiations culminated in 1976 in a three-way agreement for the development and marketing of the College Board's "College Scholarship Information Bank." That agreement and the information bank program were to survive but two years, but the decline of and dissolution of the information bank proved to be the key to the future stability of Citizens' Scholarship Foundation of America.

Under the terms of the agreement, CSFA's responsibility was to gather scholarship data within ten densely populated states designated by the College Board. New Hampshire College's role was to further refine software and to process all student applications to the program. The College Board would provide the marketing strength in all areas served by the program, including the six New England states where the Fund Finder had previously operated. CSFA could, if it wished and at its own volition and expense, bring other states on line.

Armed with the imprimatur of the College Board, some research and design money from the same source, and a $96,600 challenge grant from the Ford Foundation, Ed Lee and I set out to raise the additional $300,000 required to research and record scholarship data in the ten designated states. Three years and countless days were devoted to the task. By the time spring of 1978 arrived, more than one hundred corporations and foundations, many for the first time, had made grants to Citizens' Scholarship Foundation of America in support of the student-aid surveys. The enormity of this fund-raising effort astounds me today. On the average three calls were required for every one grant. And in states such as Texas, where philanthropy is the provincial state of art, the ratio was higher still.

Even prior to the head-to-head negotiations with the College Board, the confidence of the CSFA trustees had soared. "Not only," they reasoned, "would this new service program provide income sufficient to sustain the national operations, it could also allow for income to underwrite renewed development of state and regional Dollars for Scholars projects." The board believed as early as the Fund Finder days of 1975 that CSFA would soon be able to redirect its attention to its truly charitable purpose, the expansion of its volunteer-based community scholarship program. Income from the student-aid matching service, the trustees were convinced, would correct the major flaw intrinsic to CSFA's earlier statewide development projects in Rhode Island, Ohio, Indiana, and Northern New England. In those cases, when the seed money for those various projects was expended and the development project had ended, the local volunteers within the Dollars for Scholars chapters were then left pretty much on their own. This deistic approach left the volunteers without direct support, encouragement, and on-site assistance, resulting in an attrition rate for chapters that was understandably, but unacceptably, high.

"If," the board reasoned, "a state's private sources of student aid were researched concurrently with Dollars for

Scholars chapter development, then at the end of a three-year, foundation-supported project, income from the Fund Finder, or its successor program, would be sufficient to keep a regional director in place indefinitely." With this new model in mind, Ed Lee and I put this suppostion to the test with the help of the Bush Foundation in St. Paul, Minnesota. With renewed confidence and with $140,000 in Bush Foundation proceeds in hand, CSFA arrived in Minnesota to stay in the second half of 1976.

The nation's bicentennial year will always be viewed as pivotal for Citizens' Scholarship Foundation of America. Negotiations with the College Board, thanks to Chairman Lee, were successfully concluded. We were well on our way to raising the $300,000 necessary to match the Ford Foundation challenge grant and to underwrite the ten-state student-aid surveys. In three of those states, New York, New Jersey, and Pennsylvania, we had hired students who were scurrying over the landscape during the summer months, collecting information on state, county, and local scholarships. Our staff in New Hampshire had grown to nine, and CSFA now occupied six rooms--the entire second story--of Jean Hennessey's New Hampshire Charitable Fund building at One South Street in Concord. The 1976 operating budget was in excess of $200,000, and we knew the source of virtually every dollar. CSFA was on its way, but not to where it believed it was going.

I am not one who subscribes to divine intervention, and I am one who believes that major turning points are usually identifiable only in retrospect. So contrary to my inclination to declare that certain unforeseen events of 1976 were part of a perfectly crafted, Phelan-developed close-to-the-vest plan, I will admit up front that luck, while often a by-product of tenacity--and in the teachings of Harry Rosenberg, sometimes just sheer numbers--is luck nevertheless. Ed Lee and I found our share on one November morning in 1975.

We were in Minnesota courting the Bush Foundation in St. Paul, and slightly more than by chance we found ourselves at 7:30 a.m. in the Minneapolis offices of the Toro Company. In a sort of a "friend-of-a-friend" scenario we had been invited to meet with then Toro President David T. McLaughlin. At the close of a half-hour conversation we were asked to design and manage a scholarship program for dependents of Toro's employees. After a modicum of soul searching we agreed to do so. In May of 1976, and almost as a "favor" to the company, CSFA distributed $8,600 to fourteen children of Toro employees. The future of CSFA was assured from that day forward. We did not, of course, see it at the time. We did not experience any spontaneous revelation. In fact, we along with the CSFA board had been quite myopic. The zeal of the trustees for the Fund Finder and its successor, College Scholarship Information Bank, continued to obscure our progress with the very important other work we were doing in 1976 for the New Hampshire Charitable Fund.

Back in 1975, CSFA's New England regional director, Roger Berlinguette, had quietly developed and refined application evaluation procedures and practices in anticipation of the spring 1976 distributions from the New Hampshire Charitable Fund Student Aid Program. Scholarship and loan funds available for New Hampshire students had increased from $75,000 to more than $100,000. Ed Lee and I believe to this day that the availablility of Roger's refined procedures gave us the confidence to take on the Toro Company scholarship program. Then, purely by coincidence and within a matter of weeks of the visit with Toro, a friend in West Hartford recommended CSFA to a Bristol, Connecticut-based company then known as Associated Spring Company (now the Barnes Group). The Barnes brothers, at the urging of Keith Hinton, the administrator of the company's foundation, retained CSFA to design and manage its first-time, $10,000 scholarship program.

To almost no one's notice in the spring of 1976, Citizens' Scholarship Foundation of America distributed scholarship dollars on behalf of a statewide community foundation, The New Hampshire Charitable Fund; a highly visible and respected national corporation, The Toro Company; and a company-related foundation, Associated Spring Foundation. None of us recognized that these three prototypes represented virtually all the clients that were to follow. But outside of CSFA's board deliberations, others were taking note.

In April of 1976 CSFA hired a thirty-seven-year-old man, then living in Michigan, and in June moved him and his family back to his home town of St. Peter, Minnesota. He was our choice to direct the Bush Foundation-funded Minnesota Dollars for Scholars project. His assignment was to prove that the board's optimism for and confidence in the College Scholarship Information Bank was justified.

H. Stuart Johnson--the tall, husky, blond-haired, proven salesman, competitor, and inveterate golfer--proved to be one of the great finds of all times. Ed Lee and I often mused that once in our ignorance we interviewed scores of job candidates in Indiana and hired the wrong person. In Minnesota we interviewed Stuart as one of two and hired the right one. Stuart with the help and encouragement of his wife, Marlys, who served for a time as his project assistant, began organizing Dollars for Scholars chapters in Minnesota at a near record clip. Stuart also supervised the collecting of scholarship data throughout Minnesota and, almost as a sideline, responded to an increasing number of inquiries from Twin Cities companies who had heard of Toro's delight with its new scholarship program.

The *CSFA Annual Report for 1978* lists twenty participants in the "Corporate and Associates Program." Of that number, thirteen companies are in Minnesota including H.B. Fuller Company, International Multifoods, First Bank Systems, The Donaldson Company, The Toro Company, and The Jostens Foundation. Jostens is particularly noteworthy because, unlike the other programs, it was not intended to serve children of employees. This extraordinary program, in its first year alone, attracted some 14,000 applications in a national competition for sixty $500 scholarships.

By June 30 of 1979, Chairman Lee's last year in his leadership role, the number of corporate and associates programs numbered thirty-three, including The Johnson Wax Fund, Government Employees Insurance Company, General Mills Foundation, and Best Products Foundation. Distributions had risen from $118,600 in 1976, including the New Hampshire Charitable Fund Student Aid Program, to $259,000 in 1978, and to $824,500 in May of 1979. Of equal satisfaction to me was the fact that, perhaps for the first time, small companies as well as large could sponsor employee scholarship programs through a national service organization. CSFA's 1979 client list also included the C. A. "Gus" Johnson Memorial Education Fund and Otter Tail Power Company, both Minnesota-based. The former would have further unforeseen and positive consequences for CSFA. The donor, Mankato Attorney C. A. "Gus" Johnson II, established his dad's memorial with cash, a house lot, and a horse.

The completion of Ed Lee's eight year term also coincided with the demise of the College Scholarship

Information Bank. We all learned that as the information in the bank expanded exponentially, the reliability of data declined in the same measure. By mid-1979 more than 15,000 aid sources were collected, recorded, coded, and on file. But the problems inherent to updating the information, together with the functional limitations of the available software, portended the program's passing. Ed Lee had, as CSFA's chairman, negotiated CSFA into the arrangement with the College Board; and with the same alacrity, he negotiated CSFA out. Surprisingly very few of the myriad of funders of the student-aid surveys were upset or disappointed. Most felt the project was undertaken in good faith. In the throes of the project CSFA did, in fact, make many friends whose names would eventually find their way onto the growing list of CSFA-managed corporate and foundation scholarship programs.

At one point toward the close of 1978, when the demise of the College Scholarship Information Bank was all but certain, Ed Lee quipped to the Board of Trustees that his confidence in CSFA's future was "substantially heightened when he realized that the organization had attained the luxury to fail." He knew better than many others that during the early years of his term any failed initiative probably would have resulted in the demise of Citizens' Scholarship Foundation of America.

By the close of 1979 both Ed and incoming Chairman Ralph Seifert were convinced that the "Corporate and Associates Program," in the words of an up-state New York trustee, Thomas D. Bellinger, "would become the engine that will pull the Dollars for Scholars train." The Bush Foundation agreed, and at the close of the Minnesota Project in April of 1979, awarded CSFA an additional $60,000 to underwrite the rapid expansion of corporate-sponsored scholarship programs in Minnesota.

Ed Lee delivered his formal farewell remarks to his board.

> Citizens' Scholarship Foundation of America is ending not a year, but a decade, marked by nearly as many trials and triumphs. During these years trustees and staff alike searched for a formula for the future. In its earliest moments the nature of this search necessitated that we plan from month to month. We could seldom see clearly to the end of any year. Our survival and development were occasioned by determined leadership, excellent trustee support, corporate and foundation largess, tough negotiations, a dash of innovation, a pinch of fortuity, and not a small measure of luck. The 1980s, under Chairman Seifert's leadership, clearly will see the building of a strong financial base and a reaching out to provide many more scholarship opportunities for students throughout the country. We believe the coming decade mandates that we abandon short-term planning and subscribe rather to long-term objectives. My message today is more of a looking ahead than a looking behind. It is not a buttoning up of the immediate past, but rather an opening up for the future.

What a luxury for me as the chief staff officer of CSFA during the 1970s, to have had the time, dedication, generosity, and wisdom of Edward Michael Lee. I well recall one occasion in 1972 when I was putting together a proposal for consideration by The Lilly Endowment, I cited the commitment of my board members. I was so impressed with Ed's tally that I called him at his Westfield law office. "Ed," I said, "I just figured out how many days you were away from your law office last year working on behalf of CSFA."

"How many?" he asked.

"Sixty," I said, "what do you think of that?"

Ed paused for a moment and said: "Don't tell my wife."

Chapter Ten

Queens and Corona

The Reverend Canon Kenneth MacDonald asked for quiet, and the twenty-five or so people present that evening responded to his call and settled into their folding metal chairs. "Let us begin this meeting with a prayer." The small assembly of week-night parishioners, as one, bowed their heads.

> Let us hope, dear Lord, that we *can* make a difference in the futures of our sons and daughters. Give us the strength to place the resources of this community into the hands of our young people so that they may go forward, learn and prosper, and in turn give something to others in the generation to follow. We thank You for sending Mr. Lee and Mr. Phelan to us this evening so we may learn how we may help our children to gain important knowledge in technical schools, colleges and universities. Please give us the courage to apply what we learn here tonight to the benefit of our friends and neighbors, and by so doing, to the benefit of all who reside in our midst. We ask this, Lord, in Jesus' name. Amen.

"Amen," chorused the assembled voices.

Such was the opening of the September 13, 1974, meeting in the Church of the Resurrection Parish Hall in Corona-East Elmhurst, New York, just across the 59th Street bridge from Manhattan. The parishioners had gathered in a small Episcopal church to hear Ed Lee and Joe Phelan speak on the subject of Dollars for Scholars. And while this invocation or some variation of it might seem altogether appropriate in any locale for organizing a community scholarship program, this particular event represented a milestone in the history of Citizens' Scholarship Foundation of America.

Despite the fact that CSFA and Dollars for Scholars had its roots in the urban area of Fall River, Massachusetts, the community scholarship program had between 1958 and 1974 fared best in suburban and rural communities, chiefly in New England and in the somewhat conservative states of Ohio and Indiana.

From time to time publicity given CSFA by *The Saturday Review of Literature* and other national publications, or information included in various education-focused directories, would result in numerous inquiries directed to our national office. Whenever CSFA was permitted to exercise any advance control over the copy, the item would include the disclaimer "CSFA does not award scholarships to individuals. Please do not apply to the national office." Invariably, however, each welcomed exposure would be followed by several requests for scholarship applications. CSFA felt then, as now, an obligation to respond to any inquiry. The simple post card again carried the disclaimer with additional text that read, "CSFA helps cities and towns organize self-help local scholarship programs under the trade name Dollars for Scholars®. If you would like more information on how your community can participate, please write and request free materials." Few inquirers ever did.

One who did make a request was Mrs. Jimmie Williams of Corona, New York. She wanted to know how her black community could become a part of our program. I called and advised her that representatives from CSFA were often in New York City, and if she could pull together a few people, we would be happy to meet with them. She immediately agreed and we set a date about four weeks ahead. I needed that much time to arrange a few corporate calls in the city, and I was, I admit, not terribly optimistic that much good would come of our journey across the bridge to Queens.

My pessimism was not vested, I believe, in any inherent bias. It was rather the product of, first, my conviction that any societal problem that wasn't being righted by hundreds of millions of public and private dollars, could not be righted or even addressed by a relatively small, middle-class oriented scholarship foundation; and second, my unhappy memory of a 1970 initiative on 116th Street in New York City, that caused me a great deal of anxiety, frustration, and embarrassment.

In that episode a New York City-based *Fortune 500* company sponsored a single scholarship through CSFA in the name of a popular company officer who happened to be black, and who happened to die of a heart attack at the age of forty-six. The Charles E. Palmer Award had been endowed in 1971 with the first $500 award to be made in 1972. In a time of inner-city turmoil, I worked closely, if somewhat uneasily, on location with my contact person in East Harlem as we sought to identify the first award recipient. Once that task was completed, the president and chief executive officer of the company in question asked me to invite the young woman to his Park Avenue office in order that he might congratulate her personally.

The date was set and we agreed upon ten in the morning. My East Harlem contact person assured me the day before that both she and the recipient would be at the Park Avenue address at nine forty-five. That hour came and went as did ten, ten thirty, and ten forty-five. At eleven the photographers packed up, and the CEO left for LaGuardia to catch a plane to somewhere. My rather frantic telephone calls to East Harlem went unanswered. My long-term relationship with the sponsoring company was strained. My first venture into the minority scholarship arena was not particularly fulfilling.

So as we drove across the bridge to Queens that fall evening in 1974, I harbored no great expectations. The meeting was at seven, and Ed and I allowed extra time to locate our meeting address. As we entered the neighborhood, Ed commented on its attractiveness. At 100-117 Thirty-second Avenue we were greeted warmly and following the invocation, Ed told the story of Irving Fradkin's Dollars for Scholars program.

In these situations my role was more that of the "how to" person. I explained that the first requirement was a vote to establish a Dollars for Scholars program. I then described the three basic tasks of the local steering committee: enter into a chapter agreement with CSFA; adopt bylaws; and recruit a local board of directors. Ed and I talked about an array of fund-raising activities that had been used in other Dollars for Scholars chapter areas. We answered a few questions, shared coffee and cookies, thanked the gathering for the opportunity, and returned to our Manhattan hotel.

The next morning Mrs. Williams called me before eight o'clock at the hotel to tell me that the group had decided to go ahead. She asked if we could return in two weeks to provide a little more training. I said "yes," and we did. In its first year Citizens' Scholarship Foundation of Corona-East Elmhurst raised $4,000. Over the ensuing nineteen years it would add $89,000 to that sum and stand as a model of the concept of self-help. Indeed, the chapter officers would annually review the names of the New York-based companies that were providing unrestricted grants to CSFA and would approach them, with some success, for support for the local affiliate.

The chapter, too, was always represented in the persons of Mrs. Williams and Mr. William Goldsborough at CSFA's New York City-based annual meetings. In the 1970s and early 1980s CSFA relied on the largess of New York companies for the sponsorship of its annual meetings. Hosts in those years included JC Penney, Bristol-Myers, and General Motors Corporation. Dollars for Scholars chapters were invited *pro forma* to attend, much as stock holders are invited to attend company annual meetings. Two of CSFA's officers, the secretary and the clerk were required by CSFA's bylaws to be elected by a quorum of the chapters. This formality was accomplished by proxy vote of at least 10 percent of the membership, together with votes cast by CSFA trustees who were coincidentally residents of Dollars for Scholars communities. For several years the only other in-person vote cast was that on behalf of Corona-East Elmhurst.

I would not want to overstate the importance of either my unhappy experience in East Harlem or the joyful outcome of our adventure in Queens. But I do know insofar as the latter is concerned, as CSFA under new leadership began in earnest its urban initiatives in the 1990s, the chapter volunteers in Corona-East Elmhurst were cited as models for enthusiastic as well as skeptical residents of inner-city neighborhoods and disadvantaged communities. And on September 30, 1994, with the long-since-retired board chairman Ed Lee present, CSF of Corona-East Elmhurst was honored by CSFA for its twenty years of service to local students, a distinguished accomplishment among the now more than seven hundred Dollars for Scholars affiliates.

Chapter Eleven

A Tale of Two Martinis

A good and effective public relations program is a challenge for any organization irrespective of its budget. Any public relations program at all for a struggling, virtually insolvent nonprofit entity is a triumph. Because CSFA in its early years routinely approved deficit budgets, its public relations exposure was pretty much limited to trade publications or other periodicals that were willing to provide editorial space for the promotion of the Dollars for Scholars program. In the very early going, 1958-1963, CSFA's founder, Dr. Irving Fradkin, managed to place stories with the *Reader's Digest*, *Newsweek*, *Time*, and a host of other periodicals that were intrigued by the "one-dollar-from-everybody" idea. But in time the novelty of this notion decreased in news value, and by the late 1960s editorial space for CSFA was much harder to come by.

One publication, *The Saturday Review of Literature*, had been especially good to CSFA. The magazine's education editor, James Cass, was intrigued with both Irving Fradkin and the Dollars for Scholars program. Jim not only looked for opportunities to include vignettes on Dollars for Scholars as frequently as possible in *Saturday Review*, but he also agreed to join CSFA's board. In that capacity in the early months of 1975, he further agreed to counsel CSFA's executive director and chairman on the development of a low-cost or no-cost, somewhat coordinated, public relations program. Another CSFA trustee, Mary MacNamara of *Newsweek*, agreed to participate in a late February afternoon meeting in New York City in the bar of the Roosevelt Hotel.

Ed Lee and I had been spending another of our days visiting with various New York-based corporations asking for modest sustaining grants. By four o'clock we were ready to come in out of the chill and relax with our two compatriots. When we arrived at the Roosevelt, Jim Cass was sipping his first martini. Mary MacNamara was nowhere in sight. By four forty-five Jim was ready for a second, and Mary still had not arrived. The prognosis for a productive public relations review was uncertain.

Just ahead of five I called Newsweek and learned that Mary had been called to another assignment and could not join us for the meeting. Ed, Jim, and I were by then fairly relaxed and probably in no mood for serious planning. Jim looked up from his second olive bath and asked: "You guys ever hear of the Bush Foundation?"

"You mean the beer people?" Ed asked.

"No," Jim replied. "Bush is 3M's founding family money, and there's lots of it. I know the guy in charge there. Humphrey Doermann was for years the director of admissions at Harvard. Now he's the first-ever hired senior officer at the Bush Foundation in Saint Paul. Humphrey's a quality guy, and he'll be looking for good projects. He also owes me a favor. He might just be willing to talk to you guys."

CSFA in 1975 had almost no money in its deficit budget for travel, let alone for a jaunt for two to the nation's heartland. But Ed and I were by then at the point of induced bravado, and we agreed that a visit with Dr. Doermann was a delightful idea. Jim made good on his offer to provide us an introduction, and within a few weeks we were on our way to Minnesota. This trip marked for me, at the age of thirty-six, only the second time in my life I had ventured as far west from New England as the Mississippi River.

At Dr. Doermann's suggestion we arrived at the offices of the Bush Foundation just ahead of the lunch hour. Following our announced arrival Dr. Doermann intercepted us in the reception area and guided us rather hurriedly to the elevators and then on a short but brisk walk to the St. Paul Club where we were to have lunch. During our jaunt Dr. Doermann commented on the fact that he and his staff were in the midst of preparing his foundation's annual report. He absolutely had to be back in his office no later than one thirty. Ed and I sensed that this free lunch was seen by our host as the total repayment of whatever favor he owed Jim Cass.

We did, however, jump into our usual routine as the water was being poured at our table. Ed told the Irving Fradkin story. I talked of the success of our current Minnesota Dollars for Scholars chapters in Pipestone, Jasper, International Falls, St. Paul Park, Hinckley, and Fairmont. Ed told the story of the Spaulding-Potter Charitable Trusts' catalytic effect on the Dollars for Scholars development in New Hampshire. I spoke of a few of my minor triumphs in the wilds and not-so-wilds of Maine. And then one thirty was upon us.

Dr. Doermann looked up from his coffee cup and said, "Gentlemen, I really do have to return to my office. But this conversation deserves at least another two hours. Why don't you send me a preliminary proposal and then come back to discuss it with me. Are you able to come back?" We, of course, said, "of course," though I am certain we were both quietly contemplating the expense of a return trip. Ed had to be especially concerned, because he always traveled on CSFA's behalf at his own expense. We both knew that in 1975 airline tickets represented unusual and expensive items. And two round trips to Minnesota within the space of two months were, without contradiction, singular.

We did reschedule, and we had our two additional hours with Dr. Doermann, though we had established enough familiarity by then to address him as Humphrey. Ed and I spent the first half hour of our second meeting suggesting to Humphrey the impact Dollars for Scholars could have on the futures of young Minnesotans. We suggested that our requested grant of $140,000 from the Bush Foundation would produce minimally over $3 million in grass-roots-generated scholarships. We further speculated that the parallel development in Minnesota of our expanding computer-based student-aid referral service, The Dollars for Scholars Fund Finder, would eventually produce income from within the state sufficient for CSFA to sustain services to its community affiliates once the Bush grant had been exhausted.

With just over an hour remaining, Humphrey Doermann's time and turn was upon us. Within that time he demonstrated to us just how seriously he took his responsibilities with the Bush Foundation, and in so doing he widened our eyes considerably.

> Gentlemen, this idea sounds fine to me. But I am in no position to dictate what is good for Minnesota and Minnesotans. I have a list of sixteen people I have come to know and admire during my short time in this state. These are the people you need to convince. And once you have their confidence and conviction, I want to hear from them directly.

A Tale of Two Martinis

> In addition, the preliminary proposal you sent me following our first visit raises certain questions in my mind. I have recorded twenty or so of them here. Any final proposal you care to submit to the Bush Foundation must answer these questions in some detail. I know these tasks represent a great deal of time and probably some unanticipated expense. But you are asking for a great deal of money. My job is to see that Bush Foundation dollars are well spent.
>
> On that subject, you should also know that the Foundation is authorized under its founding documents to make grants only in five states. New Hampshire is not among them. If we are to do business with CSFA, you will have to find a fiscal agent within Minnesota. This agent must be a bona fide nonprofit organization that is willing to hold, manage, and disburse any grant we might make to the benefit of CSFA. And having said that, you must keep in mind that funding for your project is in no way assured. Once your work is done and your proposal prepared, the merits of your project will be subject to the scrutiny and action of our board of directors.

"Any questions?" he asked of the two dumbfounded individuals before him. "Good luck, keep in touch." The meeting was over. Somehow the world seemed a good deal heavier on our shoulders than it had two hours before.

The very first of the sixteen people we would come to know in our pursuit of Bush Foundation dollars advised us that Minnesota has but two seasons: "ten months of winter and two months of tough sledding." Bruce Gray, then dean of students at Gustavus Adolphus College, further advised us as we three contemplated a map of Minnesota, that "Fergus Falls was not the end of the earth, but you could certainly see it from there." He was right on both counts. We learned, too, through many of thousands of miles driven, that most of New England would fit nicely within the borders of Minnesota. We also came to understand why lodgers in areas such as Fargo-

Moorhead parked very close to stanchions where, in close proximity, electric outlets faced automobile engine blocks. We discovered what minus twenty-three degrees feels like through the clothing and on the skin even in the absence of a windchill factor. But of greatest importance we found that the warmth of the people of Minnesota more than compensated for the winter chill. In Minnesota in the company of descendants of Norwegians, Swedes, Irish and Germans, we found new friends for Citizens' Scholarship Foundation of America, and in more than a few instances, lifelong friends for ourselves.

In the space of five months and several visits, Ed and I met with all sixteen Doermann designees. We found our required fiscal agent in the Minneapolis Foundation, a community foundation that served all of Hennepin County. We even renewed a corporate friendship in the person of Bill Humphrey in the offices of General Mills Foundation. Bill secured for us a modest grant to help cover much of the cost of our interior expeditions. Of greatest importance we found among our new friends an enthusiasm for Dollars for Scholars that ranged from casual to unreserved. Some of the required testimony directed to Humphrey Doermann originated with volunteer leaders within our six existing chapters. People such as C. H. "Cap" Hegdal, a retired superintendent of schools in Fairmont, welcomed Ed and me as celebrities to School District 454. He then advised Humphrey Doermann that this district, with a population of just over eleven thousand, was raising annually, in the true spirit of Dollars for Scholars, nearly one dollar per capita in scholarships for area students.

By the end of the calendar year 1975 the required testimony was in, the twenty-one Doermann interrogatories addressed and answered, and our proposal was before the Bush Foundation awaiting action. A decision was scheduled for February of 1976.

A Tale of Two Martinis

I well remember a January telephone call from Humphrey Doermann. It came on a Saturday when two colleagues and I were in the office assigning computer codes to Fund Finder scholarship data. Humphrey had first called my home and was referred to the office. "Well," I thought as I took the call, "our cause certainly can't be hurt now that he knows he's not the only person working on a weekend."

Humphrey was calling to ask me for our preferred timing on the payment of the grant over the three-year project period. "Strange question," I thought, considering the foundation had not as yet acted on our proposal. "Maybe a little cruel, too, if the outcome was not what we hoped." I later learned that the call reflected Humphrey's firm belief that the proposal would be funded, and he wished early on to share that optimism with me. In so doing, he also wanted me to give advance thought to the actual fiscal management of the project. Four weeks later we had confirmation of our $140,000 Minnesota Project.

In years to come the grant, though the largest in CSFA's history at that time, would come to be seen as one among an impressive and still-growing series. But that grant represents in the minds of people who have a long-term association with CSFA, the true turning point in the early history of the national scholarship foundation. True, the Minnesota Dollars for Scholars project was not the first of its kind. In fact, under the able direction of one H. Stuart Johnson, the project was conducted utilizing the development strategy devised for me some ten years earlier by Eugene Struckhoff for the state of Maine. True, too, that as was the case in many projects before it, all objectives were surpassed. But unlike anything that had ever happened before, events in Minnesota during the years 1976-1979, initially viewed as only tangential to the project, ultimately provided the key to the future financial stability and national prominence of Citizens' Scholarship Foundation of America.

Chapter Twelve

Stand by Me

A single event in Minnesota in the late winter of 1975 was to change the future and fortunes for Citizens' Scholarship Foundation of America for all time. This event was the one that convinced me that good luck was not necessarily being in the right place at the right time; it is rather having enough sense to know you are there.

The importance of Minnesota in CSFA's history cannot be overstated. Minnesota, home of the Bush Foundation, is where Humphrey Doermann listened with interest to the story of Dollars for Scholars. Minnesota is the birthplace of Stuart and Marlys Johnson, the husband and wife team who helped pioneer CSFA from relative obscurity to a national identity. And Minnesota is the home of the Toro Company, a quality corporation that aspires to help lawns grow and to help throw snow.

The circumstances that brought CSFA to the attention the Toro Company were truly fortuitous. CSFA was in late 1975 under serious consideration for the $140,000 grant from the Bush Foundation for the expansion of Dollars for Scholars chapters throughout Minnesota. The regulations governing the operations of the Bush Foundation presented something of a problem for CSFA. The foundation was authorized to make grants only within North Dakota, South Dakota, Wisconsin, Florida, and Minnesota. Humphrey Doermann, executive director of the Bush Foundation, acknowledged that Minnesota alone would be served under terms and conditions of the grant, but he felt that if an exception were to be made to the allocation rule, the Bush Foundation would have to carry an asterisk in its next several annual reports. He suggested a better course of action would be for CSFA to find a qualified fiscal agent in Minnesota. CSFA could then invoice the agent for services rendered and for its related expenses incurred in Minnesota.

CSFA Chairman Lee and Executive Director Phelan agreed with the suggestion and initiated a search for an appropriate agent. Our first choice was the Minneapolis Foundation. This community foundation was headed in 1975 by Dr. James P. Shannon. I have often said of Jim Shannon that he is just what everyone would want in a grandfather: a husky, mustachioed Irishman, who was blessed with a delightful sense of humor. On the occasion of our first meeting with Dr. Shannon, Ed Lee and I arrived at the appointed hour and then waited nearly one more before our host, together with the most punished leather documents case I had ever seen, made a hurried entrance. "Gentlemen," he said, "I would like you to meet the late Jim Shannon." In Jim's inner office, framed on the wall, was "Finnegan's Law" which proclaimed that "Murphy Was an Optimist."

Remarkably, the three Irish intellects managed quickly to agree in principle on a client-agent relationship that would be wholly satisfactory to Dr. Doermann and the Bush Foundation. We three were enmeshed in the details when the telephone rang. The caller was David McLaughlin, president of the Toro Company. While Ed Lee and I were privileged to hear only one side of the conversation, we quickly realized that Mr. McLaughlin was calling Jim Shannon to seek advice in establishing a scholarship program for dependents of Toro employees. Jim listened intently for a few minutes and then said "Dave, I was a college president, not a financial aid officer. I really don't know anything about scholarships, but sitting right now in my office are two dudes from the east who think they know everything about scholarships. Do you want me to bring them over?" He did, and an appointment was set for seven thirty the following morning.

We soon learned that Jim Shannon, in addition to having been a former president of St. Thomas College, was in 1975 a member of the Toro Company Board of Directors. "The company's social conscience," he joked. Ed and I were, ahead of our appointment, fully briefed on the company products and locations. Toro, Jim assured us, had a genuine concern for the welfare of its employees. Mr. McLaughlin, in fact, made a practice of meeting regularly and informally with employees, on all three production shifts, at plants in Minnesota, Wisconsin, and California.

My sole objective going into the morning meeting was simply to offer some free advice and counsel to a company that wished to provide an in-house scholarship program. I believed Ed and I would be doing something of a favor for Toro Director Shannon in return for one we were asking of him. David McLaughlin's intentions were equally clear. Beginning in the spring of 1976, he wanted to provide scholarships of up to $500 to dependents of Toro employees.

Was he interested in technical and vocational education as well as four-year undergraduate programs? "Yes." By dependents did he mean just children and stepchildren, or would he include even parents or grandparents who were listed as "dependents" on an income tax form? "Why not?" Did he wish for the awards to be made on the basis of financial need in addition to measures of potential and achievement? "Definitely."

"Who within the company," I asked, "will be authorized to review and process the family financial information?" Mr. McLaughlin looked at his assistant, Mary Elliott, who shook her head "no." He then looked at me.

"I don't want anyone within this company, including myself, to have access to that kind of information." He paused in thought for a few seconds and then said, "Joe, why don't you do it for us? Can't your foundation process applications and select winners? Toro would pay you for the service."

At this point in the rather anemic life of Citizens' Scholarship Foundation of America I might have said, "I'm sorry, Mr. McLaughlin, we don't do that. CSFA is in the business of helping cities and towns to organize local scholarship programs." Similarly, I could have suggested he contact the National Merit Scholarship Corporation or the College Scholarship Service of the College Entrance Examination Board. But I was reasonably certain neither would give Mr. McLaughlin the program he wanted. Instead I said: "I'd like to think about it."

"Okay," Mr. McLaughlin said, "call me back in two days and tell me if you'll do it and for how much." The meeting ended.

Ed Lee and I walked back into the Toro reception area ahead of Jim Shannon who had lingered to exchange pleasantries with Mr. McLaughlin. "What do you think?" Ed asked.

"I think, Ed, we have a problem. Even if we wanted to do this, we don't have the money to set it up. We barely could afford to come back here to meet with Jim." Ed thought a minute.

"Let me talk with Jim."

The opportunity to do so came quickly and rather urgently. Both Ed and Jim had to dispose of a portion of the morning's coffee. In what I have since characterized as the "great men's room decision" or the "stand by me accords," the following conversation took place:

Ed: "Jim, we'd like to help Toro out, but we don't have any set-up money."

Jim: "How much do you need?"

Ed: "I'm not sure, but Humphrey Doermann gave us the names of sixteen people he wants to have endorse our proposal to Bush, and we don't even have walking-around money."

Jim: "Have Phelan call Dave tomorrow and ask him for a thousand dollars. I'll call Bill Humphrey at General Mills Foundation. Maybe he'll give you some walking-around money. Drop back to see me tomorrow afternoon. I'll tell you how I made out."

Ed Lee recalls the four o'clock meeting the next day.

> We were with Jim in his office for about another hour. We talked of many things, but the subject of Bill Humphrey never came up. I thought Jim had forgotten his earlier offer to help us. Our meeting ended at five. Joe went out ahead of me. As I was exiting, Jim put a hand on my shoulder, smiled, and said: "Call Bill Humphrey at General Mills and ask him for twenty-five hundred dollars." I simply nodded in relief.

Ed and I took that advice, and on the added strength of our verbal agreement with the Toro Company, ended up with $3,500, no small sum in 1975. In the course of my phone call to Dave McLaughlin, I said that CSFA would be willing to process all applications of the company's scholarship program if the company would agree to use our standard Dollars for Scholars application and Financial Aid Questionnaire, and if the company would take the responsibility of distributing the materials within its facilities. He agreed and said that Toro would authorize $10,000 for the first year of the program with scholarships renewable for up to four years. I suggested, in turn, that we would charge Toro the equivalent of 5 percent of the approved distribution plus all direct costs for materials, postage, and communications. I also said that CSFA would request of Toro a modest "sustaining" grant. He agreed again. Ed and I had been in the right place at the right time, and we did have enough sense to know it.

Chapter Thirteen

Skip, Chip, and Holly Rust

The Jostens Company, headquartered in Bloomington, Minnesota, is appropriately recognized as one of the most quality-conscious corporations in these United States. Indeed, any class ring, championship ring, insignia, lapel pin or other "recognition" product produced by Jostens is a delight to behold and a privilege to own. Fortunately for Citizens' Scholarship Foundation of America, the quality that drives the company's performance carries over to its charitable endeavors. The enlightened self-interest that drives Jostens Foundation's charitable distributions, is consistent with and even supportive of the parent corporation's quality and objectives, and as such is often imaginative and creative.

Such was the case in 1977 when Stuart Johnson and I first sat down with Skip Mooney, the internal chair of Jostens Foundation. Much of the company's success is vested in school spirit--especially at the high-school level--and in the late 1970s, as was true throughout the entire decade, school spirit was a scarce if not underground commodity. Skip, slight of frame in his early forties, shared with the two CSFA people the desire of the company foundation to recognize and reward truly outstanding high-school seniors in several of the nation's twenty thousand public and private high schools. The foundation planned to make available sixty $500 scholarships in 1978. The recipients would have to exhibit outstanding performance in community and school-related organizations, clubs, sports, and other voluntary activities in addition to demonstrating exemplary academic achievement. The foundation wanted to identify and honor America's very, very best. Did CSFA have an interest in designing and managing such a program?

The appeal of the program to CSFA's representatives was immediate. Jostens could provide CSFA its very first opportunity for national name recognition. Jostens was also held in high esteem by other major companies in the Twin Cities area, and Stuart and I, who often joked about the possibility of capturing all of the companies along either side of the Interstate 494 beltway, viewed Jostens as an important addition to our conquests. We foresaw but one major problem: the potential number of applicants. If the program was properly promoted with the twenty thousand high schools, the number of applications from this one program alone would dwarf the combined totals of twenty-seven other, chiefly children-of-employee programs, then under CSFA management. The demands on staff time would be substantial; the general program administration fee basis could not possibly apply.

That fee basis had been refined some since Messrs. Lee and Phelan had agreed in 1976 to conduct CSFA's first company-sponsored program for the Toro Company. Gone were requests for out-of-pocket expenses, a 5 percent-of-distribution fee, and a supplemental, modest "sustaining" grant. Invoking Trustee Ed Shapiro's advice to "keep things simple," CSFA's Board of Trustees approved a 15 percent-of-authorized-distribution formula for all of its employee-related, corporate accounts. The Toro Company, for example, entering the third year of its program with an authorized 1978 distribution of $15,000, would compensate CSFA with $2,250 for services rendered. CSFA's services in this instance included receipt and processing of twenty-eight applications, confirming eligibility and college enrollment of selected recipients, notifying both recipients and non-recipients, and disbursing the scholarships in two equal payments, payable jointly to each new and renewed recipient and to the college of each recipient's choice.

Clearly, at least in the eyes of CSFA, this formula was inappropriate for any scholarship program with a distribution of $30,000 that would in all probability attract applications numbering in the thousands. Forty-five hundred dollars, would not cover one-third of the estimated direct program cost. Several weeks of negotiations began between CSFA and Jostens Foundation representatives Skip Mooney and his colleague, Corporate Attorney Chip Fisher. The negotiations culminated in a very simple and straightforward fee structure: one dollar per application processed. In the first year of the Jostens Student Achievement Program, CSFA received fourteen thousand applications and accordingly CSFA received $14,000 for services rendered. The sum represented the equivalent of 47 percent of the authorized distribution. In succeeding years as the program became better known, the number of applications edged upward toward eighteen thousand. Fees paid to CSFA increased accordingly, both in dollars and as a percentage of distribution.

Skip, Chip, and others in the Jostens hierarchy understood and honored each annual fee, though somewhat grudgingly. The question was never one of fairness or equity. The company simply knew its fees as compared on a percentage basis to its corporate neighbors such as First Bank System, Toro Company, General Mills, and a dozen or so others with employee-related programs, was substantially higher. Even the fact that in the fall of 1981 Jostens increased the number of $500 awards to 140 per year, the fee-for-service amount still seemed to our friends to be disproportionately high when compared to a $70,000 distribution.

From time to time, and usually as each new annual contract was negotiated, Skip and Chip would reintroduce the question of fees with the two unyielding representatives of Citizens' Scholarship Foundation of America. I, as one of the two, would blithely suggest in the course of these discussions that Jostens could easily bring its fees more in line with others by simply increasing its annual scholarship distribution. "If," I said, "your people were willing to increase the value of each scholarship from five hundred to, say, one thousand dollars, the eighteen thousand dollar fee would compare a bit more favorably with those of your corporate friends and neighbors."

The response was always and understandably the same: other legitimate and more compelling demands on the foundation's resources precluded an increased distribution for scholarships. Stuart and I would accept the explanation, shake hands with the members of the small negotiating team, and go on our way. The Jostens Student Achievement Program would run its voluminous and demanding course, and the date for the next round of negotiations would be dutifully recorded on all appropriate calendars.

As a prelude to each annual negotiating session, every spring CSFA provided an in-person report to the Jostens Foundation Board of Directors. I and my compatriots would sit with the directors and report on the just completed program activity. We would present graphs and charts and other data that confirmed the rising popularity of the program. We would provide demographic profiles of applicants from each state. We would review the process that assured at least one recipient from each state with the remaining ninety awards allocated more or less in an array consistent with population dispersion and concentrations throughout the country. That is, California might have five recipients to New Hampshire's one. These reports, though rather dry in nature, reassured the directors that the program was being managed in conformance with the current, negotiated agreement.

In the spring of 1982 both Stuart and Marlys Johnson accompanied me on the sixty-five mile drive from St. Peter to Norman Center Drive in Bloomington. Marlys had established her own value to CSFA by, among other noteworthy achievements, signing on the first $100,000 scholarship program with First Bank System in Minneapolis. In consideration of that achievement, along with many others, she was elevated to a CSFA vice presidency in 1980. I informed my two vice presidents, Johnson and Johnson, that I planned to enliven the 1982 reporting opportunity by utilizing a prop I brought along with me.

Among the eighteen thousand current-year Jostens applications appeared an unusual presentation. A young woman, I today remember as being from Massachusetts, submitted a white, vinyl-clad, three-ring binder containing her application and all supporting and corroborating documentation. In addition, Holly Rust had painstakingly taken a pen knife and cut away a lace-like cameo opening just through the vinyl on the notebook's front cover. Into this opening she had slipped her eight-by-ten color senior picture. An attractive young woman she was.

I carried the notebook into the Jostens Foundation board meeting, and when my turn on the agenda arrived I brought it to the attention of the directors. "Today," I said, "I'm going to do something a little different. In place of the graphs and charts, I am circulating a sheet of paper containing all of the numbers and comparisons we have provided you in past years. The Johnsons and I will be happy to respond to any questions you may have relative to that information. But today, ladies and gentlemen, I want to go beyond the statistics. I want to give some life, some embodiment to your scholarship program. I want to share with you the application from Holly Rust." In the tradition of "show-and-tell," I held up the vinyl notebook, face out, so that everyone could view the attractive applicant with the equally compelling name.

"Holly," I said, "very thoughtfully provided detailed documentation, much of it in original form, for her application. Please allow me to review her qualifications with you." I did. "She is," I noted, "a member of the National Honor Society. She is senior class president and an officer in the Student Council. Holly participated in Girls' State, is a four-star, varsity-level athlete, and has received a Presidential Physical Fitness Award. Holly has numerous citations for service to her community, please allow me to share a few with you." I did. "Holly has been accepted at Harvard University and plans to enroll there in the fall. Please let me share with you a few of the comments from her teachers, advisors, and community leaders." I did. I then closed the notebook, passed it to my left for circulation among the Jostens Foundation directors, and I sat down.

For what seemed like two minutes but was probably closer to thirty seconds no one said a word. Then Skip Mooney placed his glasses on the table and said.

> Joe, if any person in this room ever harbored any doubts as to the appropriateness of this program for the Jostens Foundation, that doubt is forever erased. I don't know about my colleagues here, but my eyes are not dry. The Holly Rusts of the world are the reason for our program. I am personally grateful for CSFA and for the role that both Chip Fisher and I had in working with your people to put this program together. We are honored to have a recipient of the caliber of Holly Rust.

Everyone applauded. Smiles all around. Another brief silence. Then I said: "Excuse me Skip, did I mislead anyone? I mentioned at the outset that Holly was an applicant. She isn't included among this year's winners. She finished two hundred and seventy-third. Among the eighteen thousand received, we had 272 applicants with stronger qualifications." Another silence. One of the board members spoke up.

"I move we authorize a special award for Holly Rust on the basis of today's presentation." General agreement; a single dissent.

"Sorry," I said, "unless you're ready to fund 132 other exceptions, we cannot compromise the program criteria with any special award." General, if reluctant, agreement followed. The Johnsons and I thanked the directors who had no further questions, excused ourselves from the meeting, and headed south to St. Peter.

In the fall of 1982 Jostens Foundation directors voted to authorize the sum of $200,000 to underwrite two hundred

$1,000 awards. This decision naturally increased the allure of the program, and the number of applications received by CSFA increased to twenty thousand. But at the same time, the $20,000 fee paid to CSFA represented just 10 percent of the authorized distribution.

One significant postscript to this story is that in 1984 Jostens Foundation elected also to sponsor a CSFA-managed scholarship program for the children of Jostens company employees. Neither corporate nor foundation officials expressed any discomfort with the CSFA 15 percent fee basis. A second noteworthy postscript reveals that the Jostens Foundation Student Achievement Program continued to honor outstanding high-school seniors through the spring of 1993. During the program's sixteen year life $3.1 million was awarded to 3,160 outstanding students in the United States and, for a time, in Canada as well.

Chapter Fourteen

You Can Call Me Johnson

Marlys Johnson of St. Cloud, Minnesota, was a Johnson before she met H. Stuart Johnson of St. Peter. They met in the course of their undergraduate years at Gustavus Adolphus College, graduated and married in 1961. Long before I met Stuart in 1976, those two Johnsons had lived and taught in the Philippines and Japan, and had brought two more Johnsons into the world. The arrival of two new Minnesota Johnsons was not viewed as a particularly noteworthy event beyond the immediate family and friends, even considering that the younger of the two had been born in Japan.

Minnesota is the land of Johnsons. I have always believed that if someone wished to dine on a Friday evening at the most popular restaurant in Minneapolis or St. Paul, but had no reservation, the safest bet would be to simply approach the maitre d' and say: "We are the Johnson party of two with reservations for eight o'clock."

Seven out of ten times, I believe, the maitre d' would check the reservation list and say: "Of course; please follow me."

Another consideration about Minnesota Johnsons is that the several tens of thousands of them seem to be equally divided between the Norwegians and the Swedes. That division is important because it forms the basis for much of Minnesota's light-hearted ethnic humor. Ole, Lena, Sven, Tina, and Tiebald, will be either Norwegian or Swedish--though not necessarily Johnson--depending on who's telling the story of the moment.

At times the division runs somewhat deeper. I recall that during one of my pre-holiday shopping excursions in downtown St. Peter, I stopped into my very favorite of all stores, Swedish Kontur Imports. As I was browsing through the holiday displays--straw goat figures with red ribbons, small wooden tree hangings painted in holiday colors, blue and white traditional Scandinavian Christmas decorations, and Orrefors crystal--I came upon an elderly man contemplating a decorative Rörstrand plate. He was giving it the most intense scrutiny, front and back. When the store owner, Jan Bjöerling, asked him if something was wrong, he looked up with a scowl and said: "I don't tink so. I yoost need to be darned sure it vasn't made in Norvay."

But most of the time this supposed rift is more akin to a lilting riff that settles the old-country scores with friendly and affectionate harmony. Such was the case that sub-zero day in the winter of 1978, when Stuart Johnson of Swedish descent introduced Ed Lee and me to a Mankato Johnson of Norwegian descent. We did not actually meet Attorney Charles A. "Gus" Johnson, II in Mankato. We met him in Good Thunder, some twelve miles to the south. Gus at the time practiced the tradition of his attorney father before him and, much in the spirit of the traveling preacher, maintained four satellite law offices in small communities throughout Blue Earth County so "people who had a hard time getting around, could have the use of an attorney." I also came to know that people in the county who needed but could not afford an attorney were accorded the same courtesy.

Our first encounter with Gus Johnson brings to mind one of Ed Lee's favorite stories. It's about a character called "Big John." In it a cowboy runs into the saloon and announces: "Bad news, Big John's coming to town." Everyone scatters, save the bartender who is a prisoner of his post. Within the hour the swinging doors bang open and a seven-foot behemoth of a man clomps his way into the saloon and up to the bar. The bartender wipes his sweaty hands on his apron and asks nervously: "H-howdy st-stranger, can I b-buy you a drink?" "No time," the stranger replies. "Big John's coming to town."

Gus Johnson is something of the antithesis to Ed's story. Stuart, Ed and I were scheduled to see Attorney Johnson at two in the afternoon. When we arrived he was sequestered with a client. The clock read two forty before he came out to greet us in the Spartan waiting area. Stuart had, of course, met him before, so he registered no surprise. Ed and I had not, and we did. Here before us was a diminutive man, five feet, seven inches tall, slight of build, but compact and wiry. Attorney Johnson was sporting a swept back, light brown crew cut; a brown turtleneck shirt; and a western "string" necktie. "Gentlemen," he said, taking and shaking our hands, "welcome to Good Thunder." We were thus introduced to Gus II, the son of *"Little Gus"* Johnson.

The circumstance that had brought us into his company preceded our visit. As Stuart was casting about in Minnesota in an effort to identify community leaders to help him with the organizing of Dollars for Scholars chapters, Gus's name had come to his attention. Gus had offered to be helpful in Mankato and surrounding towns, but he was immediately more intrigued by the fact that CSFA actually managed scholarship programs for the likes of the Toro Company. Gus told Stuart that he had been thinking about a way in which he might honor the memory of his father. He had considered a scholarship fund but had decided the details would prove too cumbersome. Did Stuart think CSFA might be willing to manage a program for him? Stuart, of course, thought, "why not?" Gus then established within CSFA a modest $3,300 fund which, as time and growth permitted, would make distributions from both income and principal for scholarships for residents of Lake Crystal and for other charitable purposes.

Gus saw to the growth of the fund. His first strategy was to make contributions to the memorial scholarship fund upon the passing of a client or friend, "to provide help for the living," he said. His second strategy was to deed over to CSFA an attractive house lot in Mankato which sold for $16,000. His third strategy was one that caused Stuart to call me, and me to call my chairman, Massachusetts Attorney Ed Lee. Gus Johnson decided to give CSFA a horse, a three-year-old Arabian mare, in foal. The question before the four of us in Good Thunder that day was should CSFA accept the gift of "Lady in Red?"

Gus has since said that he was somewhat overwhelmed by the company in his office that day, and that he was embarrassed to have kept us waiting once he discovered the "pedigree" of the guests from the east. But he easily recovered his composure and suggested we go over to the farm and look at the horse. Island Farm sits in proximity to Gus's boyhood town of Lake Crystal and is some dozen or so miles southeast of Mankato. In 1978 Island Farm was owned and operated by his daughter, Suzette. As the farm's name suggests, the sixteen acre property is surrounded by the water of one of Minnesota's ten thousand lakes, thereby minimizing the need for fences to restrain the horses. The beauty of the location and the attractiveness of the several buildings were somewhat lost on Ed Lee and me, because the fading afternoon sun reduced the windless temperature to -20°, and the snow, though fifty-two degrees warmer, was better than knee deep.

Lady in Red was, however, quite unfazed by the weather. This beautiful bay mare, about fifteen hands high, was culled from about thirty other Arabians in an outside ring, and led by halter to a spot outside the barn. The lead rope was then dropped, and she stood quietly with inquiring eyes and with small puffs of moisture freezing at her nostrils. We liked the horse.

Gus made the welcome suggestion that we adjourn to the house to discuss over hot coffee how Lady in Red might become part of the Gus Johnson Memorial Fund. At the kitchen table Gus suggested that Lady in Red remain at Island Farm until late January. Suzette would continue to provide care and feeding until the time of the Arabian Horse auctions in Scottsdale, Arizona. He and Suzette would then transport Lady in Red to the auction where she would be sold to the highest bidder. The proceeds would be deposited with CSFA in the Gus Johnson Memorial Fund. This arrangement sounded more then fair, and Ed and I readily agreed to it. I could not have known at the time that I was agreeing to quite a bit more.

In early January of 1979 Gus called to inform me that because Lady in Red actually belonged to CSFA, an authorized representative had to be on hand in Scottsdale to sign the necessary papers. Without hesitation I offered to assume the responsibility. I had never been to Arizona, and my first visit would prove to be memorable. First of all I was the guest of Gus and his wife, JoAnn, in a lovely condominium on the relatively prestigious McCormick Ranch. Second, I had never in my life seen opulence and affluence so openly flaunted. And third, I arrived there with the intention of selling a horse, not buying one.

Gus said of himself that he was, among the Scottsdale crowd, a "small timer." But despite his self-estimation of personal worth, he was able to find tickets for the major auctions. Admittedly we were seated fairly far back at these events--seating was assigned by capacity to bid--but we were equal among everyone enjoying sumptuous buffets and top-shelf beverages. And when the lights went down and the full orchestra finished its opening number, we were as delighted as anyone when the stage curtains opened in the barn-cum-theater, and the unannounced Beach Boys or Bob Hope or a laser light show--in the 70s a true novelty-- served as prologue for the bidding to come. Among all of the lavish attractions, one of our favorite events was the Adam's Ranch Breakfast where ranch hands cooked biscuits in earthen ovens and brewed coffee over open fires, while Mrs. Adams passed around a breakfast appetizer of batter-fried mountain oysters as a prelude to eggs and bacon served up on plain tin plates.

Lady in Red was a "small timer," too, when it came to the actual auctions. Gus and I had been privileged over time to see the first Arabian mare to sell for $1 million and the first stallion to be syndicated for over $1 million a share. We had also attended a single auction where several million dollars had changed hands, and a song, complete with lyrics and live orchestration, was written and sung for every horse brought on stage for sale. But Lady in Red was destined for the low-end "Big Top Sale," scheduled near the close of the Scottsdale All-Arabian Show competition at Clay's El Camino Ranch. This nighttime auction was held under a red and white circus tent, brightly lighted with strings of bare bulbs. Folding, brown metal chairs surrounded the dirt auction ring. That night's free fare consisted of Kentucky Fried Chicken, jug wines, and domestic beer.

The chicken was hot and the beer was cold, and Gus and I had our free-fare share of each by the time Lady in Red was brought into the ring. She sold somewhat to Gus's disappointment for $8,900. Gus told me he had never seen the bidding so low on such obvious quality. We then elected to compensate for the perceived loss of income by maximizing the Clays' hospitality. When I reflect today on that evening, a country and western song comes to mind: "The Girls All Look Prettier at Closing Time." The horses were all looking better to Gus as the sale and evening progressed. As far as I was concerned, the horses under the "Big Top" looked every bit as good to me as those earlier immortalized in verse and melody.

At one point toward ten o'clock Gus said to me: "Joe, they're giving these horses away. If you've ever thought about buying a horse, buy one now." Well, of course, I hadn't, but his advice, like hops, had fallen on fertile soil. I was vulnerable. I had forgotten my impetuous behavior at a Dollars for Scholars art auction in Manchester, New Hampshire, where in 1970 I had bid away my savings for a new and necessary heating system for a cubist lithograph and an original Salvador Dali ink sketch. A pretty filly named Kazon came up. I started bidding at one thousand, but gave up, much to my relief, before she sold for three.

At the next bidding-and-bathroom break I was ready to return to the comfort and safety of McCormick Ranch. But the owner of Kazon sought me out, took me aside and said: "You were lucky you didn't get that mare. She's too high strung. But during the next round we'll be auctioning off her brother, a gelding named Nazon. He's a great horse, and he's also a Ferzon grandson." I nodded and thanked him, even though the Ferzon revelation meant nothing to me. It did mean something to Gus. "Ferzon," he explained, "is one of the great all-time Arabian stallions. He's still alive over at the Gainey Ranch here in Scottsdale. I think he's twenty-nine years old."

True to prediction, Nazon came under the bright lights about twenty minutes into the final round. He was special as horses go, nearly golden in color with a black mane and tail. The bidding started at one thousand and ended at three thousand. Both of those bids and the horse were mine. The next morning when the nine o'clock sun warmed me awake, amorphous evening adulation gave way to rational daytime reasoning. Despite the delight I knew Nazon would bring to my fifteen-year-old daughter, Colleen, I thought: "Joe, you are from New Hampshire. You do not live on a farm. You are out $3,000. You are two thousand miles from home. And you own a horse in Arizona. You have a problem."

Gus, the amused instigator, solved part of it. He loaded Nazon on the same trailer that had transported Lady in Red to Arizona, and took my gelding back to Island Farm, a location now only fifteen hundred miles distant from New Hampshire. There Nazon would remain until June when one of the major horse transportation companies agreed to pick him up in Des Moines and transport him to New Hampshire. Gus graciously trailered Nazon the two hundred miles to Des Moines. "It was," he said, "the least" he "could do." I heartily agreed.

But while I was out a few thousand dollars, the addition of the Lady in Red proceeds to the "Little Gus" memorial fund increased its value to over $30,000. In the next few years it would grow to $40,000, and during those years Gus and I would return to Scottsdale, partly for a little rest and recuperation; partly to satisfy his continuing interest in horses; and partly to drum up law business. "There are tons of legal issues in the horse industry," he assured me. "I'm pretty well informed in this area." We also discovered we had CSFA-related calls to make in the city of leisure. One of our long-time "sustaining grant" corporations, Callahan Mining Company, was located in Scottsdale. One of our Scholarship Management Services clients, American Compensation Association, was also there. And two of our Dollars for Scholars affiliate chapters were located outside of Phoenix and in Tucson, respectively.

The Tucson chapter was unique among our membership. It was organized in 1963 by a group of retired Jewish businessmen from Cleveland, Ohio. They had agreed as friends years before to spend their retirement years in Arizona and had further agreed to meet for lunch every Monday. According to their own testimony they soon ran out of Monday things to talk about, except for Sunday's golf game, and decided to do something useful. The something was to raise scholarship dollars for students attending the University of Arizona. Someone in the group had read about Irving Fradkin and suggested they affiliate with a national scholarship program. So they did.

Gus and I managed with no difficulty to invite ourselves to a Monday luncheon with the "Habbjach" Dollars for Scholars chapter. We, of course, thought that Habbjach was a Hebrew word of some great mystery or importance. The word in reality was the first name initials of the founding group: Harry, Arthur, Ben, Jack, and so forth. A few of the original people were still there in 1980. One, past the age of ninety, carried oxygen with him. As the years passed, new faces other than our own had been added and were represented around the table. During lunch one gentleman announced that one of his certificates of deposit had come due at a local bank, and the bank asked if he wished to reinvest it. "On the way over to lunch today," he said, "I went to the bank and said I would roll it over if the bank made a hundred dollar contribution to our scholarship fund. They said 'no,' so I took it to another bank where they did."

Gus and I were, of course, both curiosities as well as the program of the day, but the informal agenda had another item called "Any News?" One member said his wife just went into the hospital. The group leader then said: "Okay, everyone throw ten dollars into the scholarship fund to wish Charlie's wife a speedy recovery." Everyone did. Any item--a birdie on the golf course, the birth of a grandchild, a granddaughter's marriage--cost the proud announcer something. Several hundred dollars were raised around the table by some very happy people. "We ask everybody for something," the group leader said. Many people beyond their small group obviously responded, for over the years the chapter has provided $578,000 in scholarships for students enrolled at the university.

Gus, who is generally interested in everything, was, on the strength of our adventures and his relationship with the St. Peter Johnsons, developing a fascination for Citizens' Scholarship Foundation of America. He became a member of CSFA's advisory board in 1981, and by 1982 I persuaded him to stand for election to the Board of Trustees. CSFA's presence was growing geometrically in Minnesota, and with that growth came the need for on-site services, including legal counsel. His law firm provided gratis all such "unrealized expenses" to CSFA.

The ever increasing level of activity in Minnesota persuaded the CSFA trustees to hold occasional board meetings in Minneapolis as well as St. Peter. By board inclination and tradition, and in keeping with Ed Lee's "work hard; play hard" philosophy, CSFA's staff always scheduled an unusual evening of fun for the trustees. In Minnesota we looked to Gus for help. In response Gus, JoAnn and Suzette, together with other family and friends, undertook the incredible task of cleaning the big barn at Island Farm to near hospital-hygiene specifications. The Johnsons then hosted for all CSFA trustees and spouses, and all CSFA staff, a gala evening down on the farm, complete with a turkey roast, an Arabian horse show, and a barn dance. There on Island Farm I learned the delight of baked acorn squash filled with spiced hot applesauce, and of turkey roasted on a huge, covered outdoor grill. There is where we all learned that shared affection, respect, tolerance, good will, and understanding are the essential elements of compassionate productivity.

Gus, however, would do more. Settled in his oversize law office desk chair in Mankato, he tells the story best.

> Back as far as I can remember, my dad was known to everyone as "Little Gus." He stood about five feet even, but was something of a giant in the Minnesota legislature. Never one for "dressing up," he was usually seen in any setting wearing a wool cardigan and wool pants, both full of burn holes from the falling ashes of his endless chain of cigarettes.
>
> His notoriety in St. Paul brought him legal clients from all over the state. In the 1950s he had as two of his clients a Norwegian couple in Owatonna, a small city some fifty miles east of Mankato. Gisle and Eva Johnson, both then in their fifties, were of the "old school." They tolerated "Little Gus" because he, too, was Norwegian, but they begrudged him his fees. They started out with a Nash and Studebaker dealership, and eventually moved up to own what was the smallest "ma and pa" Mercedes-Benz dealership in the country.

They did not believe in credit. Everything was cash. Employees were paid in cash. Cars were purchased for cash. They lived frugally. Any profit from car sales was invested. They had no children, and they had discussed with my dad the possibility of providing funds to educate Lutheran ministers. They began by making modest annual gifts to a nearby Lutheran seminary.

When my dad died in 1977, I assumed responsibility for many of his clients. The Owatonna Johnsons were among them, and when they weren't mad at me for some reason, usually over my fees, they considered me their attorney. In one interim, when they were upset with me, they lost the Mercedes-Benz franchise in a fraudulent deal. I eventually got it back for them.

The local seminary was anxious to benefit more from the Johnsons, and despite the fact that the seminary never made much of the annual gifts, they sent some people in the early 1980s to ask Gisle and Eva for a significant gift. The Johnsons responded by giving the seminary the car dealership building in the form of an annuity. Under that arrangement the seminary would own the building, but the Johnsons would receive, during the remainder of their lifetimes, annual income equivalent to a small percentage of the value of the building. Upon their passing the building could be sold, and the seminary would receive the entire proceeds of the sale. Both Johnsons were then in their eighties.

The seminary was again weak in expressing appreciation for this gift, but someone there decided to go after the Johnsons for an advance commitment on the rest of their estate, estimated in excess of one million dollars. Mrs. Johnson was very offended. By this time the dealership had been sold, and the couple was in residence at a modest nursing home. Their money was all they had left, and neither was comfortable discussing with others how it would be distributed after their deaths. The couple asked me if they could some way benefit the city of

Owatonna. I told them of my dad's memorial scholarship fund and how it was helping students in Lake Crystal. They asked for some printed information and said they would give it some thought. They were adamant about not having any *professionals* call on them.

They both passed away in 1988, and when the will was probated, CSFA received the bulk of the estate. The established trust was worth $1.5 million dollars. The income is used for scholarships and loans for resident students of Owatonna. Up until that time, it was the largest single gift ever given to CSFA by anyone for any purpose.

When I asked Gus if the seminary was aware of this change in plans after twenty years, he said no. "I was not, as you might imagine, particularly popular with either the seminary or the Johnsons' distant relatives," Gus said. "But I had no part in changing their minds. Others deserve the credit for that."

Gus's term as a governing trustee of Citizens' Scholarship Foundation of America lasted beyond my tenure with CSFA. In 1991, when his third and final term ended after nine years, he was asked to share his thoughts with the board. He paused at one point in the course of his remarks to wipe away tears. According to witnesses to the event, he removed his glasses, found his handkerchief, wiped his eyes, blew his nose and said: "This always works pretty well with juries." More important to me was an earlier evening in May of 1986, when he and JoAnn invited me to their Mankato home for something of a farewell dinner. Conversation under the circumstances was a bit difficult, but one moment will remain with me forever. Gus handed me a glass, and raised his to mine.

"Joe, I want you to know you are my best friend on earth."

Some few Johnsons stand tall among the rest.

Chapter Fifteen

Good Call but Off the Wall

Ben G. Crosby and Ronald P. DeGregorio played handball together. Both were highly competitive and evenly matched, though Ron was the more athletic of the two. In his mid-thirties, his speed and prowess had been developed earlier when his solid five foot, seven inch frame was an asset to his ice hockey days. Ben was larger both in height and girth, but his size gave him something of a power advantage. Both were in their professional lives financial managers and investment advisors, Ben out of a large firm in Boston; Ron out of his own smaller office in Salem, New Hampshire. They were close friends.

On this particular October afternoon in 1979, the two were on the front end of a warm-up session at the Salem YMCA in anticipation of a rigorous workout to come. The small, hard rubber ball was pocking at lazy intervals off the front wall mostly above the horizontal red line. Because these high, leisurely shots came easily back to the players, neither had yet worked up a sweat. "I've got an interesting situation," said

Ben. "I got a guy down in Massachusetts with a tax problem. He needs to do something pretty quick to reduce his taxes for this year. I'm suggesting he give away some appreciated real estate. He's interested in the idea, but we don't know who to give it to."

"Does he like kids?" asked Ron.

"I guess so," answered Ben. "He doesn't have any. You have something in mind?"

"Yup," said Ron, "Citizens' Scholarship Foundation of America."

"Never heard of it," said Ben.

Such was the prelude to the first charitable remainder annuity trust given to CSFA. Ron DeGregorio just happened to be a director of the Salem, New Hampshire, Dollars for Scholars chapter. One of CSFA's more successful community affiliates, the chapter boasted among its early officers one John Sununu, then a professor at Tufts University. Ron also happened to be on the Advisory Board of Trustees of Citizens' Scholarship Foundation of America.

Ron called me the day following the handball match and asked if CSFA would be interested in entering into a life-income arrangement with a Mr. Gove W. Sleeper of Burlington, Massachusetts. At that time in my life I was completely ignorant of the more sophisticated vehicles for deferred or planned giving. My naiveté was undoubtedly a product of my long-time obsession with current income. I suggested Ron call Ed Lee who, as both chairman of CSFA and a knowledgeable attorney, would be in the best position to both understand Ron's question and to answer it. Ron explained to Ed that this seventy-six-year-old gentleman wished to make a gift of just under fifteen acres of prime real estate adjacent to Burlington's business area. The appraised value of the property was $365,000.

Ed indicated that CSFA would be very much interested and offered to meet with Mr. Sleeper to explore the matter further. Ed and I were subsequently invited to lunch at the Sleepers' retirement residence in Arlington, Massachusetts, where Ron and Ben joined us for a discussion on the proposed annuity. This discussion was not easily conducted, because as kind and benevolent as Gove Sleeper was, he was almost totally deaf. And even in the early age of electronic miniaturization, the battery pack for his hearing aid was the size of a small table radio.

Ed, in a display of patience and courtesy, educated Mr. Sleeper on the attributes of CSFA. So taken was Gove with Ed that he asked him to draft the documents establishing the Bernice McIntire Sleeper Charitable Annuity Trust. Under the terms of this trust, named in honor of Gove's first wife, Gove and his surviving second spouse, Marcia, would receive annually the equivalent of 8 percent of the value of the gift until both passed on.

The trust became a reality on December 27, 1979. The timing and the terms created an interesting situation for CSFA. The annuity contract required CSFA to begin equal quarterly payments three months to the day after the effective date of the trust. The gift, however, was land, not cash, and winter in New England is not the best time to move real estate. Ed Lee did manage in fairly short order to find a willing buyer. But the buyer's accepted offer was $325,000, and he also negotiated the right to pay off the obligation in installments over a period of three years. Gove was, however, entitled to $28,000 per year, or seven thousand dollars per quarter, beginning in March of 1980. The timing of the purchase and the terms of the sale meant that CSFA would have to invade the available principal in order to satisfy the quarterly payments to the Sleepers.

Ed in a word was a masterful manager of the trust. He not only met the quarterly obligations to Gove and Marcia during their lifetimes--Gove died in 1982; Marcia in 1989--he also divided the trust's assets among three different investors, and this strategy brought the value of the trust by 1989 to a level that exceeded the original assessed value of the real estate. But even more impressive, Ed's prowess and creativity permitted the gift to be of critical importance to CSFA during the lifetimes of the two annuitants.

At one point in the early eighties when the refreshing burden of growth caused CSFA some challenging cash-flow problems, Ed Lee suggested a unique possible use of the corpus of the trust. He sought and received opinion of outside counsel to the effect that CSFA could, under certain conditions, borrow from the principal of the Sleeper annuity trust. One condition was that guarantors would have to be secured for any loan. The second was that any loan against the principal would have to be made at a rate of interest both sufficient to satisfy the payout obligations of the trust and competitive, in terms of total return, with the unusually high interest earnings of the early 1980s economy. Five CSFA trustees together guaranteed $70,000 for any board-approved future loan obligations.

CSFA had for the first time established an internal line of credit. A small portion of the trust was converted to another asset in 1985 and 1987. In those years CSFA purchased, in two separate transactions, twenty-five acres of land, in a successful effort to expand the boundaries of its new St. Peter, Minnesota, office building and preserve the attractiveness of the building's setting. The combined purchases totaled $41,143. No trustee was ever required to make good on the guarantee. The guarantors were released following the death of Marcia Sleeper. Marcia's passing effectively cancelled any internal loan obligations, including the loan for the purchase of the land. Even with the obligations retired, the trust remainder provided CSFA full use of $348,000 in unrestricted cash assets. Over the years CSFA has kept the principal largely intact, utilizing the income to provide services and recognition awards for its Dollars for Scholars communities.

In 1993 Gove Sleeper was named posthumously a recipient of a CSFA Milestone Award. The award recognizes individuals beyond the CSFA family whose unselfish actions materially advance the programs and influence of Citizens' Scholarship Foundation of America.

Part V

Ralph H. Seifert

1980-1984

Cy
An Interlude in Chicago
J. B. Tipton is Alive and Well
Two Bills Come to Call
Three Bills Get the Call
What's Good for General Motors
Big House on the Prairie

Chapter Sixteen

Cy

On the dining room wall in a white, two-story house facing the water of Cozy Harbor in West Southport, Maine, hangs a black and white, head and shoulders, framed photograph of a sea captain. The figure is wearing a Greek fisherman's cap and is sporting a neatly trimmed beard. His age is indeterminate; could be in his forties or fifties, or maybe but most likely not, even sixties. His head is canted just a bit to the right as if he is perhaps listening to a story or a point of view, or anticipating the punch line to a well-told piece of Down-East humor. His features suggest warmth and humor even without the benefit of a smile. Somehow his visage seems larger than the picture's eight-by-ten format; larger even than the six inch black matting and the sixteen-by-twenty ebony frame.

This portrait is of Ralph H. Seifert: salesman, sailor, skier. I knew him, of course, as a long-time trustee and as CSFA's fourth chairman of the board. No one, with the understandable exception of Dr. Irving Fradkin, has a longer or stronger record of uninterrupted service to this nation's aspiring students. Cy Seifert is an exuberant man whose lifestyle might be regarded as cavalier by some and fascinating by others. But to those who know and love him, and they are legion, Cy is simply a person who has taken with gusto all that more than six decades on this earth can offer and has dedicated that lifetime to giving much of it back. A substantial portion of what Ralph Seifert has given back has benefited Citizens' Scholarship Foundation of America.

Cy's service dates back to 1961, the year Roger Williams of Carling Brewing Company hosted a meeting of community leaders from eastern Massachusetts. Roger called them together for the express purpose of hearing from the Fall River optometrist who had introduced a unique scholarship program there some three years earlier. Cy Seifert, one of Roger William's fraternity brothers at Brown University, and an already emerging community leader in nearby Mansfield, was among those invited.

Cy at that time was in his thirty-fifth year and by virtue of his age was about to retire as president of the local Jaycees chapter. Cy was not only enthralled with Fradkin's Dollars for Scholars idea, he also believed that Mansfield could become a showplace for the program. As luck and stamina would have it, Cy's retirement from the Jaycees signaled his induction as president of the Mansfield Rotary Club. He was quick to capitalize on both events. At his next Rotary meeting he convinced the forty members present to put up $25 apiece for the fledgling Dollars for Scholars program. With this $1,000 in hand, he and his fellow Rotarians recruited additional volunteers and organized Citizens' Scholarship Foundation of Mansfield. The new chapter was now the thirteenth of Dr. Fradkin's loosely affiliated community scholarship program. Cy would serve that chapter as a volunteer, a leader, and a generous contributor for the next twenty-five years. During that period the Mansfield chapter would provide nearly half a million dollars to fifteen hundred local students.

Not content with just local success, Cy carried his enthusiasm to Boston where he met with state Jaycees officials. He asked for a spot on the program of the next statewide convention, where he successfully encouraged the delegates to adopt Dollars for Scholars as a statewide project. With that mission accomplished, he asked Roger Williams to accompany him to the Newsome and Newsome advertising firm where a young account executive named Philip Webster was being paid by Carling Brewing Company to develop promotional materials for Dollars for Scholars. Phil and CSFA's first executive director, Fred Margolis, developed brochures and other items that would be suitable for use at levels as lofty as a national convention. Cy, at his own expense, carried the materials to a series of Jaycees national conventions. In between all of this activity Cy eked out a fairly decent living from his small insurance agency in Mansfield.

Cy's earlier experience with the Jaycees would serve Dollars for Scholars in other ways as well. He divided the Commonwealth of Massachusetts along much the same lines as the Jaycees' regional configuration, and then set about recruiting leaders from the handful of Dollars for Scholars chapters to help him, along with Irving Fradkin, to organize additional chapters throughout the state. Among the people he successfully recruited was a young, community minded attorney from Westfield by the name of Ed Lee.

Cy's commitment to Dollars for Scholars was not lost on Dr. Fradkin. In 1961, following the incorporation of Citizens' Scholarship Foundation of America, Cy was among those asked to serve on the first Board of Trustees. By the time I first met Cy in 1967 he had been elevated to treasurer of CSFA. In a carton somewhere I still have a Polaroid photograph of a cleanshaven, six-feet three-inch, horned-rim-adorned, thirty-eight-year-old insurance agent with a crew cut, towering over the new, and first, twenty-six-year-old New England regional director of CSFA. In that photo we are contemplating an enlarged map of the United States tacked up on the wall of CSFA's 43 Leon Street, Boston office. The map depicts, with the help of colored pins, more than two hundred Dollars for Scholars chapters in about thirteen states.

Cy would remain treasurer until 1971, the year that CSFA relocated its nomadic office from Waltham, Massachusetts, to Concord, New Hampshire. He then surrendered that position to Harry Rosenberg, who by virtue of his residence in Claremont, New Hampshire, was better located to cosign checks and spend quality time worrying over CSFA's monthly financial statements. Cy did, however, remain a very active trustee, and one who was, on the basis of his wit, idiosyncrasies, and enthusiasm, extremely popular with the CSFA staff.

By reason of seniority alone, Cy was the logical possible candidate for an earlier CSFA chairmanship when Brad Norris resigned in 1971. He was not, however, hurt or annoyed when Ed Lee was elected chairman. He knew, as did I, that if the timing for his elected term wasn't exactly fair, it was exactly right. Cy had spent much of the 1970s charting the oftentimes choppy waters of his business, New England Security Insurance Agency. Had he been elected as CSFA's leader in the early 1970s, he could never have afforded the hundreds of days CSFA required on its own course to survival. By 1979, however, both CSFA and New England Security were on the cusp of unprecedented growth and prosperity. Cy had an opportunity to "grow" two businesses simultaneously, and he was ready for both tasks. We, in fact, referred to the period of his chairmanship, 1980 to 1984, as "The Business of Doing Business."

Shortly after his election in October of 1979, Cy came to visit me at One South Street in Concord, New Hampshire. He came into my office and sat opposite me facing my desk. I was quite pleased with my desk, because among other reasons, it was new. For the first time in the lifetime of CSFA we were privileged to have new furniture. Our World Wars I and II surplus office furnishings had been recently donated to another emerging and frugal nonprofit organization.

My desk was a "conference" desk, designed so that the person sitting opposite could have both knee space and work space. The desk looked as if it belonged to someone who was terribly busy, especially if the task load was measured by the clutter on the surface. Cy looked at it for a minute, pointed to a stack of papers, and asked: "What's this?" I thumbed through the stack, and described its contents. "Are you working on any of it now?" Cy asked.

"No," I answered.

"Then," he instructed, "get it off your desk."

He went through every item on my desk in the same manner, followed by the same instruction, until we arrived at the item of my current attention. That item was permitted to stay. He then advised me that a good manager only works on one thing at a time: "Everything else is a distraction," he said. From that day to this one I have worked at a clean desk, and for many years at a table in preference to a desk. And at the close of each business day the surface is clean of paper and other debris. That lesson was the first of perhaps a hundred or more I would learn from Mr. Seifert through instruction or example in the ensuing five years.

The organization Ralph Seifert inherited at the close of 1979 was no longer terribly fragile, but it was in an organizational sense somewhat fragmented. CSFA had for so long been on a week-to-week and then month-to-month basis, that no one, trustees included, spoke of vision or long-term plans. Irving Fradkin, of course, continued to dream of his one thousand Dollars for Scholars chapters. But the costs associated with servicing that number of chapters in 1979 would have quickly put CSFA out of business.

A curious discussion, however, took place at the fall annual meeting of 1980. A gentleman named Howard A. Moreen, recently retired from The Aetna, and recently appointed to the CSFA Governing Board of Trustees, had perhaps a fresh perspective on the battle. He asked the board members to consider the concepts of "hard money" and "soft money." He noted that for the first nineteen years of CSFA's existence the national organization had been very dependent, and at times, excessively dependent on gifts and grants. "That type of money should be regarded as soft," he said, "because it is unreliable, unpredictable, and often unrenewable." Howard continued.

> In the more recent years, CSFA has been earning money, beginning with Toro in 1976 and continuing with the addition of more than thirty accounts since that time. The fees charged these companies for running their scholarship programs is "hard money." It is reliable, billable, and assuming satisfactory performance, renewable. Were I the sole guardian of CSFA's future, I would look to the hard money potential and de-emphasize over time the reliance on soft money.

That message fell on receptive ears and none more receptive than those of the newest board chairman. He noted that CSFA would in 1981 distribute more than $660,000 in scholarships out of its Concord office and another $500,000 out of its Midwest office located in the basement of the home of Stuart and Marlys Johnson in St. Peter, Minnesota. Cy expanded on Howard Moreen's observations.

> The useable income from this activity alone should be well in excess of one hundred thousand dollars. Our history suggests that an astronomical effort would be required to secure an identical sum in new, unrestricted gift and grant revenues. And while I am certainly a great champion of Dollars for Scholars, I plan to commit my term as chairman to the growth and development of our "hard money" earning potential. In addition, I plan to begin the process of restructuring CSFA at the board level in order that board members can be more responsive to an exciting and growing corporation. And, finally, I will work along with the board and staff to give this organization a truly national image.

Within a few months Cy provided the board with more detail on his third and final objective.

> For far too long CSFA has been viewed as a New England organization with a smattering of activity in the Midwest. The annual report for 1980 carries on its cover a picture of a covered bridge in North Conway, New Hampshire, and one of the Golden Gate Bridge in San Francisco. The purpose of the latter was to announce our first program activity of any consequence on the West Coast. During the five years I have committed in advance to my chairmanship, we will begin to fill in the middle.

The "filling in" of the middle was in one sense already underway. For more than three years Ed Lee and I had been raising "soft money" in the country's ten most populous states, including the likes of Texas and California, to underwrite student aid surveys for the College Scholarship Information Bank. The *CSFA Annual Report for 1979* recognized more than fifty foundations and corporations that in one way or another were supporting the survey work. But by 1980 the trustees had serious doubts as to whether the search-and-match service would ever bring significant dollars to CSFA.

Clearly the mandate was to expand the development of CSFA's Scholarship Management Services as rapidly as possible. Cy also believed that in order for this expansion to take place, certain other matters would have to be addressed. First among those matters was the makeup of the Board of Trustees and the clarification of the role of its members and the members of the Advisory Board of Trustees. Mr. Seifert asked long-time trustee, Frank E. Morin of Wilton, Connecticut, to serve as the chairman of a Committee on Trustees and to work with him and with staff to better define the respective roles of each.

A second matter was that of the internal organization of the corporation. Mr. Seifert appointed Trustee Joseph M. Hinchey, senior vice president for finance at Analog Devices, to chair a board Committee on Organization, and then to come forward with recommendations on everything from internal operations to equitable compensation.

In an effort to provide oversight for the rapidly growing financial operations of CSFA, Mr. Seifert appointed Greg J. Macri, Jr., president of Keene (NH) Products, to chair CSFA's first Audit and Finance Committee, and announced the appointment of H. Stuart Johnson as staff vice president for finance. "CSFA is now a $1 million corporation," Mr. Seifert noted. "That fact alone suggests some level of fiscal accountability. Isn't it nice to have a problem we've never had before?"

Within short order every trustee was assigned to either a committee chairmanship or a specific committee. "Now," Mr. Seifert said, "only one major problem remains. If you look around the table you will see that with the exception of David Logan Steele of Lancaster, Pennsylvania, every CSFA trustee resides in New England. I am asking Frank Morin in his role as chairman of the Committee on Trustees to address this problem. We cannot be considered 'national' in the absence of national representation."

The CSFA staff, numbering twelve in 1980--three in Minnesota, eight in New Hampshire, and one Michael Vorhaus in California--was not simply standing by in awe as the board members accepted and addressed Cy's several mandates. The level of business of CSFA was increasing at such a pace that--with the exception of he who had been elevated from executive director to senior vice president, and who was now spending up to 30 percent of his time working directly with various board members--staff was simply oblivious to the emergence of Cy's grand design.

Staff was very busy. In addition to the corporation-centered activity, CSFA had been selected by the San Francisco Foundation to conduct a major student-need study in Marin County, California. Over time the income from this project alone would exceed $100,000. The number of CSFA-administered corporation and foundation-sponsored scholarship programs had grown by the fall of 1980 from just over thirty to forty-six. CSFA's community Dollars for Scholars programs, though still secondary insofar as CSFA's priorities were concerned, had stabilized in membership at 175, and between 1979 and 1980, had increased local scholarship distributions from $711,500 to $926,000.

One event in 1980 was of particular significance to me. The board had long ago concluded that the various titles assigned me over the years were not very useful in getting me into places I had to be, such as in the audiences of high-level corporate officers. When I was elevated from executive director to senior vice president in 1978, Trustee Howard Moreen asked how the new title made me feel. "Ten years older," I replied. The problem facing us all was that Irving Fradkin, in founding CSFA in 1961, was elected president by his first board, and he had held the title as a deserved honor ever since. Only Irving could make the decision to relinquish it. He did so of his own generous volition at the October 17, 1980, CSFA board meeting held at The Aetna in Hartford, Connecticut. And in the course of a very emotional presentation I was named the first staff president of what was very soon to become a multi-million dollar scholarship corporation.

Moving us toward that stature was the establishing of the Gove W. Sleeper annuity trust at the close of calendar year 1979. At June 30, 1980, CSFA's balance sheets reflected a $38,000 turn-around, from a minus $21,023 at the close of fiscal '79 to a plus of $17,769. CSFA during my remaining years in office would not again experience a negative fund balance.

Mr. Seifert reflected on the year 1980.

> This year marks the completion of my first year as chairman of CSFA and my nineteenth as a volunteer board member of our national scholarship foundation. In my earlier volunteer capacity I helped to shape the policies and monitor the programs of the foundation. Now as a volunteer chairman, I have assumed the awesome

responsibility of providing direction for what will soon be a $3 million nonprofit scholarship corporation.

My approach to my current task is now of necessity more pragmatic. An organization of this size with its inherent responsible volunteer effort, its several innovative programs, and its growing fiduciary responsibility, must now be run by the use of the head as well as the heart. Programs of this type in our society must not only survive but must also flourish.

The year 1981 marked the 20th anniversary of the incorporation of Citizens' Scholarship Foundation of America and the 25th anniversary of Dr. Irving Fradkin's Dollars for Scholars program. In retrospect that year seems to be one in which CSFA paused briefly to catch its breath to ready itself for the forthcoming ride on the express to success. A part of that readiness was the securing of a private letter ruling from the Internal Revenue Service that gave CSFA a distinct advantage over the competition in establishing scholarship programs funded by private foundations. Another part was the fact that CSFA, because of its steadily improving financial picture, its governance reorganization, and the work of the several trustee committees, was cited as meeting all standards of the New York City-based National Charities Information Bureau, and was thereby included on a somewhat exclusive list of very high caliber, nonprofit organizations.

As part of the anniversaries' celebration, three people were seated on the CSFA Governing Board of Trustees. All were very active at the grass-roots level in addressing the needs of young people. Harold J. Hebl was a highly regarded guidance counselor in the St. Paul, Minnesota, public school system. Harold had been active during CSFA's Minnesota Project as a member of Stuart

Johnson's Midwest advisory committee. Robert Q. Baker, retired president of Bank One of Coshocton, Ohio, had for many years served as the volunteer president of the local Dollars for Scholars chapter. Barbara M. Kuzdzol of Attleboro, Massachusetts, while a New Englander, was a 1962 Dollars for Scholars recipient in her home town of Mansfield, Massachusetts. Following her graduation from college in 1966, she joined the local Mansfield Dollars for Scholars board and repaid to the chapter the full amount of her award. Barbara was the first Dollars for Scholars recipient named to the CSFA governing board.

During 1981 CSFA's number of corporate and foundation clients grew steadily to sixty. Combined scholarship distributions from all of CSFA's programs exceeded $4.5 million, and the June 30 audited financial statements reflected a fund balance of just over $95,000. In this same year CSFA ventured briefly into the publications business, producing two excellent student aid catalogs, one each for New Hampshire and Minnesota. But staff and board were soon to conclude that CSFA should focus its attention on what it did best. "Anything else on our desk was," to echo chairman Seifert's words, "a distraction."

In 1982 CSFA began to take stock of the progress it was making not only in its program growth but also with its board-driven internal reorganization. The board had become a bit more cosmopolitan with the addition of two more Minnesota gentlemen, Lloyd L. Brandt, vice president of First Bank System in Minneapolis; and Mankato Attorney C. A. "Gus" Johnson II. Of equal or perhaps even greater importance was that the two board committees on organization and on trustees had done their work well. CSFA's corporate operating structure was a study in efficiency and a model to be envied. CSFA's board structure had undergone many refinements. The number of elected governing trustees was fixed at eighteen with six terms expiring at three-year intervals. The number of annual full board meetings was reduced from five to three, all scheduled one year in advance. And the Advisory Board of Trustees, once chiefly a resting place for worn-out trustees, was redefined as an opportunity to bring people with particular interests, credentials, influence, or expertise into the CSFA family. The advisory board was also to be viewed as a wellspring for additions to the governing board.

Cy at this juncture was wrestling with one new problem. He stood before the board and announced: "We need a new name for 'surplus.' We probably shouldn't refer to it as profit. We are, after all, nonprofit by definition." Cy was referring to the fact that CSFA's revenue over expenses at June 30, 1982, exceeded $118,000, and the fund balance had grown to more than a quarter of a million dollars. I explained to both Cy and the board that the fundamental differences between a for-profit and not-for-profit corporation are first, that the board members could not benefit materially from their service to CSFA, and second, CSFA could not issue stock. We could, however, show a "profit."

Cy remained unconvinced. Howard Moreen then suggested we refer to "surplus" as "unencumbered discretionary revenues." CSFA may well have been in 1982 at the forefront of "political correctness."

Profit, by that name or any other name, is indeed sweet. It gives an organization time to think of things it would like to do in addition to the things that must be done. CSFA crossed over into Imagination Land in 1982. Irving Fradkin, pretty much on his own, had been spending his Wednesday mornings visiting the campuses of small, private colleges in and around Massachusetts. His self-assigned task was to ask college presidents if they would be willing to match, on some equitable basis, scholarships brought to their campuses by community Dollars for Scholars recipients. Richard A. Boudreau, President of Fisher Junior College in Boston, was the first to agree. "My wife was a Dollars for Scholars recipient," he said. "I'm happy to do something in return." With that simple statement the CSFA Collegiate Partners program was born.

I was soon to learn that not all colleges and universities could match student aid awarded by Dollars for Scholars or any other private sources. But we did see here an opportunity to encourage all institutions of higher learning to treat such assistance in a more equitable fashion. Under federal law, parents who save and students who successfully compete for outside scholarships are often penalized by the system. I had personally long contended that local scholarships should be viewed as part of a family's expected contribution to a child's education, rather than being viewed as part of the college-based student aid package. The rationale for this contention is set forth in detail in a 1983 document entitled "Private Aid is a Private Matter." I saw in the Collegiate Partners program an opportunity to begin a dialogue on this issue. Some small progress has been made with this perspective over the past twelve years and the dialogue continues today.

Another imaginative thought materialized in 1982 and focused on the necessity to honor and give public recognition to volunteers at all levels of CSFA's program activities. Volunteers may not be allowed to benefit materially, but they should certainly benefit emotionally if not spiritually. CSFA at the national level took note that with the advisory board pasture now closed to retired trustees, no way existed to recognize the contributions, both in performance and support, of outstanding retired, board-level volunteers. Similarly, with Irving's community Dollars for Scholars program now more than a quarter of a century old, somewhere out there in the universe of two hundred chapters, a number of dedicated folks had no doubt rendered outstanding time and service. Out of these combined reflections emerged two methods of recognition: first, CSFA's highest honor, the CSFA Trustees Honor Roll, and second, its community level counterpart, the Dollars for Scholars National Honor Roll. The latter invites local affiliates to nominate for CSFA board approval--and the resulting honor roll inclusion--those persons who were or are instrumental to a chapter's success.

By the close of calendar 1982, Mr. Seifert was euphoric. In commenting on the year just past he extolled that CSFA had enjoyed a 36 percent growth in total assets, a 58 percent improvement in the fund balance, and a 41 percent growth in actual scholarship disbursements. "Clearly," he asserted, "such remarkable growth cannot be indefinitely sustained. But," he continued, "I am optimistic enough to predict that CSFA will be a $100 million scholarship organization by the year 2003." The board as a whole chalked it up to delusions of grandeur, complicated by eccentricity. The members decided his condition wasn't serious, and permitted Cy to continue as chairman.

The following year, 1983, would prove to be the most exhilarating year in my twenty with CSFA. This year saw the signing on of CSFA's one hundredth corporate and foundation client, General Electric Foundation. GE was one of seven program sponsors making annual scholarship awards totaling $100,000 or more. Those awards in the aggregate would soon be dwarfed by a single, new account.

CSFA during the year signaled to its Dollars for Scholars affiliates that the 1970 mandate of the board, relative to restrictions on support for developing and sustaining chapters, had been lifted. Marlys Johnson, as a recently named vice president, was given the specific responsibility of reinstating chapter services including accelerated development, promotional support, and volunteer recognition. Marlys was the same person who would come to me within a few months and say: "Joe, now that CSFA is a $6 million corporation, don't you think we ought to have a formal business plan?" At the moment I thought not, but I would quickly change my mind. CSFA was getting to be big business, and was acting in a businesslike fashion. Our reputation was growing, glowing, and spreading. We were becoming better known among the *Fortune 500* corporations, and we had recently designed scholarship programs for Cray Research, Baxter Travenol, and G.D. Searle.

But neither Cy, nor Stuart, nor Marlys, nor I were prepared for three events that would define the fate of CSFA in 1983. The first was the selection of CSFA by the General Motors Corporation and the US Equal Employment Opportunities Commission for the design and direct administration of $7 million, over five years, in education grants to women and minorities in the General Motors workplace. The second was the announcement of an anonymous $325,000 grant designed to permit CSFA to open two offices in New York State for purposes of expanding both the Scholarship Management Services and the Dollars for Scholars program. The third was to initiate the strategy to construct a $1 million national headquarters facility: not in New England; not in New York or Chicago or Minneapolis; but rather in a soybean field overlooking the Minnesota River valley in St. Peter, Minnesota.

As Ralph Seifert entered his final year as chairman, nearly all he had set out to do was done. A few refinements were added in 1984. More than $300,000 was raised, chiefly in Minnesota, toward the cost of the new building. Two banks in St. Peter agreed to cooperate on a mortgage for CSFA for the $700,000 balance, permitting an early payoff without penalty--an appropriate provision as things turned out. CSFA in its board's wisdom created the position of chairman-elect, in order that the incoming chair would have a year to work with a predecessor. Board chair terms were set at two years, with opportunity to serve in that capacity limited to two consecutive terms.

Cy would preside over his final board meeting as chairman on November 17, 1984, in the not quite completed board room of the new national headquarters building. On that occasion one of the trustees who had served Cy as the architect of internal organization, Joe Hinchey, noted: "Every organization that plans to succeed has to take a quantum step." CSFA had taken that size step under the leadership of Ralph H. Seifert. But neither the effort nor the results had dulled the edges of either his personality or his appetites. When Ruth Jones-Saxey of First Interstate Bank of California was asked to comment on her first impressions as a newly elected governing trustee, she noted that because of time and distance, she arrived in Minneapolis the evening prior to her first board meeting. She joined the few CSFA people she recognized in the lounge of the North Star Hotel. As the evening progressed she took note of the activity around her. At one point she asked: "Who in the world is that crazy guy?"

"Oh," someone answered, "that's Ralph Seifert, our chairman."

Chapter Seventeen

An Interlude in Chicago

Some events seem at the time to carry no specific moral and provide no profound lesson, save the rewards of compassion and kindness. Some, nevertheless, are still worth relating, as is the tale of Leo and Marie.

I believe I am correct in my thinking that the problem of overbooking within the airline industry is a product of airline deregulation. And in the early 1980s the airlines were somewhat uncertain as to how to handle the problem. Such was the case of my second-of-July flight on United Airlines in 1982. In that year I was working in Marin County, California, under a CSFA agreement with the San Francisco Foundation. Because of the frequency and length of the coast-to-coast flights, I was authorized under the terms of the agreement to fly first class from The City by the Bay to the City of the Beans, with a change of planes at Chicago O'Hare. I was doing so that day.

My itinerary called for me to spend the night in Boston and then to meet chairman Seifert and two CSFA staff members for an informal employee recognition luncheon at Jimmy's Harborside restaurant just off Atlantic Avenue in Boston's Commercial Wharf area.

At O'Hare I was standing in the gate area a little after six in the evening when the United Airlines agent announced that the Boston flight was overbooked, and six seats were needed. The reward for those people surrendering seats included a free, round-trip ticket to any destination in the United States, an overnight stay at the O'Hare Hilton hotel, dinner at the Hilton, and a same-class departure on the next day 7:00 a.m. flight to Boston. Because I didn't especially care whether I slept in Chicago or Boston, and because I quickly realized one was free and the other was not, I slapped down my ticket on the gate counter. A tiny gray-haired woman observed my action and asked me what I was doing. I quickly explained to her the offer by United and she followed suit with two tickets. She then turned to me and said: "My husband Leo's in the men's room. Will you tell him what I did?"

"No," I said. "You tell him what you did. I'll tell him why you did it."

Leo, who was but a little larger than Marie, appeared straight away, and Marie said, "Leo, I gave away our tickets. This man will tell you why." I did manage to penetrate his look of shock, and within a few minutes we three and three others were ushered to a small room near the jetway where we were issued our free tickets, our overnight vouchers, our $10 dinner chits, and our morning flight tickets. "See, Leo," said Marie, as we walked more or less together toward the main airport lobby, "now we'll be able to go to the wedding in September in Milwaukee."

"Yeah," said Leo, still not quite fully aware of what was going on.

Neither Leo nor Marie had ever stayed at the O'Hare Hilton, a really lovely hotel considering its size. I offered to escort them to the moving sidewalk that would carry them to the hotel entrance. In turn they offered me their $10 meal certificates. They earlier had eaten a more traditional five o'clock supper in the airport. I thanked them heartily, for even in 1982 very few items on the hotel dinner menu were priced at or below ten dollars. But with thirty dollars my options increased considerably. Following check-in I did suggest they join me in an hour or so in the dining room for coffee and dessert. They were happy to do so, and appeared concurrently with my pre-dinner celebratory cocktail.

While my two tiny guests sat sipping coffee, I ordered broiled salmon. "You like salmon?" Leo asked, somewhat belaboring the obvious. "I'm a fisherman, you know?" Of course I didn't.

"Retired," Marie reminded him. Leo looked up from his cup.

"Yeah, well, the wife 'n I been in Las Vegas for a week because of salmon."

"Because of salmon?" I asked.

"Yeah," he said, "no kiddin'. Here's what happened.

My kid brother works at Logan Airport in Boston off-loadin' freight. Last week a flight comes in with a thousand pounds of salmon on it, packed in ice. Seems the trucker who was supposed to pick up the fish got lost on the way in, and when he gets there he goes to the wrong airline. Meanwhile, of course, the ice is meltin'. It's better than ninety degrees and the freight manager's gettin' nervous. Finally he calls the trucking firm that's s'posed to pick it up and says "get the fish the hell out of here." The trucking guy calls the insurance company, and a guy in a suit is out there in fifteen minutes lookin' at the fish. He don't know what to do with it, but the ice keeps meltin'.

My brother's pretty smart, so he says: "Hey, my brother Leo's a fisherman. He could use the salmon for bait." The insurance guy says "call him and get the fish outta the airport." So I went up with my truck and we loaded the pallets. Then we drove down to Quincy Market and sold the fish for four bucks a pound. We sold all we wanted to sell in two hours. We kept a hunert pounds for ourselves. Then me and Marie went to Las Vegas. Now we got tickets to go somewhere else. Pretty good, huh?

I admitted that was pretty good.

Marie said, "Leo, why don't you give Joe some salmon."

"Okay," he said, "where you goin' to be in Boston?"

I thanked him for the offer but told him the logistics would be too complicated, because I had an appointment at the First National Bank in Boston at eleven in the morning, followed by a luncheon engagement at Jimmy's Harborside at noon.

"Too bad," he said

We had dessert and parted company.

I had alerted Ralph Seifert to my change in plans, and he was on hand at Logan at ten-thirty to greet my flight. My two CSFA colleagues were in the bank lobby awaiting our arrival.

Shortly after noon we were seated at Jimmy's Harborside ordering fish fresh from the Atlantic Ocean. Just ahead of one o'clock when I was deep in a bowl of bouillabaisse, a silence fell upon the luncheon crowd. I looked toward the restaurant entrance and saw Leo, in his fisherman's overalls, working his way through the customers, obviously searching for me. When he located our table his concentration changed to relief. He came over to where we were sitting; placed a styrofoam cooler at my feet and said, "Here's your salmon; hope ya like it."

Before I could say much more than "thank you," he turned and left.

"What was that all about?" Cy asked. "That's Leo," I answered. "His brother is a freight handler at Logan..."

One day later about two pounds of salmon rounded out a holiday meal of fresh green peas and new red potatoes. Thanks to a generous spirit, I enjoyed a traditional New England 4th of July dinner. I regretted that I could not at least drop a card to Leo and Marie. I never knew their last names nor the town in which they lived. But I have mused since that holiday that inspiration, imagination, and entrepreneurial insight, are not the exclusive property of the formally educated, well dressed and suited occupants of office high-rises. Business acumen can simply be a matter of scale.

Chapter Eighteen

J. B. Tipton is Alive and Well

The call that came in that early November afternoon in 1982 was in truth not all that unusual. I had perhaps received a hundred or so similar calls in the course of my sixteen years with CSFA. The voice on the other end simply asked if I could spare him a copy of our most recent annual report. I said "sure," and the report went out in the afternoon's mail. Two weeks later on November 17, the same caller asked for ten additional copies. Again I readily complied.

The 1982 report we mailed out is a particularly handsome, understated publication entitled *Silver Dollars Two* a celebration piece for the 25th anniversary of Dollars for Scholars. The title, some two inches high, is embossed in silver on a soft gray cover. CSFA's mortarboard/book logo, encased in a laurel wreath, is plain-embossed just below the title and is centered on the cover. Within the report's pages is a memorial tribute to Gove W. Sleeper who had provided CSFA an annuity trust some three years before his death. On the very same page appears a "Private Sector Initiative

Commendation" from President Ronald Reagan, one of five awarded out of a competitive field of two hundred applicants, and the only one presented to a national organization.

The three major sections of the report are separated by full-page, stunning, black and white photographs, one each of maple trees in the fall in New England, the new office building of Northwestern National Life Insurance Company in Minneapolis, and a sun-drenched clearing in the redwood forests of California. The latter prefaces a section on CSFA's strengthened organization and improving financial picture. The balance sheets reflect that for the first time ever, CSFA had managed-assets exceeding $1 million and had ended the year with an unrestricted fund balance of more than a quarter of a million dollars.

This information was not lost on my fall caller. He called me again in mid-December; reminded me of his earlier request; and gave me a bit more detail on the basis for both it and the current call. "I represent," he said, "a very quiet and totally anonymous group of philanthropists. I shared your report with my board, and I sense an interest there. If you have occasion to be in my neighborhood, I would be interested in talking with you."

Unfortunately his "neighborhood" was on a pathway to nowhere, and even the near completion of the interstate highway system did not provide any reasonably direct access. Chances were something less than likely that I would somehow coincidentally find myself within his environs. I called Ralph Seifert. "Well," said Cy, "no problem. Melissa is home from college for the holidays. Her college is quite close to where you need to be. Call your new friend out there and set a date in early January. We'll take Melissa back to school."

With my "Of course I'll be in your neighborhood" ruse established, I set a date for January 11. Melissa was kind enough to agree to return to college a few days early. My plan was for Cy and me to rendezvous for dinner with my caller, his wife, and one other person, at a restaurant close to Melissa's destination. The other person was Tom Bellinger, a CSFA advisory trustee who, as time revealed, had introduced our evening's host to the subject of Dollars for Scholars. Tom was this gentleman's financial advisor. Tom was also in the throes of trying to organize a Dollars for Scholars chapter within his local school district.

I spent the night of January 10 at the Seifert residence in Mansfield, Massachusetts. By eight the next morning we were on our way in Cy's customized van with Melissa at the wheel. We were certain to arrive at our destination in plenty of time or not at all, because, as is true of the mail carrier, neither the snow, nor the sleet, and--in our particular case-- also the gray pall of the day, would keep Melissa from her appointed task. Though we couldn't see much else in the snowstorm, we could see the speedometer reading sixty miles per hour. For much of the eight hour drive, Cy and I sat at a round table in the rear of the van and discussed CSFA business. My agenda included my wish to build a CSFA headquarters building, and I wanted to build it in Minnesota. This idea might have seemed heretical to any New Englander other than Cy, but he found it "interesting."

We agreed that even though we knew nothing about our evening's host or the people he represented, we should consider asking for funds for a state project similar to the one successfully concluded in Minnesota in 1980. The two hundred thousand dollars the Bush Foundation had invested there had already returned $2.4 million in new, direct scholarship aid. CSFA had in Minnesota thirty-seven affiliated community Dollars for Scholars programs where once there were six. And our CSFA Midwest office was in

1982 distributing over $1 million annually on behalf of thirty-six companies and foundations.

Cy and I, as we earlier suspected, reached our travel objective in plenty of time. We took up residence in Melissa's off-campus apartment where the one bed remaining for her yet-to-arrive apartment mate was available for one of us. Cy graciously granted it to me. He chose the floor.

At seven thirty that same evening, clad in our business attire, Cy and I arrived at an elegant restaurant with the warmth and charm of a 1700s colonial mansion. Where the outside evening had been bitterly cold, the fire on the upstairs hearth warmed us as we sipped a beverage and awaited the other members of our party. The day's storm had reduced itself in the darkness to occasional half-dollar-size snowflakes floating featherlike, in the illumination just beyond the multi-paned windows.

The remaining three members arrived promptly at eight. We five were ushered downstairs to a private, corner table in the low-ceilinged, dark-wood-paneled dining room. Cy and I had already choreographed the evening in a manner that would give us both an opportunity to eat. During the appetizer course Tom Bellinger spoke of his fascination with the Dollars for Scholars program. He noted that his two present CSFA friends were scheduled to address a group of interested citizens in his community the very next evening in hopes of starting a chapter for the school district. He then mentioned how his friendship with a fellow named Ben Crosby had led to a generous gift for CSFA from one of Ben's clients, Gove Sleeper.

During the main course Cy spoke of his long association with Citizens' Scholarship Foundation of America. He told of the incredible success of the Mansfield, Massachusetts, Dollars for Scholars program. When my plate was clear, he turned the program over to me and attacked his cooling dinner. I spoke briefly of the growth of CSFA over its first quarter century, and as the dinner plates were cleared and dessert arrived, I spoke in some detail on the Minnesota project. I then turned my attention to my double-chocolate German layer cake.

Our host expressed his personal admiration for our combined presentation and then asked: "How much would it cost to do for a major East Coast state what you did for Minnesota?" The perfect question. Without hesitation, Cy looked up from his dessert fork.

"Four hundred and eighty-four thousand dollars."

I dropped mine.

"Where, pray tell," I thought, "did he get that number?"

This, to me astronomical, number did not seem exorbitant to our host. In fact, as we parted company at the restaurant exit he said simply: "Send me a proposal."

Cy and I stayed behind for a nightcap. I then asked: "Cy, considering what the Minnesota project cost, where pray tell *did* you get that number?" He smiled.

"It just came to me, and it felt good, so I used it."

The number as things turned out was a bit troublesome for me. Now that I had it, I felt obligated to use it, because after all, my chairman had uttered it. The proposal for the envisioned state project included a "scaled down," three-year budget of $478,000. Within its pages was a wish list that included such things as a thirty-minute documentary film on CSFA and the Dollars for Scholars program. That one item had been estimated at more than $90,000 by the media department of a prestigious university. The proposal went back and forth for three or four iterations. My new friend was something of a grammarian, and I credit him today with teaching me all I know about the proper and creative use of hyphens. That new knowledge was reflected in our proposal of March 16. We heard little more until April 20, when my friend called and asked for copies of CSFA's current year unaudited financial statements.

At that time in the life of CSFA, I was dividing my time between our national office in the frame house in Manchester, New Hampshire, and CSFA Midwest in the home of Stuart and Marlys Johnson in St. Peter, Minnesota. The latter office had quickly outgrown both their ten-by-eight wine cellar, and then their larger, paneled basement playroom. We had determined, in fact, that income to that office was sufficient to permit CSFA to rent a few rooms downtown on the second level of the two-story Minnegasco building. In occupying those four rooms we did not deny ourselves the occasional pleasure of using the 726 Lower Johnson Circle residence as a place where Stuart, Marlys, and I would meet informally to consider the needs of and the outlook for our growing organization.

In the early afternoon of May 8, 1993, we were sitting on the Johnsons' spacious sun porch involved in one of our many discussions. The telephone rang. The call was for me, and the caller said simply: "Joe, I'm calling to tell you that my board yesterday considered your proposal, and I'm pleased to tell you it was accepted for funding."

Stu and Marlys could sense that something important was happening.

"But," continued my friend, "we are not going to give you everything you asked for. I need to meet with you as soon as possible. Can you fly to New York City tomorrow and meet me to discuss the project?"

We met the next day for lunch and our "negotiations" at the University Club on Fifth Avenue. My friend sat across from me with his copy of the proposal.

"Let's see what items we can take out," he said. The negotiations began in earnest. Two hours later almost nothing had been accomplished. He thought, for example, that the film was just a nifty idea. I thought it was fluff. Finally, at about four o'clock my frustration began to surface.

"Look, we're not really getting anywhere," I said. "Why don't you just tell me how much your people are willing to give us. I'll then go home and re-tailor the project to that sum."

"Okay," he said, "Three hundred and twenty-five thousand dollars." This very tidy sum was the largest grant by more than half again that we had ever been given for a statewide project.

"Great," I said, "we can do it. But would you mind sharing with me just how your people arrived at that figure?" He smiled.

"Sure," he said. "In your materials you made mention of a gift of that size you had received from a gentleman in Massachusetts. I believe Tom Bellinger spoke of him, too, at our dinner meeting in January."

"Gove Sleeper," I said.

"Yes, he's the one," said my new benefactor. "Apparently Mr. Sleeper knew you and your organization. One of my people said: 'Hell, we don't know either, really, so we'd be crazy to give them one penny more.' I guess his logic made sense to everybody else."

Well, it certainly didn't matter if that logic made sense to me or to CSFA. We had chosen New York State as our project of preference, and the anonymous donor had agreed with our choice. By June 30, 1986, the date of the official end of the project, CSFA and its people generated $3.8 million in new scholarships through the efforts of thirty new community Dollars for Scholars chapters and through the largess of twenty new corporate and foundation-sponsored scholarship programs. These numbers became even more impressive with each passing year.

Income from the project permitted CSFA to maintain a permanent metropolitan service center on Long Island. The center was ably staffed by Bernard T. Coté, who claimed he was given the assignment because he was the only person on staff who came from an urban background. He was raised in Biddeford, Maine. CSFA was also able to fund, with its "earned" income originating with area corporations, a permanent Dollars for Scholars regional office in upstate New York.

So pleased were the people whose initial gift was made partially on the basis of not really knowing Citizens' Scholarship Foundation of America, *per se*, that subsequent gifts from the now quite friendly and knowledgeable anonymous source have totaled almost $2 million. This seed money has produced equally impressive results all along the East Coast and in other parts of the country as well.

Cy Seifert and I like to sit on his harbor-facing porch in West Southport, Maine, and reminisce on the "Melissa Ride of Terror." Cy considers that January excursion the apex of his five year chairmanship. "After all," he said, "on that one trip we decided to build a national headquarters; we made a presentation that got us the largest project grant in CSFA's history; and we convinced the people in Tom's school district to start a Dollars for Scholars chapter. Not too shabby for two days work."

Chapter Nineteen

Two Bills Come to Call

Among the corporate friends of Citizens' Scholarship Foundation of America, none has been more faithful than General Electric Company. GE's unrestricted support for CSFA dates back to a $1,000 gift in 1962 and has continued almost uninterrupted until today. Memory tells me that my very first corporate call, predating my 1968 appointment as executive director of CSFA, was in Crotonville, New York, a few miles north of New York City. A white frame building there served as home for both the GE Management Institute and the GE Educational and Charitable Fund. My predecessor, Dan Walker, and I called on one J. Moreau Brown to either thank him for the $1,000 gift for 1967 or to request a renewal for 1968.

In the early 1970s the fund moved to the huge mill-like General Electric production facility located in Bridgeport, Connecticut. I said of that move that the foundation must have been going into hiding, because Bridgeport, like so many other early New England cities, is a maze of streets paved apparently on whim, and even a structure as large as General Electric proved a challenge to find. But during the Ed Lee CSFA chairmanship of the 1970s, we did indeed persevere, and in each of those eight years we found a friendly host in General Electric.

The faces would change over the years. J. Moreau Brown left GE in 1972 to serve as a vice president of the Council for Financial Aid to Education in New York City. And in 1980 when GE occupied its new corporate headquarters in Fairfield, Connecticut, the GE Fund was among the GE family tenants. Despite the changes, the support for CSFA remained constant, and from time to time the amount of annual support increased. This support was consistent with the company's demonstrated philanthropic interests. GE sponsored a very generous educational loan program for the children of its employees, had an impressive history of support for engineering programs in colleges and universities, and had long participated in the National Merit Scholarship program.

Over time General Electric's charitable contributions program increased in complexity and size. Within the new Fairfield facility CSFA's contact person became William Stoddard, the fund's program manager for administration. His boss and secretary of the foundation was William Orme, a gentleman regarded in his time as one of the most distinguished people in corporate philanthropy. Bill Stoddard for whatever reason was a very strong advocate for CSFA and its Dollars for Scholars program. He was also fascinated by the fact that in the mid-1970s, CSFA found itself in the business of managing company and foundation scholarship programs. In fact, he told Ed Lee and me during our 1979 visit, that General Electric had hosted a meeting of corporate contributions officers wherein everyone in attendance heard of the "wonderful job" Citizens' Scholarship Foundation of America was doing for the Toro Company in Minneapolis.

Bill Stoddard's welcomed fascination with CSFA was occasionally expressed by his successful attempts to include Bill Orme in our Fairfield-based conversations. I was always flattered to have Mr. Orme in my presence, because in terms of scale of support CSFA was a very small fish in General Electric's contributions pond. I was often also frustrated, for despite his apparent awareness of CSFA's progress, Bill Orme evidenced very little interest in our Scholarship Management Services. He said he believed General Electric Company was doing enough in that area. He held the National Merit program in high regard and could see no real need for increasing direct aid to individuals. His position seemed to me to be resolute and unyielding.

Then, in July of 1983, a call from General Electric came into CSFA's Manchester, New Hampshire, office. Bill Orme was on the other end. Following the exchange of friendly greetings he asked me when I expected to again be in southwestern Connecticut.

"We are thinking," he said, "about expanding our scholarship commitment for children of employees."

"How about tomorrow?" I asked somewhat facetiously.

"Great," he replied. "Come in and visit with Bill Stoddard and me at two o'clock. We'll see if we can talk business."

The next morning I left New Hampshire with a good supply of both optimism and materials. Upon my arrival at General Electric I learned that the company was considering a new $100,000 scholarship effort. Bill Orme wanted to know what I had to offer. I told him that the hallmark of CSFA's corporate programs was that each one was tailored to the sponsoring company. The program design was based on responses to thirteen questions, and even then the company was free to add its own nuances and eligibility requirements, assuming such additions were consistent with good program design and with federal law. Bill Stoddard asked me to describe a few of our larger client programs. I was happy to do so. The hour slipped by, and at its close Bill Orme said: "Sounds too complicated to me. With National Merit we're not required to design anything. Kids take the PSAT and that's that. I guess I still don't know what you bring to the process that's any better."

"Just imagination," I said, but my optimism had faded, and my hopes were deflated. Shortly thereafter I was again on the Merritt Parkway on the front end of a four hour return trip. My disappointment ran deeper than my ego damage. CSFA was at that time very much in need of a high-recognition client in the northeast. Among our ninety-nine clients in 1983 only United Parcel Service stood out as a household name east of the Hudson River.

Then on August 11 another call originating with Fairfield came in. This time the caller was Bill Stoddard. "When can Bill and I come up to see you?" he asked. "We have an exciting idea."

"How about tomorrow?" I replied. And the date was set for August 12.

The two Bills arrived like twins with new tricycles. Their obvious excitement was not diminished by our humble headquarters. They sat down with me at the table in the former dining room of our white frame house, accepted our offer of coffee, and then Bill Orme said: "Listen to this. We've decided to make one hundred $1,000 awards to high-achieving sons and daughters of GE employees. Our recipients will be high-school seniors in public, private, and parochial high schools. You people will pick the winners.

But here's the twist. The scholarship recipients will each identify the high-school teacher who had the greatest impact on their lives and education. That teacher will receive five hundred dollars to be used to purchase classroom equipment or supplies unavailable from the school or district. We call it the STAR program. STAR translates to 'Student *and* Teacher Achievement and Recognition.' How's that for imagination?"

"Outstanding," I said. "We'll be honored to manage it for you." The remainder of the visit was dedicated to details and procedures. CSFA had its one-hundredth client.

The *CSFA Annual Report for 1984* has on page four a full-page, full-color photograph of Bill Stoddard and me visiting with two of the first one hundred STAR program recipients. We are all on the rear terrace of the General Electric headquarters building in Fairfield. Both students, Dennis Hughes who was bound for Notre Dame and Michael Fuller who would attend Brigham Young, are wearing navy blue wool crew neck sweaters. Each sweater has a small white star embroidered on the left breast. The sweaters, along with recognition plaques, were gifts from General Electric to all one hundred recipients. In the picture we all look relaxed and comfortable, but part of that memory is the fact that the temperature on that August 8 date was 104°, and our suits and their sweaters made the one hour photo session seem interminable. The two young men were rewarded for their suffering and endurance with GE "walkman-type" radio/cassette players. I happily settled for iced tea.

The STAR program is noteworthy for reasons that transcend "imagination." Some early concern expressed by General Electric officials was that the program might be viewed as elitist, because financial need was not a criterion, and some suspicion existed that the awards might gravitate to children of high-income employees. If that outcome were to be a consequence of the program, CSFA would be powerless to change it. The CSFA selection process is "blind" insofar as no-need based programs are concerned. Information on family income is not required in such instances and is therefore unknown. The selection process is weighted heavily on academic performance, meaningful participation in school and community activities, and corroborating testimony.

GE's contributions people took a careful look at the program's first one hundred recipients. The distribution both amazed and pleased them. Three of the awards represented employee incomes of $80,000 or more. The same number represented employees with incomes under $20,000. Thirty-seven of the awards represented incomes of $50,000 to $80,000; and fifty-seven represented incomes of $20,000 to $50,000. The awards on the whole were reflective of the distribution of incomes throughout General Electric Company.

So pleased was GE with the program that in 1986 GE Foundation extended STAR to Canada under an Internal Revenue Service ruling that eventually could permit the program to go worldwide. The idea of a global program moved closer to reality in 1994 when, according to Phyllis McGrath, the GE Fund's programs manager for pre-college programs, General Electric made use of the IRS approval by creating an "Asian STAR program for children of GE employees in all Asian countries where the company has operations."

Today in retirement Bill Stoddard still reflects wistfully on the STAR program. "Interviews I had with the recipients," he remembers, "proved time after time that they were most proud of the $500 awards to their high schools, for that 'sorely needed laboratory microscope' which was never covered by the annual school budget. To allow their favorite Biology teacher to make the selection was the frosting on the cake."

Bill speaks, too, of certain GE memorabilia he has on display in his home. The enlarged and framed photo of the Hot August Day occupies, he says, "an honored position in my house." And when his oldest son, himself a high-school principal, learned the story behind the picture he said: "Gee, Dad, all I thought you did at GE was make money. You were actually involved in something worthwhile."

Chapter Twenty

Three Bills Get the Call

Wakefield, Massachusetts, a north-of-Boston town with twenty-five thousand residents, was comfortably settled in 1644 and remains so today. Idyllically nestled between Quannapowitt Lake and Crystal Lake, Wakefield seems an unlikely place for a local police chief to be involved in a showdown. So, as I sat in October of 1994 with Patricia A. Mooney and J. Kevin Lally at lunch in a restaurant bearing the city's name, I was somewhat incredulous as they shared the saga with me. Sitting at a private table in Wakefield's, they nevertheless assured me that on July 7, 1967, at nine o'clock in the morning, Chief of Police Merritt Wenzel did indeed face an adversary. And when it was over, the local folks who showed up to witness the event counted 120 or more holes drilled on the spot where the battle had raged. Of the encounter Chief Wenzel was quoted as saying: "I had to do it for the kids in town. I knew the deal was going down before I left home in the morning. It was time for me to play my hand. The citizens of Wakefield rightfully expected me to do my job. There were no heroes. Let's just say I survived the experience, and this community is all the better for it."

Michael Collins, then manager of the Municipal Light Department and one of the eyewitnesses, agrees. "It wasn't so much a firefight," he says, "as it was a face-off with a firefighter. And besides, we had to get some good publicity or we'd never sell the rest of the cribbage boards." Police Chief Wenzel and Fire Chief William Hurton met on that Friday morning to decide the local open-air cribbage championship. In a community as cosmopolitan and refined as "Wakefield on the Lakes," the three hundred-year-old game, a product of the genteel English poet and soldier, Sir John Suckling, was viewed as a preferred way to settle old scores. The playing card and pegboard game was also regarded as an okay way to corral community spirit. It was viewed by Michael Collins, co-chair of the special committee on cribbage boards, as a way to raise a few more dollars for Wakefield's Citizens' Scholarship Foundation.

The day of combat had been made possible by a local resident, Harold N. Comins, who had spent nearly all his life's leisure time producing eighteen hundred Formica-topped, felt-bottomed, hardwood cribbage boards. The boards could be purchased at three dollars each at the Municipal Light Department, the offices of *The Wakefield Daily Item*, Wally's Cleaners, and American Mutual Liability Insurance Company. "And each one comes with six steel pegs," Mr. Collins had been quick to note.

Pat and Kevin, both who had served as presidents of the local Citizens' Scholarship Foundation, paused in their storytelling to suggest we place our orders. Kevin pointed out to me that the "fish and chips" menu item was called "Cy's Choice," a selection apparently unrelated to either CSFA's colorful past chairman, or the equally colorful story at hand. Wakefield apparently had been first settled by a gentleman named Cyrus.

Pat handed me a green scrapbook, well over an inch thick, filled with hundreds of articles and pictures detailing the first thirteen years of the local scholarship foundation's thirty-four year history. The scrapbook revealed that the open-air cribbage championship was apparently one of many events organized in the mid-1960s by local residents to benefit the graduates of Wakefield High School and the Academy of Our Lady of Nazareth. "In fact," Pat said, "the whole scholarship program was kicked off by a very special event. A Mr. John Nilan, who worked at American Mutual, wrote an original musical comedy called *Make It for Two*. A friend of his, Alice Valkenburg, composed the score, and more than seventy Wakefield residents made up the cast. Three performances raised nearly four thousand dollars in January of 1960."

The local Rotary Club subsequently sponsored two other major musical events, the first in 1966 involved the very popular disc jockey, Jess Cain of WHDH in Boston, together with "243 voices and 103 instruments." The second, a high-school band concert, played to a sell-out crowd. A Columbus Day auction at American Mutual raised over two thousand dollars, despite "the prevailing cold weather." An art exhibit was held at the high school. And in May of 1966 an appeal went out to parents asking not for bucks, but for books...of "trading stamps." *The Item* reported: "Five thousand letters appealing to parents to donate a book of trading stamps... have been given out to pupils in the local schools. How many of them have been read by the parents remains a mystery. They have been found in shirt pockets in....weekly washings, in bureau drawers between socks, rock collections, nails, comic books, and other treasures..." On the strength of a separate effort the local teachers' club received *The Item*'s editorial praise for "being solidly behind a move that helps local young people get an education." The teachers had contributed one thousand dollars from the proceeds of their own fund-raising events.

Over Cy's fresh Dover Sole and curly fries my noontime companions told me a great deal more about Citizens' Scholarship Foundation of Wakefield. I concluded that those early events--cribbage tournaments, band concerts, auctions, and city-wide appeals for support--did not in and of themselves distinguish the Wakefield Citizens' Scholarship Foundation from its 187 counterparts raising scholarship dollars in 1966. Neither was the chapter's genesis particularly unusual. Seven years earlier a local attorney, William J. Lee, who had served as chairman of the Wakefield school committee, expressed his belief to the Chamber of Commerce and to others that something needed to be done to raise the level of scholarship dollars in the community. He had no specific plan in mind until a friend, Catherine Simpson, showed him an article in *The Boston Globe* extolling the virtues of something called "The Fall River Plan." Bill Lee and the chamber president, John McCarthy, Sr., traveled the sixty or so miles to visit with Fall River optometrist Dr. Irving A. Fradkin. They came away with a kernel of a plan for Wakefield. On November 7, 1959, Dr. Fradkin sent Mr. McCarthy a handwritten note expressing his hope that Wakefield would move ahead. The community did move ahead in August of 1960, but did so independent of Irving Fradkin's small cadre of loosely affiliated chapters. The graduating class of 1961 shared over $1,500 in locally sponsored awards.

In 1962 the local scholarship group elected to join Citizens' Scholarship Foundation of America. The national organization had formally incorporated in May of the year before. By 1964 the chapter was raising more than $7,000 a year, and by 1970 the success of its first year had been surpassed tenfold to over $15,000. In fact, in that year one hundred Wakefield High School students canvassed the town and raised $1,500 in a single day. But again, this steady progress was being emulated to greater and lesser degrees by other CSFA affiliates in the commonwealth, throughout New England, and in more isolated areas around the country.

What does distinguish Wakefield is that as early as 1964 this Citizens' Scholarship Foundation of America affiliate was on its way to becoming the largest citizen-supported scholarship program of its kind in the United States, and by extension, the world. Perhaps somewhat obscured by the fanfare of the fashion shows and flower shows was a string of spontaneous events that would, first by chance and later by design, account for the laudable success of this citizen movement.

Soon after the 1963 assassination of President John F. Kennedy, residents of Wakefield established a permanent scholarship fund in his memory. Then in May of 1966 a small group of parishioners working with Attorney William J. Lee created a $10,000 permanent fund as "a living testimonial" to the Reverend Frederick J. Deasy, "a man of God whose personal interest in the welfare and education of young people was well known and appreciated by the members of his parish."

In September of 1968 *The Item* reported that Wakefield had lost a third son to the Vietnam War "when a sniper's bullet...ended another promising life," and that Lieutenant Peter B. Rich would be permanently memorialized by his friends through the funding of an annual scholarship in his name. In October of 1968 Dr. Cornelius Thibeault, a local veterinarian, walked unannounced into a meeting of the directors of the local scholarship foundation and presented the first of two checks, one for $10,000, the second for $15,000, to fund permanently a scholarship which might "be used to help students interested in careers connected with the care of animals."

The untimely passing in 1971 of the woman who had nearly a decade earlier called to Bill Lee's attention *The Boston Globe* article on the "Fall River Plan" served as impetus for a "stunned community" to mourn the passing of Catherine E. Simpson. Her will provided for a permanent fund in her name. And then in 1974, the maker of cribbage boards, Harold Comins, bequeathed his house and car to the local Citizens' Scholarship Foundation. His memorial was ultimately funded with $36,000.

Other permanent funds had been established within the chapter as well. Among them, one funded by a local manufacturing firm, D.S. Greene Company; another by the Wakefield High School Class of 1929; and still another by the Greenwood Women's Club as its final formal action when it turned over its treasury on the day in 1969 the club disbanded. By the time Wakefield Citizens' Scholarship Foundation held its quarter-century celebration in 1985, one hundred and forty funds, worth in the aggregate over three-quarters of a million dollars, were under the management of the local chapter.

A local banker, William R. Spaulding, at the urging of his wife Gertrude, a CSF director, agreed to assume the volunteer role of funds manager. "Bill Spaulding," says Pat Mooney, "is still serving the chapter as its funds manager after thirty years." Now retired as president of the Wakefield Savings Bank, Bill speaks of Fidelity Funds with the same deference as the uncle in the film, *The Graduate*, spoke of plastic. And apparently with some justification as today the foundation holds and manages 327 permanent and accumulating funds worth $3.65 million. "Any new accumulating fund," according to Pat, "must grow through additional contributions to a level of three thousand dollars before awards will be made in a fund's name."

As coffee is served to us, Pat speaks with affection of still a third Bill. "And then we had Bill Jones, a chapter faithful for almost twenty years. He served for many years as chairman of our awards committee, and was our president in '68 and '69, following his retirement. He had been the business and financial editor of *The Boston Globe*. Bill became our writer and historian. Up until he retired from chapter service and moved to New Hampshire in 1983, he would write the little stories describing each of the permanent funds. He wrote the history of our chapter that's in our twenty-fifth anniversary booklet, and authored our annual appeal brochures. Bill is very much a gentleman; he still tips his hat to the ladies. I just love him. We miss him."

Bill Lee is missed as well. His name and that of his granddaughter, Laura A. Lee, appear in the list of memorial funds in the 1994 chapter brochure. The same brochure reports that in that year 229 scholarships averaging over $900 were apportioned among forty-seven high school seniors, 165 enrolled undergraduate students, eleven graduate students and six adult continuing education students. The chapter has in a single year surpassed one hundredfold the success of its first scholarship year.

I personally enjoyed the privilege of meeting Bill Lee when he was honored in 1982, along with Bill Jones and Bill Spaulding, by Citizens' Scholarship Foundation of Wakefield. In that year the chapter had nominated "The Three Bills" to the newly established Dollars for Scholars National Honor Roll of Citizens' Scholarship Foundation of America. The CSFA Board of Trustees unanimously approved the nominations, and I, as president of CSFA, was invited by the chapter to present individual awards to the three Bills during the afternoon of June thirteenth.

We gathered for the occasion at the Hartshorne House, the oldest house in Wakefield, where I recall the ceilings were so low that the two taller Bills, Lee and Jones, had to duck down to pass through the doorways and could barely stand at full height in the corner-posted living room. Standing with me in a picture taken by the ever-faithful and supportive *Wakefield Daily Item* is the then chapter president, Patricia Mooney. She along with Kevin Lally and fifty other directors of Wakefield Citizens' Scholarship Foundation would carry forward the spirit and dedication of the three Bills being honored that evening. Pat and Kevin today represent together more than thirty years of service to the local scholarship effort. Both are today also involved at the national level, Pat as a governing trustee; Kevin as a long-term advisory trustee. "I'm in it for the excitement and feeling of accomplishment," Pat says as we await the luncheon check. "Imagine, since 1960 this town has given almost $6 million to our cause. We have awarded $2.5 million to almost three thousand students. Our permanent funds will approach $4 million in the current year. How could I not be excited?"

"How about you, Kevin," I asked as we stepped out into the bright October day and paused to appreciate the autumn colors visible over the storefronts and extending far back to one of the lake shores. "What got you involved?" Soft-spoken by nature, Kevin paused a moment.

"Well, if you look in the brochure, you will find the name John K. Lally, Jr. John was my son. He was killed in a motorcycle accident in New Hampshire while going up for a job interview in 1978. His friends and our family established a scholarship fund in his name in the same year.

From that point on I just wanted to be a part of the local chapter." I thanked my friends for lunch, tucked the borrowed scrapbook under my arm, and headed for the nearby parking lot. I thought to myself as I worked my way up Route 128 to Interstate 95 north, that I, too, had enjoyed a very high noon in the town square.

Chapter Twenty-one

What's Good for General Motors

Some debate still exists over which of two CSFA employees actually brought in to our Manchester office the article from *The Wall Street Journal*, but whether it was Peter Whitman or Yvonne Gosselin is of little consequence. The fact that one or the other person called it to my attention was of great consequence indeed. The article in the October 8, 1983, edition described in some detail a settlement between General Motors Corporation, the United Auto Workers, and the United States Equal Employment Opportunity Commission.

The settlement was the result of a class action proceeding charging General Motors with discrimination in the workplace. The entire settlement was in several tens of millions of dollars. Of greatest interest to me, as I sat at the conference table in the former dining room of our Manchester, New Hampshire, facility, was the description of plans for the distribution of $7 million in education grants to women and minorities represented in the General Motors workplace. The article noted that the principal use for these dollars would be vocational and technical training, but nowhere in the text appeared a description as to how the allocations would be made. The names of two General Motors officials appeared in the article, so I made a quick choice of Alfred S. Warren, Jr. and prepared a letter to his attention. In it I said.

> Citizens' Scholarship Foundation of America is, we believe, the fastest growing scholarship service organization in the country. While we trail Educational Testing Service and National Merit in dollar distributions, our hallmark, the design and development of tailored scholarship programs, accounts for the wide acceptance of our services by more than one hundred companies, foundations, and associations nationwide. And lest you think our size inhibits our capacity to handle large volume programs, I would like you to know that one program alone, The Jostens Student Achievement Program, attracts over fourteen thousand applications each year for CSFA to process.
>
> I do not know what plans you have, if any, for the design and administration of the women and minorities scholarship program envisioned under the settlement. I would respectfully ask, however, that if outside assistance is to be considered, CSFA be given an opportunity to show our mettle before a decision is made. You will see on pages 13-15 of our Annual Report for 1983, that many have earlier decided that CSFA was and is the way.

Within the annual report, the clients listed included General Electric Foundation, General Mills Foundation, Scott Paper Company Foundation, CIGNA Corporation, and a number of other household names. The letter went out of Manchester that very afternoon.

Nothing happened for three weeks. But then in October I received a telephone call from a Mr. Tom Gawel of General Motors Corporation. He told me that he, his boss Chet

Francke, and one of two other GM people would be arriving in Philadelphia that very afternoon. Could I meet them at their hotel for a discussion over breakfast the next morning? I readily agreed to do so.

The hotel of the GM people's choice was the Four Seasons, something of a luxury spot in downtown Philadelphia. Because of the early morning appointment hour and my fear of logistical problems if I stayed at say, the airport Holiday Inn, I asked my secretary, Maryanne Martin, to book me into the Four Seasons. She placed the call; then placed the call on hold; and informed me that the only room available was the presidential suite. The price was dear, of course, but the rationale for staying there was even more compelling. "Please book it," I said. I then drove home; packed enough clothes for two days; and headed for Boston's Logan Airport and thence to Philadelphia.

The presidential suite was in a word, well, "Presidential." I called Tom Gawel's room and left word that I was indeed in the hotel. I then foresaw a thorny problem. I knew that I had the ideal spot for a breakfast meeting, given my large and attractive living area atop the hotel. On the other hand, to offer this forum might give CSFA a wastrel image to the people who were staying on the ground floor. My worries were soon assuaged, for when Tom Gawel called me that evening, he simply gave me a room number for the eight o'clock meeting. As matters turned out the room was rather small and certainly cramped. I wondered why we had not met in the hotel dining room. I soon found out.

Chet Francke took the lead. He said, "Look, we have something of a problem here. We cannot discuss the GM/EEOC agreement with you. We cannot even permit you to ask questions about it. Our situation is that we know nothing about you or your organization, and we won't bring you to the attention of our counterparts in Washington unless and until we are convinced of your credibility." The rest of the hour was mine.

When I finished my discourse on CSFA, Mr. Francke said, "Okay, here's what we're going to do. You take a train down to Washington this afternoon. Make a reservation at the Mayflower Hotel. Tom and I will try to find someone from EEOC to have dinner with you and us. If we do, don't greet us like old friends. If we don't, the meal's off. In either event," he continued, "Tom and I are scheduled to meet with Jim Finney and his people at EEOC tomorrow morning. If everything works out, we will get you on the agenda for a half hour or so at the morning meeting. We'll see what happens from there."

Things did work out, and the next morning I found myself at the first of what were to be a series of meetings in Washington over the next several weeks. Looking back I can say that the conference room atmosphere at EEOC--with GM people on one side of the table and EEOC people on the other, and James N. Finney, director of EEOC, at the head of the table--was far from hostile, but on the other hand I sensed no camaraderie. But there I sat at the other end of the table, the prototypical, white, Anglo-Saxon, Protestant male, offering up my services and those of CSFA for the design of and management of the Education Grants Program for Minorities and Women.

Following that initial meeting my family and I left almost immediately for Florida to visit Disneyworld and Epcot Center. During our stay in an Ed Lee-provided condominium, a call came in from General Motors and EEOC inviting CSFA to compete by way of a proposal for the program rights. I immediately called my two colleagues in Minnesota, Stuart and Marlys Johnson, and invited them to Florida for the purpose of drafting the proposal.

The three of us always had extraordinary rapport in preparing proposal drafts. Many such documents were constructed around the dining room table at their home in St. Peter. We often said that if one day CSFA had a museum, that dining room table would have a place in it. We could in the space of three or four hours develop a complete proposal package. I would describe the concept and rationale in general terms. Marlys would give these two considerations the necessary substance. She would then identify all necessary procedures. Stuart would estimate and tabulate costs as we went along. Then the three of us would construct a timetable and calendar. Marlys and I would then agree on specific writing assignments. Stuart would devote the rest of his day to building a budget. On the following day, barring the need for further research, the proposal and supporting documentation would be on its way. This process was almost magical in its efficiency.

None of us knew then who our competition was for this program, nor do we know for certain today. But we suspected with good reason that the largest names in national scholarship service agencies had an interest in the GM/EEOC program, and all the others had something of a name-recognition competitive edge.

Our three-page letter proposal went out to General Motors and EEOC on November 29, 1983. Jim Finney and his colleagues had asked CSFA for some early sign of "good faith." Both EEOC and General Motors were concerned over any possibility that levied administrative costs would disproportionately dilute the number and value of the program grants. We, on the other side, were equally concerned that the unpredictable volume of activity within the program might put CSFA out of business if the fee basis was not equitable. CSFA addressed this impasse by offering to do all of the program design work at no up-front cost, and then amortizing the real cost of this activity over the five year life of the agreement. That offer was not insignificant in that CSFA had identified ten major program-related tasks and each of the ten had multiple subsets.

For three weeks we waited like expectant parents with a past due date. Then on December 13, 1983, a call came into our Manchester office. Maryanne advised me it was from the Washington offices of the Equal Employment Opportunity Commission. The caller was Chet Francke: "Joe," he said, "we're going to put you on the speakerphone here. I'm with Tom and Jim and the other folks who have been reviewing proposals. We want you to know we have selected CSFA to do the final design work and to manage the Education Grant Program for Minorities and Women."

I do not recall my reaction other than I advised the callers that our preference would be to manage the program out of St. Peter, Minnesota, because of our growing technological capacity in that office. We then agreed to meet in St. Peter after the first of the year to review the proposal and calendar and to plan for the first of the five years of the program. I called Stuart Johnson at CSFA Midwest with the news. I well remember his reaction, as it was an interesting variation on a traditional holiday greeting. My next call was to CSFA Board Chairman Ralph Seifert. We all sensed that this news was the biggest event in the life of CSFA. We were right. The formal agreement for CSFA management of the program was executed on January 10, 1984.

This program would tax the time and talent of CSFA, for it proved to be far more elaborate and complex than any of us--including the GM and EEOC people--had ever imagined. Sparing much of the detail, I would note that the eligibility pool represented not only 140,000 women and minorities among General Motors' more than four hundred thousand employes, but it also included dependents of those eligible employes, plus another universe of former employes who were in the General Motors work force at the time of the filing of the discrimination charges. The dependents of this latter group were included as well.

The overwhelming share of the $7 million distribution was slated for vocational and technical training. This program objective posed unusual problems of its own. Accredited junior colleges, community colleges, and public vocational and technical schools were without question viewed as appropriate and eligible training locations for the eventual participants. But many other legitimate schools for specific skills development, such as welding or computer operation and repair were without accrediting standards. And other "training institutes" and schools of the not so legitimate variety would be, we believed, anxious to exploit the GM participants.

The program eligible people were to be selected on a first come, first served basis, so a means of time dating each application had to be developed. The application and supporting material would have to describe the program clearly, devoid of any hint of ambiguity. The greatest challenge was a requirement that every enrolled eligible person be tracked, to at once demonstrate that the letter of the GM/EEOC agreement was being honored by CSFA, and that the program was providing the desired results. This program, we concluded, would require unique, tailored, extensive, and probably expensive, software. We had no prototype.

These daunting requirements notwithstanding, Stuart, Marlys, a young computer programmer named Tom Dennison, and I spent the first two weeks of the new year reasoning through the management of this incredibly complex and potentially cumbersome program. Our anxiety level was high, as we had never attempted anything of this scope, and we knew the GM people would be on location in St. Peter during the third week in March for the review and planning session.

The visitation day was soon upon us. Stuart and I rented a new Oldsmobile from a local car dealer for our early-morning sixty-five mile drive to Minneapolis to pick up the visiting contingent. Until this time no representatives of either General Motors or EEOC had visited CSFA's modest facilities in either New Hampshire or Minnesota. We picked up our guests and chatted amiably as the IDS tower in Minneapolis gave way to the silos of rural Minnesota. Our new friends seemed puzzled by our distance from the Twin Cities. By the time we arrived at the CSFA offices at 315½ Minnesota Avenue in St. Peter, we believed we saw looks of incredulity. I do not know what our guests had surmised about our facilities as a result of the several earlier sessions in Washington, but clearly they did not anticipate the CSFA-Midwest office would occupy four rooms above the Minnegasco office and Domino's Pizza, at a location that might best have been described in the writings of Sinclair Lewis.

We of confident air and nervous stomachs ushered the GM people to the second floor; introduced them around to the support staff of three; and joined Marlys and Tom Dennison in a makeshift conference room, which was actually Marlys Johnson's office redecorated and rearranged with borrowed furniture for the day. As we were taking our places--Chet Francke and Tom Gawel to the right, Tom the computer person at the foot, Stuart and Marlys on the left, and me at the head of the table--Tom Gawel said: "We have a hundred and one questions for you people. They're all in my briefcase."

"That's fine," I said. "I would like to suggest that we present our recommendations to you during the remainder of the morning. We will then break for lunch and then return here to respond to your questions. Okay?" It was, and I began by asking Tom Dennison to outline the parameters of the necessary software. For forty minutes or so he did. I then asked Stuart to display detailed budgets for the start-up costs and the first full year of the program. Stuart, always a man of few words, made his presentation in the space of ten minutes. I then directed everyone's attention to Marlys. I said: "I asked Marlys to prepare a sequential, task-defined overview of the program. She has it available for your review."

Marlys then opened her folder; presented each conferee with a document; and said: "Gentlemen, I have identified 130 sequential tasks. We will cover as many as we can before lunch and then come back to the remainder if necessary." She then went through the litany in a paced fashion. When she finished the hour was approaching one o'clock. No one had interrupted her. Marlys closed her folder and observed that we were a bit behind schedule. I suggested we break for lunch and then return to address GM's "one hundred and one questions."

"No need to," said Tom Gawel. "They've all been answered. Let's go have lunch, and then Stu and Joe can take us up to the airport. We can probably get an earlier flight to Detroit."

Elation made its quiet masterpiece.

A few postscripts on this program are in order. The first one is that because this program with its $1.4 million annual distribution was not technically a scholarship program--it was a non-competitive entitlement program--it became the impetus for a new business component of Citizens' Scholarship Foundation of America. We borrowed somewhat loosely from the Greek language and named the component EGIS. The acronym identified CSFA's "Education Grants and Innovative Services." Throughout the 1980s, and well into the 1990s, this business unit managed similar if much smaller EEOC settlement programs. The unit also worked with smaller EEOC settlement programs. The unit also worked with companies such as Burger King to provide employee-incentive savings, or "set-aside" programs for college education.

The second noteworthy item is that CSFA much later learned that the entire GM/UAW/EEOC settlement was unique and precedent-setting for future resolutions of similar discrimination charges. Prior to the GM settlement, such agreements generally called for the distribution of large sums of money over the universe of "wronged" employees in the form of relatively small amounts of direct compensation. The GM/EEOC agreement was forward-looking in that the "paid-and-gone" approach was replaced by activity that had potential for far greater future earning power for the participants. Over the life of the program, nine thousand General Motors people benefited from the education grants program. Chet Francke is quick to credit Clarence Thomas for the introduction of the program: "As the then head of EEOC, Clarence Thomas immediately saw the merits of the aid to education approach. His enthusiasm and stewardship made it happen."

The third and final postscript cites the impact of this program on the future of Citizens' Scholarship Foundation of America. What was good for General Motors was certainly great for CSFA. During the life of the education grants program, 1984-1990, CSFA's corporate and foundation client base grew from just over one hundred accounts to 324. In the same period annual distributions on behalf of corporate clients rose from just over $3 million to nearly $14 million.

To be sure a good deal of hard work and enlightened leadership by CSFA's current president, Bill Nelsen, contributed to this progress. But I recall with pleasure a luncheon hosted by First Interstate Bank in Los Angeles in program and a CSFA trustee, had invited a few Los Angeles corporate counterparts and friends to hear the CSFA story. When I had finished my more or less formal presentation, Fred Nelson of Arco posed a question. "Joe, this is all very interesting, but you have to realize that Arco is big business; very big business. What is the size of the largest employee base you serve?"

I paused for a very long moment, placed my right hand over my chin and mouth and appeared to ponder. Then I said: "Four hundred and sixty thousand." Fred smiled.

"Okay, okay, General Motors. Who's your second largest client?"

"Chrysler Corporation," I replied.

Chapter Twenty-two

Big House on the Prairie

From the very beginning we called it simply, "The Building." Long before Jim Kagermeier placed his tools on his architect's table; long before Buhler Construction Company submitted the low bid; long before the St. Peter School Board made possible the transfer of two and one-half extraordinary acres to CSFA. Long before all of these events, we had talked of building a building. We wanted a permanent home for our itinerant organization. For between CSFA's founding year in 1961 and the winter of 1982 the national office had been headquartered in six different locations, three each in Massachusetts and New Hampshire. During those mean and lean years Trustee David Logan Steele, a bank trust officer from Lancaster, Pennsylvania, who handled *pro bono* CSFA's very limited investments, remarked: "Hell, whenever the Allis Chalmers certificates came due, I never knew where to send the money. Those guys sure moved around a lot."

The first five moves were the products of expediency and affordability. The sixth, the 1981 move from Concord, New Hampshire, eighteen miles south to Manchester, was a consequence of CSFA's rapidly growing Scholarship Management Services. By that time CSFA was managing sixty company-sponsored scholarship programs, up from forty-six in 1980. Distributions on behalf of these clients approached $2 million. CSFA had completed its eighth year as Jean Hennessey's tenant at the New Hampshire Charitable Fund in Concord and had outgrown all of the space the benevolent landlord could provide. The answer to this problem was an affordable, single-story, white frame house on Londonderry Turnpike, a rural route running north and south on the eastern outskirts of Manchester. The house's most distinguishing interior feature was bright red bathroom wallpaper, flocked with six-inch black fleurs-de-lis.

CSFA Governing Trustee Edward Shapiro, president of nearby New Hampshire College, agreed that, at $1,000 a month, the Londonderry Turnpike location was a reasonable interim solution for CSFA. The open basement with a bit of redesign and some staff handiwork would prove suitable for Dollars for Scholars mailings and other chapter services, and the same area would accommodate the managing of corporate scholarship programs. The upper level housed the CSFA president in the dining room, the receptionist-secretary in the living room, and the financial officer and one program officer in each of two small bedrooms. We as a staff painted and wallpapered the "office" areas--leaving only the bathroom unmolested--and built all of the tables, shelf space, and mail-cube "cubby holes" required for the basement work area.

But as 1982 neared its close, the volume of business increased again by more than 30 percent. Some inner voice cautioned me that the walls of the little house just would not hold the business ahead of us. That voice outwardly expressed itself to Chairman Seifert in the course of our treacherous van ride in January of 1983. I was a bit tentative in my proposal to him, because I not only wanted to build something, I also wanted to build something well beyond the borders of New England. I was suggesting a building in Minnesota.

Ralph Seifert was, however, always open to new ideas, and his mind, much like the van we were in with his daughter at the wheel, was very quick. "Okay," he said, "assuming it's a good idea, let's consider the issues. Would you move your personal household to Minnesota?" "Not necessarily," I replied. "I travel nearly 80 percent of my time now. I would want a management structure that would continue to allow me to do so. We have Stu and Marlys Johnson already out there. I think they could run CSFA on a day-to-day basis."

"Do you want your offices to be in Minneapolis?" Cy asked.

"No," I said, "I think CSFA's strength and appeal are vested in its rural and reliable-work-ethic image, the industrious kids out in the country. I don't want to change that. We have good people in St. Peter. We should try to stay in that general area." Cy thought a minute more.

"Okay, here's what you have to do. First, convince Irving. That will be the toughest task. Second, get together with Gus Johnson. See what he can bring to the table. Third, get Stu and Marlys on board. This plan has major implications for those two.

"What we won't do," he continued, "is raise the issue of a new headquarters building at the January 21 board meeting. It's too soon, and the trustees never like big-issue major surprises. What you will do following the January meeting is prepare and distribute a 'white paper' on the subject of CSFA's migrations and then come to the April board meeting prepared to defend it. We'll see what happens. But first you've got to convince Irving." We then turned our attention to more immediate business.

Cy's sensitivity to Irving Fradkin's probable reaction proved to be adroit. Cy knew, as I knew, that if a new headquarters building was on the agenda for the January meeting, Irving Fradkin, as CSFA's founder, would immediately envision the fulfillment of a lifetime dream. He had advocated since 1969 that the permanent offices of CSFA should be returned to his "Scholarship City" of Fall River. From time to time Irving shared with me his discomfort when residents of Fall River challenged him on CSFA's various moves. "Why not here?" They reportedly asked. "It's your program, Doctor Fradkin. It started here." But to my way of thinking the reasons for excluding Fall River, or Massachusetts, or the rest of New England for that matter, were far greater in number than the good reasons for building in the midwest.

I knew I could not in any event delay my session with Irving. He had to be the second to know. I called him just as soon as I returned to New Hampshire, and in keeping with my belief that serious business should be discussed with people on their own turf, I set up an appointment to visit with him near Fall River. We met during the late morning of January 13 at a Dunkin' Donuts shop on Route 24. I explained to Irving that CSFA was now playing in the big leagues, and the history of moving from place to place, renting various properties, was not in the organization's future best interest. I showed him statistics on our growth and detail on our projections. And finally I said: "Irv, I want to build a national CSFA headquarters building in Minnesota." He sat thoughtfully for a few minutes, sighed, and said: "I'll pledge ten thousand dollars to get you started."

Within another few days, I called Gus Johnson, and confirmed that he and I would spend another one of our coveted weeks in February in Scottsdale. All of the usual appointments and activities were more or less scheduled, and time was blocked out for nothing in particular. During one of our at-leisure afternoons we motored down to a shopping center on Bell Avenue to pick up the makings for authentic nachos. As we pulled up to the supermarket, I said: "You know what, Gus? I've been thinking about moving CSFA's headquarters to Minnesota." Gus turned off the ignition, and we sat in his 1980 Seville and talked for the better part of an hour. I told him of Cy Seifert's interest and of Irving's acquiescence. I told him the chances of getting it done were unknown. CSFA had improved credit but very little disposable cash. I reminded him that CSFA had a strong East Coast orientation and a provincial board that might well resist dramatic change.

Gus listened in his usual attentive fashion: his head tilted back and cocked just to the left--a slight hearing problem, I think. He then said: "It's a great idea. I'll put five thousand in with Irving's ten. I can be helpful, too, in finding a good location, and maybe an architect. My law firm will handle all of the legal matters. And I'll give some thought as to how we might convince the easterners." We then went in and purchased our corn tortillas, jalapeño peppers, Monterey Jack and cheddar cheeses, hot salsa, black olives, and a six-pack of chilled Bohemia Beer, and headed back to our microwave oven at Camelback resort. Gus had brought a great deal to the table.

My next assignment was with my compatriots, Stuart and Marlys Johnson. I could never really keep anything from them, and I had hinted to them at the time of the

January board meeting that something had to be done about our nomadic and disparate nature.

February in Minnesota stands in brittle contrast to the arid desert landscape of southern Arizona. But Stuart, Marlys and I did have one method of compensating for the cold. Stuart had built a redwood sauna in the basement of the Johnsons' Lower Johnson Circle home. The dry-heat bath experience was new to this New Englander, and even though we were always toweled to a level of acceptable decency, some time was required for me to win the war with my puritanical upbringing. I learned to enjoy the sauna and the cleanliness and relaxation that came with it.

The Johnsons' sauna was far more than a Scandinavian bath. It was a social experience. It was also a hotbed, so to speak, for great ideas and discussions, and accompanying good decisions. In fact, when any of the three of us had a business issue of any significance, that person could call for a "Sauna Summit." I did so call during my mid-winter visit to St. Peter.

A sauna promotes a certain equality among its participants. The trappings of office are very much absent. Hair, once neatly combed or coiffured, is matted on the forehead. Exposed skin glistens as the pores open and get busy with the cleaning regimen. Residual eye shadow cuts its colored concourse down the cheeks and drips from the chin. This five-feet, by six-feet, by six-and-one-half-feet enclosure provided our venue for corporate democracy.

Five minutes into the first of three fifteen-minute sauna sessions Stuart said: "What's up?" I paused only for the sake of dramatic impact. "I want to build a national headquarters for CSFA."

"I thought so," said Marlys. "Where?"

"Here," I said.

"Saint Peter?" she asked, just a bit incredulous.

"Well, here or somewhere nearby," I said, "maybe Mankato or LeSueur. Someplace where we will be welcome. Gus is willing to help us find a good location at a fair price. What do you think?" Stuart looked up.

"How will we pay for it?" He asked. He had taken over the financial operations of CSFA in 1980 and he knew the looks of the books.

"I don't have a clue," I responded.

In and out of the sauna the discussion continued. We soon got beyond "whether" and moved on to "how."

"I'll bet," said Marlys, "our Minnesota clients would help. Do you think the board will help fund it?"

"I don't know," I said. "They may not even like the idea."

Marlys laughed and said: "Let's go for it," and the decision was made. Following our respective showers Stuart opened a bottle of his treasured 1976 Jordan Vineyards Cabernet Sauvignon, the king of the cabernets, and the rest of the evening on into the early morning was dedicated to dreaming and scheming. We had a big selling job ahead of us. We three had to be the embodiment of enthusiasm.

The April 1983 board meeting went exactly as Cy and I envisioned. Ahead of the meeting I prepared and distributed my "white paper," one of only three I would draft during my twenty years with CSFA. The paper was entitled "CSFA, The Next Twenty-five Years: National Office and National Image." The board members were generally intrigued with the thought of a physical national identity. David Steele once again suggested the CSFA nomad should find its peaceful valley, settle in, and till its fields. Cy permitted some discussion of possible locations and then called on me to speak directly to the question of Minnesota. I noted that St. Peter was on this very spring day the *de facto* location for many of CSFA's fundamental business operations. Marlys Johnson was in charge of the national development of the community-based Dollars for Scholars program. Stuart Johnson was overseeing more than 70 percent of all of CSFA's financial operations.

The state of Minnesota, with the aid of the Bush Foundation and the persistence of the two Johnsons, had provided CSFA with its first reliable long-term survival model. The Johnsons had effectively proven that while new Dollars for Scholars programs could be organized as an evening activity, companies could be enlisted in CSFA's Scholarship Management Services during daylight hours. The "hard dollar" income from the latter, we learned, could support the volunteer efforts of the former. "We should consider," I suggested, "working from within CSFA's geographical center of strength." Cy then noted that ahead of the meeting he had received four phone calls on the "white paper" from trustees who were unable to attend. Three had endorsed the concept; one had expressed reservations. Cy then requested and received trustee approval for the staff to further pursue the concept of a Minnesota-based national office in anticipation of the June meeting. The chess pieces were on the table.

Marlys, Stuart and I decided that our preferred strategy was to structure the best possible case for *our* location of choice, as opposed to eliminating other possibilities or offering the board other options. We knew geography would favor us. Minnesota is the nation's heartland, almost equidistant east and west from both shores, and Minneapolis is due north of Dallas. We knew demography would support us as well. The resident Scandinavians, Irish, and Germans were widely regarded as conscientious, reliable, and industrious workers. The quality of public and private education at all levels was in the aggregate perhaps the best in the nation. Voluntarism, as it had come to be called in the Reagan presidency years, was integral to the culture. And the philanthropic bent of Minnesota's citizens and corporations fired the envy of nonprofit outlanders.

The infrastructure supported our case. The Minneapolis-St. Paul airport had become both cosmopolitan and international and was doubling in size about every five years. Republic Airlines was flying everywhere. Every major industrial center in the United States was no more than four air hours away. The drive from St. Peter to the airport was an easy hour and fifteen minutes, and parking was available on both ends. CSFA's corporate reality was another asset. Thirty percent of CSFA's ninety corporate and foundation clients were within the borders of the state, and the Midwest office was serving clients as far west as California. Twenty percent of CSFA's 193 Dollars for Scholars chapters were serving Minnesota school districts. Every case was made save the emotional one.

The emotional mine, we felt, needed salting. The Johnsons and I paid a call on a CSFA trustee who just happened to be a vice president of First Bank System in Minneapolis. Lloyd L. Brandt was also the gentleman who oversaw the bank's charitable programs. Three years earlier First Bank System had retained CSFA to help celebrate the bank's fiftieth anniversary. Bank President Don Grangaard rejected the notion of big parties and other internal celebrations. He wanted to do something of substance for both the employees and other people who resided in the five states served by First Bank. Lloyd had somehow heard of CSFA and invited Marlys Johnson to talk about the possibility of scholarships. The outcome was CSFA's first $100,000 scholarship program.

The birthday celebration would continue at that level for five years, and during that period we would capture a master of understatement and dry wit. We told Lloyd that we believed we needed something in our back pocket for the June meeting. We asked if First Bank System might support the building project. He said he couldn't promise anything, but he would try to secure before June a bank commitment of fifty thousand dollars. With that assurance and some rough cost numbers on a building of ten thousand square feet or more, we began our search for a site.

That search fell to Stuart and Marlys who were soon to be aided by the St. Peter Economic Development Corporation. Clete Schroepfer, vice president of the Nicollet County Bank, and a member of the corporation, approached Stuart and asked him how many jobs he thought CSFA could bring to St. Peter within five years. "I guessed forty," Stuart remembers, "and that number was impressive enough to capture the corporation's interest." During the next several evenings Clete showed the Johnsons twenty-one possible sites. They settled on one, and when I next visited St. Peter, without prologue, they loaded me into their car and took me on a brief "mystery ride" to the crest of a hill in the south end of town. The crest overlooked the Minnesota River valley.

The sensation I experienced on that day was identical to one of some fifteen years prior, when in New Hampshire I was searching for my first family home. Following six frustrating months of uninspiring house showings by real estate agents, I followed up an advertisement in a Sunday newspaper by driving to the location of a home listed in the classified section as a private sale. As I approached the driveway and looked at the property, I turned to my wife and said: "This is the place." When I stepped out of the Johnsons' car into that field of bending grasses and wild flowers, I turned to my friends and said: "This is definitely the place." We were, as one, prepared to face the board.

We certainly appeared to be ready as we joined the CSFA trustees as guests of New Hampshire College President Edward Shapiro in the college board room. We had charts. We had graphs. We even had overhead transparencies. We had a helping of Irving's chutzpah. Following the general housekeeping items on the meeting agenda, Stu, Marlys and I made our presentation and our proposal. The response was as anticipated: some support, some skepticism, and a bit of hostility. "Why not New York?" someone asked.

"Because," I replied, "the city is inconsistent with our corporate image, and we have the general area covered by our Metropolitan Service Center on Long Island."

"Why not Chicago, if you want to be in the big-time Midwest?" "Because we have almost no presence in Illinois, and there is no compelling reason to go there."

"How about Boston?"

"Out of the question. CSFA has never been able to raise serious money in Massachusetts. We'll need help with the funding. We'll never get it there."

Trustee Joe Hinchey, in an effort to provide beleaguered staff a respite, advised the board that it was simply impossible for staff to prove "there is nowhere else for CSFA to locate." But the debate raged on. One trustee doubted the advisability of owning real estate at all. Two believed the project to be just too ambitious.

Chairman Seifert withheld his personal position and carefully choreographed the discussion. Everyone at the table, save Mr. Seifert and one other, had a say. Cy had saved Lloyd Brandt for last. Cy finally turned to his immediate right.

"Lloyd, you're a Minnesotan. Your bank is a client and your foundation has contributed to CSFA. We haven't heard from you. What's your informed opinion?" Lloyd leaned back in his chair, brushed back with his right hand his thinning black hair, and appeared to reflect for a moment. He removed his eyeglasses and placed them on the table in front of him. He then addressed his colleagues in his measured way of speaking.

"All of the arguments I've heard here have merit. I've listened carefully, and I'm now prepared to offer you a compromise." Everyone else at the table, including the staff members, leaned forward and looked his way.

"I think," he said drolly, "the very best option is to have a Park Avenue address...somewhere in Minnesota."

Everyone laughed, the tension dissipated, and Chairman Seifert called for a vote.

The board, at the urging of Trustee Frank Morin, actually took two votes. The first was to establish a permanent headquarters facility. This motion carried unanimously. The second was to locate the facility in St. Peter, Minnesota. This motion carried by a vote of twelve to two. We had climbed the first mountain, but as the bear discovered, other Matterhorns materialize before success appears within range.

When the board next assembled in Minneapolis in October, the Audit and Finance Committee recommended that in view of the estimated $700,000 price tag on the project, the "trigger," or go-point should be $350,000 in gifts and firm pledges. The board agreed. The early fund raising had gone pretty smoothly. We had First Bank's $50,000 gift, and the Bush Foundation announced a like amount. The trustees and senior staff had also pledged $50,000 and had raised the board participation goal to $100,000. The preferred site had already been purchased from the school district by the St. Peter Economic Development Corporation. The corporation stood ready to deed the land to CSFA.

Gifts in kind helped. Marvin Windows offered $40,000 in top-of-the-line, insulated refracting windows. General Electric Company offered every one of several appliances the building would require. Digital Equipment Corporation assisted with the computer mainframe and peripherals. Office Interiors of Minneapolis, through a special arrangement with DICOMED, committed first-quality movable office partitions. Cash gifts were provided by thirteen other corporations including Jostens, Norwest Foundation, Illinois Tool Works, Otter Tail Power Company, and Weyerhaeuser Company Foundation. We were well in sight of the "trigger" figure, and our optimism was reshaped as conviction.

Our co-conspirator, Gus Johnson, was exhibiting his confidence as well. Gus had earlier introduced us to the Mankato architectural firm of Wick, Kagermeier, and Skarr. The firm agreed to do all of the design work and preliminary drawings at no cost, with the understanding that if the project went ahead, the firm would be hired as its architect. The firm had already suffered an earlier false start when CSFA came close to occupying the original, but long out of use Carnegie Library in downtown Mankato. Undaunted by the wasted effort on the library's redesign, the firm assigned the "new building" project to a young architect named Brian Paulsen. Brian in turn produced a building design incorporating all of the features and requirements the Johnsons and I described for him. This "envelope," as it is called, was the basis for the first architect's drawing, a last-minute addition to the *CSFA Annual Report for 1983*. The initial design was essentially utilitarian and Californian, predominately stone and redwood, with long, sloping roof sections and clerestory windows along the peaks. The report was distributed with accompanying fanfare to the trustees in the course of the

October annual meeting. The Johnsons and I were for some reason vaguely dissatisfied.

Throughout the winter of 1983 and into 1984 Stuart Johnson and I carried the design and accompanying blueprints around Minnesota as part of our fund-raising arsenal. Then on one rainy March day as we traveled up Highway 169 en route to Highway 18 and General Mills Corporation, I glanced to my right as we crossed over Interstate 494, and exclaimed, "Stuart, that's it; that's the building I want." Stuart stopped, turned the car around, and returned us to the site of my inspiration. We were at the entry gate of one of two buildings owned by the Naegle Company of Minneapolis. The wood-frame building we were facing was a curious and very attractive mix of Victorian and Colonial American architectures. "It's perfect," I said. Stuart thought a minute.

"I'll go in and see if they've got a picture we can have."

"Don't bother," I advised. "It's pouring, and even if they have a picture, they won't give it to you."

"No harm asking," Stuart said, as he opened the car door, stepped into the sheets of rain, and dashed through the developing puddles in the parking lot. Five minutes later he came out carrying a large manila envelope. Inside it were two, eight-by-ten, full-color photos of the Naegle building.

Stuart and I called on both General Mills and Jostens that day, but our minds were on Mankato. We left Jostens at three o'clock, drove the hour and a quarter to St. Peter, bypassed that city, and hurried into the offices of Wick, Kagermeier, and Skarr. Jim Kagermeier was in with Brian Paulsen. I dropped the photos on Brian's desk and said: "Here's what we want." Once again, rather than being frustrated or offended, both architects studied the photos and became very excited. "Great," said Brian. "You shall have it." And have it we did. The firm not only quickly redesigned the entire exterior of the building but also built a wooden scale model of the new design for the Johnsons and me to use to convince the board of the necessity for the design change. We three were ecstatic. We authorized the architect to go out to bid.

Everyone involved with the building project in 1983 believed that CSFA was in an excellent position to enjoy maximum value for each construction dollar. The Minnesota economy was very depressed. Foreclosures were pretty much a daily occurrence for farmers who had used inordinately inflated land valuations as the equity basis for incurring huge debt for farm expansion. But the grain loading docks in Duluth fell silent when national policy closed the lucrative doors to the Soviet market. The economy tumbled, expansion projects were interrupted, foreclosed on, or canceled, and the building trades became idle. Given this scenario our architect estimated that the CSFA building could be constructed for well under fifty dollars a square foot. We had based our total project cost of $700,000 on that assumption. Our number included all of the necessary equipment and furniture. The board was prepared to seek financing for half that amount. The St. Peter banks, despite several setbacks in the agricultural market, were amenable to that level of financing. Then the bids came in.

Stuart called me at my New Hampshire home during the first week of April. You're not going to like the numbers," he said. "The low bid for construction is $684,000, roughly seventy dollars a square foot, and nearly what we estimated for the entire project." We were suddenly facing a project approaching $1 million. I called Ralph Seifert with the disheartening news. Cy, as usual, was unfazed. "Meet with the architect," he said. "See if you can cut a few items or change some specs on the building. Then go get Gus and talk to the banks. Keep in mind" Cy said cheerily, "if you borrow a hundred thousand, the bank owns you. If you borrow a million, you own the bank. Call me back and tell me what you find out. I'll deal with the board."

In short order, we "found out" two things. First we could not alter the construction specifications or downgrade the materials requirements without compromising the beauty or quality of the building. Second, we discovered that two local banks, Nicollet County Bank and The First National Bank, were willing to share in a $700,000 mortgage. I have always felt that this offer was courageous in view of the prevailing economy and the fact that the building, while serving as collateral for the loan, was essentially 100 percent financed and was tailored to CSFA's very specific needs. Under the best of circumstances the building would not move quickly in a foreclosure sale. The banks' decision could not have been predicated on CSFA's minuscule assets. It had to have been based on CSFA's potential to grow and to serve the best interests of the city of St. Peter. I have often thought, too, that the decision was made in part as an expression of confidence in the intelligence, tenacity, and resilience of our resident vice presidents, Stuart and Marlys Johnson.

Ralph Seifert's optimism never wavered. On a gray and windy April 7, 1984, standing near the center of the two and one-half acres atop the hill in St. Peter, he presided over the dedication of the land to the purposes of Citizens' Scholarship Foundation of America. In contrast to the cold bleakness of the day, St. Peter school children, dressed in their colorful winter jackets and hats, framed the presumed location of the building, each holding firm, in defiance of the prevailing winds, huge circus-like bouquets of red, yellow, and blue balloons. Ralph Seifert, spurning a winter coat, addressed the fifty or so townspeople and local dignitaries who, along with representatives of Minnesota's Dollars for Scholars chapters, had gathered on the hill.

> Today, my friends, CSFA is a healthy and vibrant company. No doubt about it. Our business plan has worked. Each segment of our business is expanding. CSFA's staff is without peer in its understanding of private scholarship management. Our new facility will enhance even further our staff's effectiveness. I thank Joe, Stuart, and Marlys and all of their colleagues for their efforts in bringing us here today.
>
> But there are others who have made this day possible...those of you representing all ages and walks of life working at the local chapter level providing financial aid for people in your communities. I salute each of you. I wish I could shake every hand. To the east, south, west, and north, the pulse of the volunteer quickens across this land of ours.
>
> I salute, too, the men and women in the corporate world who have directed charitable dollars to scholarship purposes, and who have selected CSFA to manage those programs and funds. I salute companies and foundations, particularly in Minnesota, that have underwritten a good portion of the cost of this building project, thereby demonstrating their belief in CSFA's mission.
>
> I salute especially the people of St. Peter who have welcomed us here and coordinated their efforts to make this day happen. In your collective names, I dedicate this land and its future building to assisting those who seek enlightenment and the lifelong learning skills provided in a free society through higher education.

Upon his return to New England Cy infused his Board of Trustees with the spirit of the dedication. He involved the most skeptical among that body in the mortgage negotiations with the two St. Peter banks. During the April 13 board meeting in Syracuse, New York, he spoke eloquently of the event of April 7 and of the attitude, cooperation, and determination of the leadership of St. Peter. He had asked the Johnsons to bring the heavy and somewhat unwieldy building model to the meeting. The model survived just long enough to carry the day with the trustees. It was the focal point of the meeting and the first to-scale evidence that the building would be a reality. Within twenty-four hours two American Airlines freight handlers at the Syracuse Airport would drop the crate and reduce the model to blue and white kindling. No one had the audacity to request the architects to rebuild it, and besides, its purpose had been admirably served.

The heavy equipment of Buhler Construction Company, out of Butterfield, Minnesota, stood ready to move in just as soon as the frost was out of the ground. Popular Minnesota lore suggests that this event can take place any time before the Fourth of July. But spring came early to St. Peter and construction was well underway by the first of May. By mid-June Stuart and Marlys and I were able to enjoy a sunset and a glass of wine seated on a pile of two-by-sixes in what would one day soon be Marlys's office. By October first we began to believe the 1984 annual meeting, scheduled just five weeks away, might be held in the building rather than in offered facilities at nearby Gustavus Adolphus College.

The interior beauty and quality of the building are impossible to describe in any detail. But late one afternoon, two days before the somewhat delayed November board meeting, the Johnsons and I were arranging the hastily purchased folding tables on the concrete of the as yet uncarpeted board room floor. We heard the sound of a laborer working overhead. He was putting finishing touches on the exposed beams that concealed the indirect lighting, positioned to reflect off the cathedral ceiling. "You're working pretty late," Marlys said.

"Yah," he acknowledged.

"We appreciate it," Marlys said. "We want to be ready for our board meeting on Saturday."

"Oh, you bet," he said. "It's a privilege to work on such a beautiful building."

So intent was Chairman Seifert to hold the board meeting in the new structure, that he postponed it for two weeks to allow for construction delays. Cy arrived at the Johnsons' home during the afternoon of November 16. He had intentionally stayed away from the construction site since the day of the April land dedication. For this occasion he borrowed Stuart's black and white 1957 Chevrolet Biscayne, a car that had belonged to Stuart's late grandfather. At dusk he drove the route I had traveled with Stuart and Marlys on our "mystery ride" more than a year before. We three in that late fall evening stood outside the building awaiting our chairman. He drove in from Jefferson Avenue along a dirt road through the soybean field. He stopped the car facing the building, emerged from the classic Chevrolet, and stood before the double paneled, dark oak doors. He said aloud, "Oh my!" Then he literally ran around the building repeating, "Oh, my! Oh my! Oh my!"

"That," I said to my two colleagues, "is about as emotional as Mr. Seifert gets."

With the sun high the next day in the brisk fall morning sky, other board members shared Cy's excitement. Some few were speechless. As we toured the exterior, I took Lloyd Brandt aside and confided to him that I had hoped to have a paved access road to the building come in from Jefferson Avenue. From that direction the road would border land set aside by the city for swings and slides and picnic tables, and other trappings of recreation.

"I wanted our road to come in over there," I explained, "so we could name it 'Park Avenue.' But," I went on, "we ran out of money, so we have to use Riverview Road coming up the hill from the south. I'm sorry we couldn't get it done, Lloyd." I said. But we do have an alternate plan to recognize your part in the project. We plan to name a large section of the building in honor of First Bank." Lloyd reacted immediately.

"You can't do that!" He said. "The bank made it clear it wanted no recognition whatsoever for its gift."

"Yes, I can, Lloyd," I insisted, "and I'm going to. We plan to call this whole ground level the First Floor."

The building, as originally designed, would be able to accommodate the management of $25 million in scholarship distributions on behalf of companies and foundations. When CSFA's Minnesota-based staff of thirteen took up occupancy between the December holidays of 1984, CSFA was managing just over $9 million on behalf of 152 sponsors. Both board and staff believed the space available would suffice for operations into the late 1990s. The growing popularity of CSFA as the scholarship program manager of choice dictated otherwise.

CSFA reached the $25 million benchmark in 1993. And despite the fact that a tasteful and complementing addition was made to the building in 1991, the original structure has fallen victim to progress. The board room and library in the east ell are now partitioned for offices. File cabinets obscure the impressive Kasota stone fireplace. The small, attractive guest quarters in the west ell now house members of the ever-growing professional staff. The kitchen table is a sometimes conference table. The living room is crowded with two sections of the original board-room table. The tasteful decor competes with current use and purpose. The two small bedrooms are offices. The sauna sits cold, a storage closet. Open areas of the main building, such as the hallways, have been relegated to additional storage space or are dedicated to office machinery and work tables. Progress, CSFA's constant companion, has been no friend of the building. "Today we say we're going to the office," Marlys says a bit plaintively. "Stuart and I almost never call it 'the building' anymore."

The circumstances of today, however, can never in our collective minds diminish the joy and exhilaration of the evening of January 31, 1985. On this occasion we invited the Buhler Construction crew back to St. Peter for a "Builders' Night." Almost to a person, the carpenters, masons, plumbers, electricians, painters and laborers appeared, some nervously, in their Sunday best. With beverage of choice in one rough hand and hors d'oeuvre of choice in the other, they wandered through the furnished offices on the upper level and down the central circular staircase to the open work areas below, stopping now and then to admire their personal handiwork or to point out a feature to a spouse or friend. The job foreman, Al Tadd, was close to tears when he told us that no one had ever done such a thing for the crew before. "This building," he said, "is a treasure. Marlys, Stuart, and I, sharing his emotion and his moment, agreed.

Part VI

Edwin B. Knauft

1985-1988

Burt
The Lesson of the Half-Mile Bridge

Chapter Twenty-three

Burt

"My earliest recollection as a Board member of CSFA," says Edwin B. "Burt" Knauft, "was a time in 1977 or '78 when we met up in Reading, Massachusetts, at Addison-Wesley Publishing Company. You remember the guy there, what was his name, who designed and published that first CSFA annual report in about ten years."

"Don James," I said.

"That's right, that's right; he's the one. The report had a picture in it of the horse Gus Johnson gave us. The Red Lady, or something like that?"

"Pretty close," I said. "Lady in Red."

"That's right, that's right; but that's not what I remember best about that meeting. What I remember is that we were having a CSFA board meeting, and we had to bring our own lunch."

Burt smiles on this October 1994 day as he busies his way around his modest but attractive Washington, DC, condominium, preparing lunch for today's guest.

"I think the pizza Ruth left for us is going to be pretty good. Is it too early in the day for you for a beer?"

"Not at all," I assured him, "I'm on my last assignment."

Burt Knauft, fifth chairman of the board of Citizens' Scholarship Foundation of America, is one of those seemingly ageless people who in their seventies appear to carry unmarked by time the features of two decades before. At six feet, Burt, with his lean figure and gray, trimmed and wavy hair, satisfies today the "preferred" 1970s criteria for the senior corporate officer. This executive profile was first described to me by CSFA's second chairman, Brad Norris: "You have to be at least six feet tall, and you have to weigh less than one hundred and eighty pounds," Brad had said of those who then dwelled on the mahogany rows.

Burt was in fact a long-time corporate officer in Aetna Life and Casualty Insurance Company in Hartford, Connecticut. He has since had the distinction of having retired on schedule from The Aetna at age sixty-two, following thirty years of service, and from two other executive-level positions in the private sector. On this day as he moves with dispatch from the tiny kitchen to the glass-top dining room table, his energy level suggests that if called upon to do so, he stands ready to undertake a fourth. When I met Burt late in 1976, he was Aetna's vice president for Corporate Social Responsibility. "Some people think that's an oxymoron, like airline cuisine," he quips, "but at The Aetna it was serious business."

My first business with Burt Knauft was serious as well, in that I was engaged at the time in a quiet, personal altercation with the National Information Bureau in New York City. NIB was then, and is today under a slightly altered acronym and title, the quasi-accrediting agency for charitable organizations around the country. Now known as the National *Charities* Information Bureau or NCIB, the organization keeps track of such things as what percentage of receipts from contributions actually address the charitable purpose of a nonprofit organization. Prior to 1976 CSFA had no trouble finding itself on the NIB "approved list," because virtually all contributions receipts at both the local Dollars for Scholars chapter level and at the national level were earmarked for either local students or for the ongoing proliferation of Dollars for Scholars chapters.

In April of 1976, however, NIB announced its decision to make its reports available to the general public and to revise and tighten its "Basic Standards in Philanthropy." Organizations not meeting the revised standards were placed on notice. Citizens' Scholarship Foundation of America was among them. The notification was more than just troubling, because in the nation's bicentennial year CSFA was still about 50 percent dependent for its survival on gift and grant income.

I needed serious, but of course, *free* counsel. A friend of a friend, Bob Merriman, president of the Coordinating Council on Foundations for the Greater Hartford Area, arranged a luncheon meeting for me at the Hartford Club. His other guest was Edwin B. Knauft. Over lunch I explained my dilemma to Mr. Knauft.

> CSFA works just fine. We have a Board of Trustees numbering at any given time between forty and fifty members. The full board meets once a year, usually in New York City, and ratifies the actions of the Executive Committee. The Executive Committee is made up chiefly of people from New England who can get together several times a year at very little expense to them or CSFA. NIB wants us to change all that. My chairman, Ed Lee, and I have been to New York on at least three occasions to try to convince the people at NIB that CSFA ain't broke, from

a management point of view, at least. Their position is that the only way we can get back on the list is to fix it anyway.

Mr. Knauft asked me a few questions about the makeup of the board and of the Executive Committee and about the number of meetings per year and the average attendance at each. He then reacted.

> Well, okay, the first thing you have to understand is that for many major companies, and especially those whose contributions programs are understaffed, and that's a lot of them, the NIB listing is the first screening procedure for new grant requests. If you're not on the list, you won't make it past the wastebasket. You don't have to conform to NIB standards, but you do have to weigh the risk of exclusion. The second thing you need to know is that the standards are viewed by the corporate giving community as necessary and reasonable. You won't find much sympathy as you try to justify your erstwhile independence and resistance. You will, in fact, raise the specter of suspicion. My advice is go along. You may not like what you have to do, but I'll bet when you're finished, you'll have a better organization.

Clearly the advice was not as I sought, but I stopped thirty miles north of Hartford in Westfield, Massachusetts, on my route back to New Hampshire and shared the news with Chairman Lee.

I have since decided that much of my resistance to NIB's standards was a product of my then to-date thirty-six years of upbringing in New Hampshire, a state that resists any type of outside intervention in its affairs. Witness today no Martin Luther King holiday, no motorcycle helmet law, and no seat-belt law for people over twelve years of age. Few people in New Hampshire stand opposed to the three concepts, but the mind-set in the Granite State is "nobody's goin' to tell us what we gotta do."

Resigned to Mr. Knauft's advice, I decided I needed still another ally in the reform process, and I found one in another of my CSFA trustees. I had met Frank Morin some seven or eight years before when he, in his early thirties, headed up the counseling program in the Salem, New Hampshire, high school. Frank, who I much later learned had the nickname "Chub" in his youth, was an exuberant man of average stature who always seemed on the edge but never over the edge of being overweight. Of initial interest to me and to CSFA, Frank was, in addition to being an exemplary public-school guidance counselor, immediate past president of the American School Counselors Association. In 1974 I decided that this friendly fellow with the near perpetual five o'clock shadow would be a logical addition to the CSFA board and, because of his proximity to CSFA's administrative offices, to the Executive Committee as well.

By 1976 Frank had left public education and had joined a private employee-relocation firm in New Canaan, Connecticut. There he continued to use his counseling skills. New Horizons assisted families who were relocating to southwestern New England at the behest of any of a number of the major national companies, many of which had slipped away from Manhattan in the early seventies to establish headquarters in more pristine and less volatile environments. Frank also spent his evenings working out of his home with local young people and their parents who were hoping to find the ideal and most prestigious higher education match. Both Frank's office and home were on my frequent route to New York, and I was always welcomed as a guest at either. His office was just off Exit 37 of the Merritt Parkway, my preferred scenic four-lane highway to the city. At this location, with the blessing and support of his employer, we began a seven year process that would intersect fortuitously and favorably with Burt Knauft's growing interest and involvement with Citizens' Scholarship Foundation of America.

Frank and I discussed in great depth and detail just how an organization such as CSFA should be structured. In the process he became my counselor, and we became the closest of friends. He agreed essentially with NIB's standards and considered our new initiative as historically important to the future of CSFA. Frank had an enviable understanding of organizational dynamics and of the various motivations of people who wish to serve. He cautioned me that organizations, large or small, are resistant to dramatic change, and I realized that my own behavior was the personification of that kind of resistance. Frank knew intuitively that CSFA was going to grow, and that the days of board meetings being little more than a handful of volunteers listening to staff reports and commiserating over budget shortfalls would soon be behind us. He was the second person to advise me that the challenge to a chief executive officer of a nonprofit agency was to keep the board focused on governance and the staff focused on programs. Trustee Ed Shapiro had earlier warned me to keep my trustees busy or "they would soon be into my programs," where, he said, I would definitely "not want them." Frank helped me to discover that the chief executive officer is the fulcrum between board and staff and the liaison between policy and practice.

The pace of our internal reforms, however, was not in synch with NIB's reporting schedule. In November of 1977 NIB announced a further revision of its standards, and in May of 1978 released a report on Citizens' Scholarship Foundation of America critical of its governance and its financial reporting procedures. CSFA, despite its generally acknowledged high ethics and commitment to purpose, was dropped from NIB's "approved" listing. Ed Lee and I in short order again journeyed to New York to ask for more time to refine and implement our reorganization plan. NIB agreed to reinsert CSFA in its listing within a category called "In Finding," a temporary classification, that put me on notice that I, as the chief engineer, did not have the luxury of being a reluctant drag-on.

Frank and I began by recommending to the Executive Committee on July 19, 1978, that the governing board of CSFA be limited to fifteen members, all but one with fixed three-year terms. Five terms were to expire in each of two years, and four would expire in the third. Dr. Fradkin, as president and founder, occupied a permanent place on the board. The Executive Committee itself would be a subset of this body with a membership never to equal or exceed in number a quorum of the governing board. The full board would meet a minimum of three times per year to address the governance responsibilities of CSFA. The Executive Committee would be empowered to act on behalf of the board--within certain boundaries--in the interim between board meetings.

We also, at the urging of then Chairman Lee, did away with a curious, but not at all unique to CSFA, procedure provided for in the bylaws: the practice that required all actions of the Executive Committee to be subject to ratification by the full board in the course of the annual meeting. Ed Lee reasoned successfully that "what has been done with proper authority should not be undone. You cannot," he said, "logically, empower a body to take action on your behalf, and then permit the authorizing body to reverse that action. What if, for example, the Executive Committee authorizes the filling of a position or the purchase of a piece of equipment? Such actions are not easily or appropriately reversed. If the full board is not enamored with the actions of its Executive Committee, it has the option of electing new officers or otherwise changing the nature of the committee. Don't tie the hands of those who are empowered to govern."

What of the thirty or so former board members who would not find a place on the fifteen-member governing board? The temptation was to simply assign them to the Advisory Board of Trustees, made up originally of a handful of people who were willing in the early 1960s to lend a name as a small favor to CSFA Founder Irving Fradkin. For a time, Frank and I and the board yielded to that temptation. By 1978 the Advisory Board of Trustees had grown to number thirty-four, including holdovers from the old and defunct board structure, past and retired chairs and other former officers, and a smattering of new faces of people who had some interest in the future of CSFA. But in that same year when Burt Knauft attended his first meeting as a new face among CSFA's governing trustees he saw firsthand where his earlier counsel at the Hartford Club had led. Little did he know how far it would go.

By 1979, as time was closing in on the last of Ed Lee's eight years as chairman, he and I were feeling pretty smug about our progress with the governance of CSFA. Meeting attendance was up; a quorum was common. Every governing board member was assigned to one of six functioning board committees: Trustees, Publicity, Audit and Finance, Aid Distribution Policy, Organization, and Special Projects Review. Provision had been made for the outgoing chairman to serve as a voting *ex officio* board member to provide continuity in the change of leadership. Ed Lee and I were ready and anxious to call on our friends at the National Information Bureau. We did in the fall of 1980 and learned those folks were not done with us yet.

"While you technically meet the NIB Standards," we were told, "you do not yet have a 'Statement of Functional Expenses' as part of your audited financial statements."

"What's that?" we asked, somewhat abashed.

"It's a breakout of administrative costs, fund-raising costs, and programmatic expense. Essentially, it's little more than a time and expense allocation, on a horizontal axis, of all of the things you do."

"How do we get to those numbers?" we asked.

"You will have to work that out with your auditor," we were told.

But "working it out" took considerable time and not a little expense. We sensed the urgency of conformance, for the Council of Better Business Bureaus, a long-time indirect ally of CSFA, was now insisting on the same type of financial data. We were on a reconnaissance mission without a map. The only immediate upside to the task was that it was, perhaps, tangentially related to the self-imposed mandate of incoming Chairman Ralph Seifert. Cy had previously announced one intention, among others, to streamline the business operations of CSFA. The task of Functional Expense Accounting proved, however, to be formidable. Assigning personnel costs to specific programs was simple enough when someone's work was limited to one program, but allocating bookkeeping, secretarial support, and the supervisory time of senior staff, tended to be onerous. The same problems held true with insurance and rent, and the division of travel expenses when any of us would in the course of a single day make a fund-raising call, market a scholarship program to a corporation, and help a community set up a new Dollars for Scholars program.

The exercise ultimately required eight new audit columns, encompassing eighteen expense categories, supported in turn and verified by purchase and expense specific documentation. We devised a system for recording on a weekly basis a percentage-of-overall-activity analyses, a fixed-cost allocation schedule--including depreciation-- and, the least popular of all documents, a fifteen-minute-interval personal time sheet. I felt as if the federal government had paid me one of its "I'm here to help you" calls. I quipped to the board that the cost of documenting our general administration was seriously aggravated by the burdensome requirement that we keep track of it.

The birth of Functional Expense Accounting in at least one small way justified the gestation and discomfort. We learned, for example, that CSFA's combined general administration and fund-raising costs ran less than 10 percent of overall operating expense. And when compared, say by 1983, to the more than $4 million in allocated scholarships, those costs were both highly competitive and relatively insignificant. We were able, too, for the very first time, to determine how we as employees actually spent our time and to consider how it might be better spent. Such documentation proved very valuable as CSFA in 1983 entered the world of strategic planning.

Burt Knauft had been absent during a good part of CSFA's new governance and accounting gyrations. In 1982 he was granted a leave of absence from The Aetna and the governing board of CSFA in order that he might accept a position with President Reagan's "Task Force on Private Sector Initiatives." The task force was established ostensibly to aggrandize the role of the not-for-profit sector in the United States and to encourage that sector to assume an even greater role in meeting the charitable needs of our society. Burt and I agreed in retrospect that the mandate was not particularly well served. "The administration believed," said Burt, as he cleared the table of pizza crumbs and brought on the sugar cookies and peppermint-stick ice cream, "that foundations, corporations and voluntary organizations could reduce government's burdens and, along with those reductions, relieve some of the tax dollars committed to welfare, education, and other charitable causes. This belief," Burt continued, "was not founded in any basis of reality."

Indeed, as was true of prior administrations and those to follow, at the same time a President was urging on private philanthropy and "voluntarism," each Congress was being particularly punitive to charitable giving from any source with a clear oxymoron called "tax reform." Over time nonitemizing taxpayers lost their short-lived privilege of deducting charitable contributions. Severe limitations were placed on tax credit for gifts of any kind of appreciated property and for original works of art. The introduction of the "Alternative Minimum Tax" computation dissuaded some wealthy people from making significant gifts to qualified charities. Nothing that the various administrations were doing or advocating was reflected in the reality of the activities on the Hill. "All of this stuff," asserts Burt, "was essentially a public relations effort."

I, of course, knew full well that scholarship programs had not escaped the attention of the policy makers and rule writers. I have always contended, insofar as the Internal Revenue Service is concerned, that when people are hired to write rules, they will invariably spend all their time writing rules. Thirteen years earlier The Tax Reform Act of 1969 had established somewhat arbitrary limits on the number of scholarships that could be made available to company employees through company-related foundations. The resulting IRS Revenue Procedure 76-47, finally published in 1976, complicated the process even further. And the rules were virtually immutable, irrespective of the "blindness" of the recipient selection process or the qualifications of the applicants.

"But," Burt admits, "life was heady here in Washington. Ruth and I loved it. So when my stint with the task force ended in 1983, and I had completed an interim assignment as a research associate at the Program on Nonprofit Organizations at Yale, I elected to take the position of executive vice president with Independent Sector." IS was in December of 1984 the still young, but decidedly prestigious, private national organization established to look out for the best interests of grant seekers and grant makers alike. Burt remained with IS until his third retirement in 1992, and during this stint he co-authored with two associates *Profiles of Excellence: Admiring Success in the Nonprofit Sector*.

Burt's anticipated return to active duty on CSFA's Governing Board of Trustees coincided with the final months of Ralph Seifert's five-year commitment to the chairmanship of CSFA. Once again I was given something of a free hand in selecting the successor to the chair, but this time around my choice would be hoisted on his own petard. I flew to Washington in the spring of 1984 where Burt met me in a restaurant at National Airport. I asked him if he would consider the chairmanship, and following some brief reflection and a nondescript meal, he said "yes." I then explained that the selection process had been streamlined a bit. The CSFA Committee on Trustees, chaired by one Frank Morin, now reserved the right to interview all prospective trustees and potential officers. Would he agree to an interview by members of the committee. Again he said "yes."

"That interview," says Burt while clearing away dessert dishes and serving up coffee, "is one I'll never forget. I caught up with Frank and Irving Fradkin at the Steak Loft in Mystic, Connecticut. I expected a decent meal and an informal, somewhat social evening with old friends. The meal was, as I remember, pretty good, and the friends were still friends, but the interview was tough. Those two fellows asked me hard questions about my commitment and availability. They told me how far CSFA had come during my leave of absence and asked if I thought I had the ability to maintain or even accelerate that pace. They asked what I felt I could bring to the chairmanship that qualified me above anyone else. I thought to myself 'this is a rugged but wonderful process.' CSFA had become in the space of two years a real organization."

On November 17, 1984, Burt accepted the gavel from Ralph Seifert in the unfinished, unfurnished CSFA board room on the hill in St. Peter, Minnesota. He had inherited an organization representing scholarship distributions nudging $8 million. The operating budget was balanced at just under $800,000, and the outlook was favorable that "unencumbered discretionary revenues" of $52,000 for the year just ended would be exceeded by the close of fiscal year 1985.

"The stability of the organization," Burt says, as we carried our second cup of coffee into the living room, "gave me, as chairman, an opportunity to build on the reforms I encouraged when you and I first met at the Hartford Club." He continued.

> Cy had done wonders with the staff, and he had made great progress with board membership, especially in its geographic representation. He had a good committee structure, too. Board meeting attendance was superb, over

90 percent if I remember right, even though the majority of the members continued to pay their own way.

I believed that the quality of the board was as vital to the future of CSFA as the qualifications and dedication of the staff. My chief responsibility as chairman was to focus on the board's *behavior*. As chair-elect I headed up at Cy's request CSFA's first long-range planning committee. That plan was almost entirely board-driven. You remember when Joe Hinchey came in with about fifty feet of computer paper containing various possible growth scenarios for both Dollars for Scholars and the scholarship management program. The long-range plan was predicated on one of those scenarios. It fueled the annual plans developed by staff. We as trustees were able to structure broad performance goals based on recent history and anticipated conditions and circumstances. The plan draft was reviewed and reworked by all board committees, so that each board member could assess the long-range plan's impact on committee work and on individual commitment.

One of the most important things we did was the board 'Self Assessment.' That exercise not only pointed out how the nature of CSFA trusteeship had changed, but its outcome also clarified board and staff responsibilities. I, too, shared the notion that the key to everything was to keep board members governing and staff members performing.

Burt carried the empty coffee cups to the kitchen and spoke over the sound of dishes being loaded into the dishwasher: "As soon as the long-range plan received board approval, I replaced the *ad hoc* committee on planning with a permanent board Planning Committee charged to monitor the progress of the plan and to recommend modifications in the face of unexpected developments. Do you remember the 'purple tab'?"

"Oh, sure," I said. "You asked me to document the history of CSFA as background information for the long-range planning committee. One of the sections contained information on unanticipated events that either helped or hindered our progress. It was identified by a purple tab."

"That's right," said Burt. "I told the Planning Committee to be always alert for 'purple tabs.'" Burt returned to his chair.

> Another interesting thing that happened was that the Committee on Trustees came to be viewed as perhaps the most important of all committees, because people alone determine the fate of an organization, and members of nominating committees generally select people most like themselves. Frank Morin continued to head it up. His committee in short order recommended term limits for trustees. That was a particularly difficult decision, because it meant the mandated eventual departure of the likes of Ralph Seifert, Ed Lee, and Gus Johnson. The committee also recommended that in addition to the immediate past chairman being an officer of the board, the officer position of chair-elect also be established. We then had solid continuity in our leadership changes.
>
> As the board went about its new business, I stressed to you and Stuart and Marlys the importance of keeping the board informed. Your pre-board meeting materials improved dramatically both in substance and in quality. The information became resource material for the committees, as opposed to reports to the board. I knew that committee meetings are where the work of an effective board really takes place. Our board meetings ran crisply, and we scheduled them over two days, one weekday and one weekend day. I wanted the board to socialize for at least one evening, because I believe it is just as important that members know each other as it is for them to know the organization. I remember that Frank Morin in a rare moment of mock impropriety actually appointed Gus

Johnson and another trustee, Bob Baker, as social co-chairs of CSFA. These appointments were made very late one evening in the lounge of the North Star Hotel in Minneapolis. I felt it politic to confirm the action in the course of the next day's board meeting.

I checked my watch and saw that our afternoon was slipping away. "Beyond your work with the board, Burt," I asked, "what else of importance comes to mind when you think of your chairmanship?"

"Well," he replied, smiling, "right in the middle of my term, you resigned."

That resignation was a surprise to everyone, including me. In the spring of 1986 I was completing my twentieth year with Citizens' Scholarship Foundation of America and my sixth year as its president. CSFA was financially secure. The income from the management of nearly $9 million in sponsored scholarship programs was permitting CSFA to do things, not always unique things, but things certainly new to the organization. In keeping with CSFA's mission the board had instituted an educational assistance program that would provide employees up to $4,800 per year in college-cost reimbursements for dependent children. The program was based solely on years of service. The board had also approved a nonprofit, incentive-pay program, predicated on formal performance evaluations. Our staff of sixty had shared $55,000 in additional compensation in December of 1985. The outlook was far better for 1986. Trustee Joe Hinchey had arranged for an independent executive salary survey, and CSFA employee compensation was set at competitive levels. CSFA was also providing incentive grants to its local Dollars for Scholars affiliate chapters. The program had grown from $12,000 in distributions in 1984 to an anticipated $48,000 in 1986.

All trustees for the first time could, on request, be reimbursed for expenses related to board meetings, though the majority continued to either decline reimbursement or to contribute back the payments. The reimbursements were even extended to members of the Advisory Board of Trustees who were actively serving on board committees. The advisory board, at Frank Morin's urging, had been trimmed of the sentinels of the past, and its membership became both a screening ground and training platform for future governing trustees.

CSFA's imagination and innovation remained intact and attractive to America's corporate community. The growth rate for CSFA corporate programs compounded at 33 percent. Every year we would be warned by Trustee Hayden W. Smith of the Council for Aid to Education not to plan for a growth rate that was unsustainable. As each year passed I would joke with Ed Lee, Ralph Seifert, and Burt Knauft by saying that "Hayden was right: we were unable to sustain it. We again surpassed it."

Near the close of fiscal year 1986 CSFA's corporate and foundation client list reflected 184 sponsored programs. Notable among recent additions was Burger King's "set-aside" program that provided higher education grants to student employees on the basis of time worked for the company. Also noteworthy was the Bank of America California Student Achievement Awards program. This program was especially memorable in that in 1978 when CSFA successfully solicited a $5,000 grant from Bank of America in support of its scholarship survey work in California, I was told by Ed Truschke--whom I had known from years earlier when he was a contributions officer at Xerox--that the bank would probably never call on CSFA for the management of its scholarship programs. But in 1985 following an internal cost analysis of the achievement awards program, CSFA was invited to assume its administration. CSFA sustained the spirit and quality of the statewide program and at the same time reduced the administrative cost by two-thirds.

CSFA had made internal managerial moves that were also working remarkably well. In March of 1985 shortly after the new headquarters building in St. Peter became a reality, Stuart and Marlys Johnson convinced me that the growth of administrative burdens had finally outstripped their combined capacity to manage CSFA's internal operations and at the same time continue to generate new business. We spent the first half of a morning at the Johnsons' kitchen table at 726 Lower Johnson Circle, where my colleagues of ten years recounted the difficulties they were facing. At ten o'clock the two of them left for the headquarters building. I remained at the table, reviewed my notes, and catalogued thirteen specific areas requiring attention. At eleven thirty I called Marlys and asked her to bring home at lunch time a supply of easel-size newsprint paper. I then called Burt Knauft in Washington to tell him what I had in mind and to secure his blessing for it.

Following a hasty lunch, we three moved to the dining room table. The newsprint paper was spread out on the larger table, and I suggested that we each draw a large circle, and then segment each circle into our individual current responsibilities. That task accomplished by two o'clock, I then asked, "what are we willing to give up; to turn over to someone else?"

The combined list was a compendium of internal operations. We divided the list into three management areas. I then asked the Johnsons to identify with me three people currently on staff who could in all probability manage the areas. The three named were then invited to the Johnson home at half-hour intervals beginning at three o'clock. By five o'clock we had named Carrie Dauner national director of Dollars for Scholars, Marilyn Rundell manager of Scholarship Management Services, and Beverly Swenson manager of our newly designated Education Grants/Innovative Services program, which included the $7 million General Motors Education Grant Program for Minorities and Women. The appointments were made on a Wednesday afternoon; announced to the staff on Thursday morning; and became effective on Monday. CSFA's new "middle management structure," a product of four days' deliberations and action, would last virtually intact for nearly ten years.

The new structure permitted the Johnsons and me to concentrate on external marketing. Stuart retained his responsibility for financial operations, but now with some trained assistance; Marlys maintained her responsibility with program promotion and public relations. We were able to develop an internal/external management configuration that proved to be very efficient. Any one of the three of us, for example, could meet in, say, California with officials of Levi Strauss on the upper corporate floor; secure the answers to the thirteen questions that effectively tailor-designed a company scholarship program; take the elevator to the ground floor and the pay-telephone bank; then call our remarkable administrative assistant, Jolene Christensen with the answers to the thirteen questions. During the return flight to Minneapolis we could draft a personalized cover letter and arrive back in St. Peter to find a program proposal awaiting our review. The normal turnaround time was four days; the results almost always favorable.

All of this national office activity was augmented in 1986 by the complementary activities originating with CSFA's five regional service centers. The Long Island-based Metropolitan Service Center, under the direction of Ben Coté continued to stimulate new corporate programs in New York City and New Jersey. The remaining centers were focusing on the renewed commitment to the development of Dollars for Scholars chapters. Much of this activity was supported by grants earmarked for chapter development, but increasing amounts of what Trustee Howard Moreen had identified as CSFA's "hard money" were being assigned to this purpose. And as Trustee Tom Bellinger had predicted, those dollars were indeed "pulling the Dollars for Scholars train."

As to my personal decision not to continue to travel on that train, or the entire CSFA railway for that matter, I reassured Burt: "You must never regard my resignation in any way as a personal affront. I was certainly happy with your chairmanship. I made that decision over a period of five days. Then I needed another two years to figure out why I made it. Actually, Marlys Johnson figured it out for me. She told me I was bored, because nothing since 1983 and 1984 rivaled in magnitude the General Motors program, the anonymous benefactor, and the building of 'the building.' What else would you like the world to remember about your chairmanship?" Burt thought a minute.

> Well, I think I was helpful in keeping CSFA focused on its mission. We were offered opportunities to get into the student loan business and to possibly manage the matching gifts programs of some of our corporate scholarship clients. The lesson of the Fund Finder and the College Scholarship Information Bank was for me a good one. Being too interested in new ideas is sometimes counterproductive. An organization with a wealth of talent must be able to tell the difference between what it can do and what it should do. That's not always easy, but CSFA

was well beyond the point of taking on diversions out of a sense of desperation.

We found Bill Nelsen, too, and that was a great accomplishment. And the board decision in 1986 to ask Lloyd Brandt to step down temporarily from the board and take on the interim presidency of CSFA was astute. You have to remember that the organization had you as its executive leader for almost all of its history. The potential for confusion and disarray was pretty great. By keeping the interim position in the family, so to speak, we avoided any major upheavals. Oh, and the activation of the Trustees Honor Roll in, I think, 1988 was another good thing.

Indeed it was. In the spring of 1988 CSFA President Bill Nelsen called me to ask if I would work with former Trustees Lee, Seifert, Moreen and Morin, to develop guidelines for a more formal role for the twelve people named to the honor roll. I agreed to do so, and in July we gathered at Ralph and Sandra Seifert's summer home in West Southport, Maine. We worked through the day and following a prepared-on-the-shore Down East Shore Dinner, complete with lobsters and corn-on-the-cob, we decided in the spirit of continuing respite to call another of the honor roll inductees. We located former Trustee Greg Macri, at his home in Walpole, New Hampshire. Greg is first among his peers to enjoy a good joke, but at times he is a little too trusting and perhaps a bit gullible, so I suggested to Sandra that we place the call in a particular way.

We dialed his number, and when he picked up, Sandra said: "Good evening Mr. Mackree."

"It's Macri," Greg corrected.

"This is your AT&T operator," Sandra continued. "I have a collect conference call from a Mr. Feelin in West Southport, Maine. Will you accept the charges?"

"I guess so," Greg replied, and I came on the line.

"Hi, Greg," I said. "This is Joe Phelan. I'm up here with Cy and we got to thinking about you and thought you might like to renew a few of your old CSFA acquaintances. I've got Ed patched in from Westfield, Massachusetts; Frank from Wilton, Connecticut, and Howard Moreen from Hancock, New Hampshire. They all want to talk with you."

"That's great," said Greg, and I started the parade of voices.

"How ya doin'?" asked Ed Lee. And the conversations went on from there. Howard Moreen took his turn at the telephone.

"Howard," greeted Greg. "Great to hear from you. What are you up to?"

"Well," Howard replied, "I'm not here, Greg; I'm in Hancock."

"So I understand," acknowledged Greg.

The call encompassed the better part of an hour and when my time came around again, Sandra carried out my next instruction. She came on the line and said: "Mr. Mackree."

"Macri," Greg reminded her.

"Mr. Mackree, this is your AT&T operator. I must inform you that you have reached your AT&T credit limit, and I must have your permission to continue the conference call."

"How much is it so far?" Greg asked.

"One hundred and forty-eight fifty," she replied.

Greg reacted with a loud epithet and slammed down the phone. The next day I dropped him a note apologizing for running up his phone bill and offering him the ten dollars I said I was willing to collect from the callers.

The serious business of the Honor Roll Trustees had just been partially completed during our July stay in Maine. In the spirit of the old days I drove down to Wilton, Connecticut, and spent an evening with Frank Morin finalizing the membership guidelines and defining the limits of the group's responsibilities. We wanted everyone to know that the Honor Roll Trustees had no governance role with Citizens' Scholarship Foundation of America. With those tasks completed, I then agreed to attend a September 23 meeting of CSFA's Executive Committee in Minneapolis. The meeting at the Hotel Sofitil was a bit difficult in that our *ad hoc* honor roll committee had decided that the proper place for the founder of CSFA was with his honor roll peers. Irving Fradkin was the first person elected to the honor roll and the only member who was not retired from active trusteeship. He sat in as a member of CSFA's Executive Committee that Friday afternoon, and while he agreed in principle with the recommendations of the *ad hoc* committee, he knew he would have difficulty relinquishing his voting membership on the Board of Trustees. By five o'clock Irving's concerns had been fully addressed, and the Executive Committee voted to adopt intact the proposed guidelines. We then adjourned to the hotel dining room.

My day with Burt in Washington was nearing its close as well. "That was a rough meeting, as I remember it," he said, "but things lightened up at dinner."

"Yes," I said. "Do you remember I had taken pictures at the July meeting, when Cy took everyone out in his Cape Dory for a sail off the coast of Maine? I was passing the pictures around the dinner table that evening. Two of them were very colorful head and shoulders shots of Pat and Ed Lee. Do you remember what Irving did? He held up the two pictures together.

"These are great pictures of Ed and Pat," said Irving. "Has Ed seen them?"

"Yes," I replied.

"Well," Irving continued, "didn't he want them blown up?"

"Oh, no," I insisted. "He really liked them." Trustee Penny Wilson almost fell out of her chair. Irving remained nonplused.

On that bit of recalled mirth I took my leave from the Knaufts' condominium. "Keep in touch," Burt admonished, as he hailed me a cab on 25th Street. Honoring that request proved to be inevitable. In September of 1994 Burt was named, along with Gus Johnson, to the National Trustees Honor Roll of Citizens' Scholarship Foundation of America.

Chapter Twenty-four

The Lesson of the Half-Mile Bridge

The timing of the call that came in that March morning just after seven, suggested that someone on the East Coast had forgotten about the one-hour time differential with Minnesota. At any rate I was awake and was contemplating my corn flakes in the dining area of the CSFA guest quarters. Whoever was placing the call had direct access to my telephone, because in between normal business hours the main switchboard automatically forwarded calls to the apartment. "Good morning," I responded cheerfully, half expecting the caller to be a scholarship applicant who had either lost some piece of an application package or who was otherwise checking up on the status of an application already submitted.

"Good morning to you," came the equally cheerful reply. "This is Muriel Knecht at the University of New Hampshire. Please hold for Dr. Haaland." This call was not entirely unexpected. For two months the university had been coaxing me to become its first vice president for alumni and development. In the course of my fifth meeting with President Gordon Haaland, just the week before, he had asked if I thought I could duplicate for the university's fund-raising program the success of Citizens' Scholarship Foundation of America. I said "maybe, but I would hope it wouldn't take twenty years this time around." He laughed and said the university might be willing to accept that risk.

Until this point I had exhibited no real enthusiasm for the vice presidency. I had very much enjoyed the courting process, and I was flattered to be considered. At the close of this interview, Dr. Haaland said: "I need to check with a few people, but I wouldn't be surprised if we called you in a week or so and offered you the position." I thanked him for his confidence and said if the offer was extended I would want at least ten business days to think it over. He said, "Fair enough."

Here, then, at the close of March, 1986, was the anticipated call. President Haaland wasted no time on preliminaries. "Joe," he said, "this is Gordon. The trustees have authorized me to hire you for the vice presidency. Your university needs your help. Will you come back to Durham and work with us?"

"Sure," I replied, and that was that. Well not quite "that," because as I sat contemplating my soggy cereal, I immediately began to consider the consequences of my action. Now I had to tell people of my decision. I suspected some protocol existed in these situations, but I was uncertain after twenty years as to what it might be. Clearly, though, Burt Knauft was at the top of the list. I called Independent Sector in Washington, DC. When Burt came on the line we exchanged the customary greetings and the "how are you's," and then I said: "Burt, I've been offered a vice presidency at the University of New Hampshire."

"Uh oh," he responded, "did you accept it?"

"Yes," I said rather sheepishly.
"Effective when?" Burt asked.
"July 1," I answered and realized at that moment that my CSFA clock was in a very late hour.

Within a few days the difficulties of informing everyone were behind me, and the planning for my send-off began. By coincidence alone my final board meeting was scheduled in New York City at the end of May. Ben Coté, director of CSFA's Metropolitan Service Center had for months been making preparations for the meeting. He had found among CSFA's Manhattan corporate clients sponsors for luncheons and receptions. JC Penney and New York Telephone Company led the list. All of the arrangements were in place. I was determined that we would have a celebration.

New York City was the ideal place for my impending exit. Midtown recalled for me the disheartening and depressing days of the late 1960s and early 1970s when the country boy wedged his way through crowded streets and avenues in the cold February rain, looking for the elusive corporate grants. A decade later New York was a source of inspiration and elation for me, as we added corporate scholarship clients from along Park, Madison, and Sixth avenues. I remembered with particular fondness the day in 1983 when my newspaper horoscope read "Time will prove you lucky," and on that very same day Time, Inc. called me to announce its plans for a $100,000 CSFA-managed children of employees scholarship program. I contrasted once again my unhappy adventure on 116th Street with the satisfaction of an evening in a church just over the bridge to Queens. I reflected on the negotiations with my generous, anonymous benefactor at the University Club. I recalled the marvelous dinners and evenings out with Ed and Pat Lee, as well as a particular luncheon, very early in my career, with Irving and Charlotte Fradkin.

Given my belief that the success of Citizens' Scholarship Foundation of America was the embodiment of the "Tom Sawyer Theory of Management"--a good many wonderful people doing a good deal of hard work while believing they were enjoying it--the entertainment Ben Coté had scheduled for the evening before the board meeting could not have been better chosen. All trustees and staff had tickets, courtesy of JC Penney, to see George C. Scott and John Cullum in *The Boys in Autumn*, a theater-in-the-round depiction of Huckleberry Finn and Tom Sawyer reunited in their much later years.

The setting for my farewell remarks, the DeWitt Wallace Room at the New York Public Library, was appropriate as well. Nearly two decades before I had shared a picnic lunch with Mr. Wallace on the beautiful grounds of the *Reader's Digest* in Pleasantville, New York. There following a sandwich and soft drink, he reached into his jacket pocket, took out his checkbook and wrote a check payable to CSFA in the amount of $10,000. I had never seen anyone do that before.

In great contrast to the stature and demeanor of the late DeWitt Wallace, the story I elected to share with my assembled colleagues and friends in the library on that Friday afternoon involved an ephemeral figure, a craggy elderly man who, simply by chance and circumstance on a foggy Maine day, provided me with one of the great lessons in life. I stood behind the podium in the cherry-paneled meeting room and said: "My friends, I'm pleased to share with you the story of the half-mile bridge." I recalled for them a time in Maine in the spring of 1968.

The Lesson of the Half-Mile Bridge

US Route 1, or the Post Road as it is sometimes called, begins its journey along the Atlantic Coast in either Florida or Maine depending on your preference or perspective. Within the state of Maine US Route 1 runs a somewhat ragged line two hundred and fifty miles east-northeast along the coast until it bumps into Eastport, the easternmost community in the continental United States. From there it turns due north and works a straighter line for an additional hundred and fifty miles where it terminates on the Canadian border.

Eastport sits at the noteworthy bend in the road, a town of nineteen hundred souls once famous for its sardine industry. But as is true of Monterey, California, the sardines apparently decided to summer one year in Norway and never returned. Eastport, however, was not to be denied entirely some continuing notoriety, and I recall, as I was growing up in New Hampshire, the radio weather forecasts were always bracketed from "Eastport to Block Island." I had heard, then, of Eastport, Maine, long before I ever had occasion to know exactly where it was located, and even longer before I visited there. Eastport is, as we say in New England, "a fur piece from anywhere," about as far Down East as any point up north can possibly be.

Despite its geographic extremity Eastport may not be the place of origin for "Down East humor." I'm certain, however, that many of its residents could serve as caricatures for the personalities immortalized on vinyl and mylar by Robert Bryan, Marshall Dodge, and Tim Sample, to name but a few. My friend Ed Lee loves to tell the story of the camera-laden tourist in Kennebunkport who exclaims to the yellow-slickered lobsterman, "Wow, mister, there's sure a lot of funny characters around here!" "Ayuh," replies the old salt, "but they all go home come Labor Day."

Ralph Seifert prefers the story of the traveling salesman who drives into East Millinocket and stops bewildered at a fork in the road. One road veers to the left;

the other to the right. The sign between them points straight ahead and says "Millinocket 6 Miles." The puzzled salesman is relieved to see a seasoned farmer leaning on his fence just this side of the intersection. He rolls down his window and says: "Say old-timer, does it make any difference which of these two roads I take to Millinocket?" "Not to me it don't," comes the crusty reply.

Both Eastport and Down East humor are important to the story of *The Half-Mile Bridge*. I am privileged to have visited the first on at least three occasions. I am even more privileged to have lived within a real-life experience of the second. In the spring of 1968 I departed my home in Alexandria, New Hampshire, and headed for Eastport, Maine. I believed at the time I was completing my final professional assignment with Citizens' Scholarship Foundation of America. My eighteen-month letter contract was about to expire, and with it my tenure as Northern New England regional director. My assignment at hand was to raise one hundred thousand dollars to keep the regional office going following my departure. I had made good headway with the fund-raising project, and I was in the process of following up on my last few prospects.

On this particular March day I was on my way to meet with Mr. John Pike Grady, a member of a very prominent Eastport family. The family, as I remember, had made its fortune during the roiling days of the sardine industry. Both Mr. Grady and the sardines were no longer particularly active, but he had expressed for many years his interest in the Dollars for Scholars program. He was living comfortably on Moose Island just off Eastport. I planned to ask him for one thousand dollars, a sum that would in no way compromise his lifestyle. I was en route to make the ask, and I had allowed two days for the 350 mile trip.

I had learned early on in my career that morning is the best time to ask for money, so I planned my itinerary accordingly. My schedule called for me to drive to Machias on the first day, so that I would be but fifty-eight miles west of Eastport by nightfall. I scheduled my appointment with Mr. Grady for ten o'clock the next morning. I would, I believed, wake up refreshed in Machias to complete the shorter part of my journey.

I arrived as anticipated at the Bluebird Motel in plenty of time to go into town and have dinner at Helen's "Famous for Pies" Restaurant. I returned to my comfortable, eleven dollar room and slept soundly, confident of my next day's plan. But when I awoke at seven in the morning, any thoughts of enjoying a leisurely continental breakfast and free newspaper were scuttled. The morning fog was so dense that I could not see the motel office in the ell just a few doors down to the right of my room. By seven twenty-five I was in my Pontiac Tempest, orange juice, coffee and donut precariously balanced on board, once again heading east.

Driving in a cloud, especially a literal one, is no fun. At no point in my journey did I know exactly where I was. By nine fifteen, I was certain I had missed my right turn onto Route 190, and I believed I was on my way to Presque Isle or the province of New Brunswick. I also noticed I was almost out of gas. I turned right at the next available intersection, and began my search for a filling station. One materialized out of the fog, a gray and weathered swayback general store with two glowing globes seated atop two orange gas pumps.

Out of the store and mist came a figure out of *Down East* magazine. He was slim, better that six feet tall in his red and black, checkered wool shirt and liberally stained coveralls. The flaps on his dirty blue bill cap did not quite obscure the cotton wads in both of his ears. He was bewhiskered with a goodly spray of salt-and-pepper hair, fashioned by the barber of B.O. Plenty. His boots were a mess.

"Fill it up, please," I said, "regular gas." He went about this task as if it was the only one scheduled for the day. While he pumped, I pondered my map of Maine. I was on

Route 189, so that fact held out some hope, but not much in rural New England. At about four gallons I exited the car and asked: "Where am I?"

"Lubec," he replied.

"How far to Eastport?" I inquired.

"Haffa mile," he rejoindered.

"Great," I said with obvious relief, "I've got an appointment there in twenty minutes."

He looked up from his work. "You ain't gon'ta make it," he advised.

"How come," I asked, "you said it's half a mile, and I have twenty minutes."

"Well," he measured off, "because it's haffa mile over the watta, and there ain't no half-mile bridge. It's twenty-three miles around."

Well, of course he was right, so I left the peninsula I was on and drove around to the next one on my right. I was both agitated and late, but Mr. Grady whose residence was also sharing the morning's lack of visibility was very understanding. He and I chatted for a time, and just before noon I left Moose Island with a check for one thousand dollars in my pocket. Only in the course of my long drive home did I begin to appreciate the humor of my whiskered friend in the fog.

The adventures of that day did not end with my departure from Eastport. When after ten hours I arrived home in New Hampshire, three pieces of mail awaited me. The first was a letter from David Williams, president of the local International Packings Corporation. With it was a check for five thousand dollars. The amount astounded me. Harry Rosenberg and I, in accordance with a regional office funding formula, had asked him for five hundred. The second envelope contained an offer of a doctoral fellowship at Indiana University. The third was a firm job offer as assistant headmaster at Hebron School in Maine-- a job I knew would lead to the headmaster position within a year if not sooner. My wife and I were discussing the two offers when the telephone rang. The caller was Dan Walker, my boss. He was calling to tell me he had resigned as executive director of CSFA to accept a position at Yale. He asked me if I wanted his job.

We all know how that turned out. But over the next twenty or so years I would come to appreciate, with the help of my friends, my staff, and my board, that anything worth doing in life is worth any monumental effort that might be required. There is in our lives no half-mile bridge. My time with Citizens' Scholarship Foundation of America was twenty-three miles around.

Author's Afterword

October, 1994. I am sitting with Leslie S. Hubbard at his home in Walpole, New Hampshire. I try to visit him at least once a year, and fall is best, for his living room windows overlook the brilliant foliage of the Connecticut River valley. Les, by his preference and by my design, has not received the attention he deserves in the story of *The Half-Mile Bridge*. He has done much during his ninety years with and for so many, but he prefers his quiet anonymity, and I respectfully honor his wishes. Les is as always curious about the status of the people who sat with him at the board table during his twelve-year trusteeship with Citizens' Scholarship Foundation of America. Because for the most part I have kept in touch with his many governing contemporaries, I am able to provide him with reasonably accurate information.

Les mentions to me that he continues to see **Greg Macri** when Greg picks him up once or twice a month to take him to breakfast at the local diner.

Irving Fradkin continues at age 71 to practice reduced-load optometry in Fall River, Massachusetts, and continues to envision programs he deems as useful and inspirational to the young people in his city.

Jean Hennessey and husband John maintain their home near Dartmouth College in Hanover, New Hampshire, but Jean has taken on a three-year assignment in Montreal, PQ, as director of the North American Commission for Environmental Cooperation.

Ed Lee still practices law in Westfield, Massachusetts, but on his own terms. He and his wife Pat spend the winter months in Jupiter, Florida, where Ed's batting average in the seniors' softball league hovers around .480, and his infield fielding percentage is better than .900.

Bert Knauft since his retirement from the Independent Sector in 1992 has not succumbed to the lure of a fourth career. He and Ruth continue to enjoy the vitality of Washington, DC, and life in general.

Howard Moreen, quite unexpectedly to everyone but himself, passed away, at age 81, in May of 1993 in Hancock, New Hampshire. He collapsed at the bridge table just after making a grand slam. He had written his own obituary and had left his personal papers and documents neatly arranged in his home on his desk. A memorial fund at CSFA bears his name.

Brad Norris is retired from the practice of law. He and his wife, Doris Elizabeth, divide their time between Rapid City, Michigan, and the Dominican Republic.

Author's Afterword

Frank Morin did not live to see his 60th birthday. Just ahead of it, in May of 1994, he grudgingly surrendered to Lou Gehrig's disease. A CSFA memorial scholarship fund pays homage to both Frank and his dear wife, Betty Jo.

Ralph Seifert and Sandra summer and sail in West Southport, Maine, and winter and ski in North Conway, New Hampshire. At age 67 Cy's energy and proclivities continue unabated. Cy, in the winter as a volunteer, teaches skiing to small children. He is chairing CSFA's national fund-raising campaign.

Gene Struckhoff and Norma live in Timonium, Maryland, just outside of Baltimore. Struck seems to be taking a breather from setting up community foundations all over the world. He now has more time to spend at Oriole's Park at Camden Yards.

Les also mentions how he continues to be amazed at what happened to "the good Dr. Fradkin's little scholarship program." We talk and joke a bit about the "Tom Sawyer Theory of Management," and he asks me how the book is coming along.

"Well," I say, "I've got about eighteen chapters done, and I estimate maybe a half dozen to go. All the stuff you probably remember is written down. I'll be happy to send you a copy of the manuscript."

"No," Les says, "I'll read it at the same time as the rest." He then sits back in his chair and winces slightly because of a "little problem" he's been having with his back.

"Do you know, Joe," he asks, "what the greatest thing was you did with all of us?"

"No," I say, "what?"

Les smiles and says, "you brought us along."

Index

-A-

Academy for Educational Development 57
Addison-Wesley Publishing Co. 245
Aetna Life and Casualty Co. xxiii, 164, 168, 246, 254
Agnes M. Lindsay Trust 28, 47, 49
Airline Deregulation 177
Alden, Dr. Vernon 57
American Airlines Foundation 53
American Automobile Association 77
American Can Co. 48
American Compensation Association 145
American Express Co. 50
American Mutual Liability Insurance Co. 200, 201
American School Counselors Association 249
Analog Devices 166
Angel of endowment 69
Annuity-Related Internal Line of Credit 154
Anonymous Grant 183-190
Arco Foundation 219
Arthur Andersen & Co. 49, 56
Aroostook County, ME 34, 78-80, 84-86
Associated Spring Co. (The Barnes Group) 104
Augustana College xvii
Avoiding distractions 163, 170, 264
Avon Products Foundation 53

-B-

Baker, Robert Q. 170, 260
Bangor Daily News 30
Bank of America xxxv, 261
   California Student Achievement Awards 261-262
Bank One, Coshocton, OH 170
Baxter Travenol 174
Bellinger, Thomas D. 106, 185, 186, 189, 264
Berlinguette, Hilda 86, 87
Berlinguette, Roger L. 81-87, 103
Bernice McIntire Sleeper Charitable Annuity Trust 153, 168
Better Homes and Gardens 7
Best Products Foundation 105
Björling, Jan 138
Blue Earth County, MN xii, 139
Boston Company, The 57
Boston Globe, The 202, 204, 205
Boudreau, Richard A. 172
Boys in Autumn, The 272
Brandt, Lloyd L. xxiii-xxiv, 170, 229-230, 231, 232, 239-240, 265
Brigham Young University 195

Bristol Enterprise, The 13
Bristol-Myers Co. 113
Bristol-Myers Fund, The xxxv
Bristol, NH 10, 11, 82
Bristol Memorial High School 11, 20
Brown, Carl F. 79-81
Brown, Helen 52
Brown, J. Moreau 51, 52, 57, 191, 192
Brown University 21, 160
Buhler Construction Co. 221, 238, 241
Burger King xxxv, 218, 261
Bush Foundation 102, 103, 106, 116-121, 123-124, 228, 232

-C-

C. A. "Gus" Johnson Memorial Fund 105, 140-144
CBS Foundation 52, 60
Cain, Jess 201
Callahan Mining Co. 145
Carling Brewing Co. 20, 21, 25, 44, 45, 48, 59, 161
Cass, James M. 57, 115-116, 117
Cattle Baron Restaurant, NYC 53
Charles E. Palmer Award 111-112
Chicago O'Hare Airport 177-179
Christensen, Jolene 263
Chrysler Corporation xix, 219
Church of the Resurrection 110
CIGNA Corporation 210
Claremont, NH 63, 64, 65
Cogswell Trust xxxvi
Colby College 23, 29, 33, 37
Coleman, James xxvi
College Entrance Examination Board (CEEB) 100-102, 106, 126
College Scholarship Information Bank 100, 105-106, 264
    Student Aid Surveys 166

College Scholarship Service 126
Collins, Michael 200
Cologne, Germany 65
Comins, Harold N. 200, 204
Computer-based student aid referral service 73, 99-100
    see also NH Scholarship Locater Service, The Fund Finder, College Scholarship Information Bank
Concord, NH 20
    Orr & Reno 21, 44
    NH Charitable Fund 70
Connecticut River valley 279
Continental Can Co. 53, 57
Coordinating Council on Foundations for the Greater Hartford Area 247
Corona-East Elmhurst, NY 110-113
Corrigan, Jean 33, 35
Coté, Bernard T. 190, 264, 271
Council for (Financial) Aid to Education 51, 192, 261
Council of Better Business Bureaus 253
Council on Foundations 19, 51
Cray Research 174
Crosby, Ben G. 151-152, 186
CSFA Advisory Board of Trustees 146, 166, 171, 252, 261
CSFA Board Committees
    Aid Distribution Policy 252
    Audit and Finance 166, 232, 252
    Executive Committee 68, 86, 95, 247, 249, 251-252, 267
    Organization 166, 252
    Planning 258, 259
        Board driven 258
    Publicity 252
    Special Projects Review 2
    Trustees 166, 167, 252, 256, 259

Index

CSFA (Governing) Board of Trustees 24, 57, 131, 149, 162, 164, 165, 169, 170, 171, 205, 223-224, 227-228, 231-232, 237-238, 239, 247, 250, 251, 258, 259-260, 267
  Chair-elect 259
  Immediate Past Chairmen 252
  structure of xviii-xix, 5, 68, 252
CSFA Board Self Assessment 258
CSFA Charter Members 6
CSFA Collegiate Partners Program 172
CSFA Composite Program Distributions 170, 257
CSFA Corporate and Associates Program 105
  see also Scholarship Management Services
CSFA Corporate Sustaining Grants 48, 96, 97
CSFA Date of Incorporation 6
CSFA Development Office xxv
  National Fund-Raising Campaign xxv
  see also *Vision 2000*
CSFA Educational Assistance Program 260
CSFA Education Grants and Innovative Services 217-218, 263
CSFA Employee Incentive Program xx, 260
CSFA Financial Aid Questionnaire 128
CSFA Fund-Raising Campaigns 58-61
  Endowment Fund Drive 68
  see also Gale Associates
CSFA growth and development of xvii, xxiv, 27
  origin of 5
  see also Fall River Scholarship Plan
CSFA Honor Roll Trustees xix, 173, 265, 266-267, 268
CSFA management structure and style xix-xx
CSFA Metropolitan Service Center 190, 264, 271
CSFA middle management structure 262-263
CSFA Midwest Office 165, 185-186
  advisory committee 170
CSFA National Headquarters Building xv, 175, 185, 230
  builders' night 241
  guest quarters 269
  land dedication 236-237
CSFA National Office Locations 221-222
  100 Purchase St., Fall River, MA 6
  43 Leon St., Boston, MA 16, 25, 44, 162
  195 West St., Waltham, MA 56, 67, 162
  One South St., Concord, NH 102, 162, 163, 222
  Londonderry Turnpike, Manchester, NH 193, 209, 222-223
  1505 Riverview Rd., St. Peter, MN 154, 257
CSFA New England Regional Office 47-48, 79-87, 101
CSFA performance motivation 50, 84, 172
CSFA Scholarship Management Services, 166
  description of xvii, xxi
  score corps xvi
  program fees 128, 130-136
  growth of 98, 103, 104, 105, 165, 218, 240, 260, 261

CSFA Student Aid Catalogs 170
CSFA The Next Twenty-Five Years: National Office and National Image 227, 228
CSF of NH 64
CSF of Maine 23, 92
Cullum, John 272
Cushman, Darby and Cushman 61

-D-

Dartmouth College 25
Dauner, Carrie 263
Deasy, the Rev. Frederick J. 203
DeGregorio, Ronald P. 151
Dennison, Tom 215, 216, 217
DICOMED 233
Digital Equipment Corp. 233
Doermann, Humphrey 116-121, 123-124, 127
Dooley, James M. 61
Dollars for Scholars xvi
    chapter incentive grants 25, 260
    early anonymous gifts 6
    origin of 3-4
    philosophy of xxi-xxiv, 14
Dollars for Scholars Chapters
    Caribou, ME 84
    Chittenango, NY xxi
    Claremont, NH 24, 63, 66
    Corona-East Elmhurst, NY xxxv, 112, 271
    Coshocton, OH 170
    Fairmont, MN 117
    Fall River, MA 3
    Hinckley, MN 117
    International Falls, MN 117
    Jasper, MN 117
    Lebanon, NH 66
    Manchester, NH 143
    Mansfield, MA 160-161, 170, 186
    Newfound (NH) Region 14-15
    Parkers Prairie, MN xxii
    Pipestone, MN 117
    St. Paul Park, MN 117
    Salem, NH 152
    Skowhegan, ME xxxv, 37
        SAD #54 39
    Tucson, AZ (Habbjach) 145-146
    Wakefield, MA 200-207
        endowed funds 203-206
    Westfield, MA 92
Dollars for Scholars Fund Finder 98-99, 101, 102, 118,
Dollars for Scholars National Honor Roll 173, 205
Dollars for Scholars Projects
    Indiana 43, 49, 97, 101
    Maine 28, 33-39, 45, 79
    Minnesota 104, 106, 121, 123, 185, 187
    New Hampshire 27, 64
    New York 189-190
    Ohio 28, 49, 101
    strategies of 29-31
Dollars for Scholars, status of 6, 28, 43, 67, 95, 160, 167, 229
Dollars for Scholars trademark 56, 61
Dollars for Scholars 25th Anniversary 169
Down East Humor 273
Durfee High School, Fall River MA 4

-E-

East Harlem, NY 111-112
Eastport, ME 273
Edison Hotel, NYC 53-55
Educational Renaissance xxvi
Eisenhower, Dwight D. 6
Elliott, Mary 126

-F-

Fairmont, MN, School District 454 120
Fall River Herald, The 3
Fall River, MA 3, 25, 110
Fall River Scholarship Plan, The 4 5, 7, 20, 44-45, 59, 202
  see also Dollars for Scholars, philosophy of
Fargo-Morehead, MN 119
Farmington Teachers College 29
Fergus Falls, MN 119
Fiddler, Robert 37
Finney, James N. 212, 213
Fisher, Chip 131, 132, 135
Fisher Junior College 172
First Bank System (MN) 105, 132, 170, 229-230, 232
First Bank System (MN) 50th Anniversary Scholarship Program 133, 229
First Interstate Bank of California 175, 218
First National Bank of Boston 180
First National Bank of Cleveland 58
First National Bank (MN), The 236
Ford Foundation, The 6, 25, 100, 102
Four Seasons Hotel, Philadelphia 211
Fradkin, Charlotte, xxvi, 4, 5, 53-55
Fradkin, Dr. Irving A. xxiii, xxviii, xxxvi, 3-7, 9, 20, 24, 38, 53-55, 59, 74, 91, 95, 96, 97, 98, 112, 115, 145, 159, 161, 164 168, 171-172, 202, 223, 224-225, 251, 252, 257, 267, 280, 281
Francke, Chet 210-212, 214, 218
Fuller, Michael 195

-G-

Gale, Bob 58
Gale Associates 58, 59-61
Gardner, John xxvi
Gardner, Maryanne 211, 214
Garroway, David 6
Gawel, Tom 210, 216, 217
General Electric Co. xix, 48, 191, 233
General Electric Foundation 51, 57, 173, 210
General Electric Fund 192
  STAR Scholarship Program 195-197
General Mills Corp. 234
General Mills Foundation 105, 120, 127, 132, 210, 234
General Motors Corp. xxxv, 113, 174, 209-219
  Education Grants Program for Minorities and Women 212-218, 263
Genetti, Albert D. 11-12, 15
  see also Bristol Memorial High School
George Gund Foundation 57, 58, 61, 69
Goldsborough, Mr. William 113
Good Thunder, MN 138
Gosselin, Yvonne B. 210
Government Employees Ins. Co. 105
Grady, John Pike 274, 276
Grangaard, Don 229
Gray, Bruce 119
Gressel, Kay 44
Gund Guarantee 58, 59, 69
Gustavus Adolphus College xiv, xvi, 119, 137, 238

-H-

Haaland, Dr. Gordon A. 269-270
Hague, The, Netherlands 65
Half-Mile Bridge, The xxxv, 273-277
Hard Money vs Soft Money 164-165, 228, 264
Harold Cabot & Co. 59
Harry S. Truman Scholarship program 99
Hartford Club, The 247, 257
Harvard University 134
Hatfield, Robert S. 57
H.B. Fuller Co. 105
Hebl, Harold J. 169-170
Hegdal, C. H. "Cap" 120
Hennessey, Jean L. 69-75, 83, 102, 222, 280
Hinchey, Joseph M. 166, 175, 231, 258, 260
Hinton, Keith 104
Hotel Roosevelt, NYC 92
Hotel Sofitil, Minneapolis 267
Hubbard, Leslie S. 86, 94, 95, 279-281
Hudson, NH xxxi, 9
   Alvirne High School xxxi, 9
   Benson's Wild Animal Farm xxxii-xxxiii
Hughes, Dennis 195
Humphrey, Bill 120, 127, 128
Hunzeker, William A. 73
Hurton, Fire Chief William 200

-I-

IBM 53
Illinois Tool Works 233
Independent Sector xxiii, 256
Indiana University 276
Iococca, Kathy xxxvi
Innovative Scholarship Programs 74, 105, 130-136, 194-197, 212-218, 229, 261
Internal Revenue Service 255
Internal Revenue Service letter ruling 169
International Multifoods 105
International Packings Corp. 13, 276
Island Farm, Lake Crystal, MN 140, 147

-J-

Jaycees
   Mansfield, MA 160
   Massachusetts, Commonwealth of 161
   National Convention 161
James, Donald 245
JC Penney 113, 271, 272
John H. Pearson Trust 71-72, 73
Johnson, C. A. "Gus" II 105, 138, 149, 170, 225, 233, 245, 259, 260, 268
Johnson, Gisle and Eva xxxv, 147-149
   Owatonna Scholarship Endowment 149
Johnson, JoAnn 141, 147, 149
Johnson, "Little Gus" 139, 147
Johnson, Marlys C. xxiv, 104, 123, 133, 137, 165, 174, 188, 212-213, 215, 216, 217, 225-227, 228, 229, 230, 236, 238, 239, 241, 259, 262, 263, 264
Johnson, H. Stuart xxiv, 104, 121, 123, 129, 133, 137, 138, 139-141, 165, 166, 174, 188, 212-213, 214, 215, 216, 217, 225-227, 228, 230, 234, 235, 236, 238, 241, 259, 262
Johnson, Suzette 140, 147
Johnson Wax Fund, The 105
Jones, Bill 205, 206

Jones-Saxey, Ruth 175, 218
Jostens Co. 129
Jostens Foundation, the 105, 129-136, 233, 234
   Board of Directors 133-136
Jostens Foundation Children of Employees Scholarship Program 136
   Student Achievement Program 129-136, 210

-K-

Kagermeier, Jim 221, 234
Kaufmann, Liesel 65
Keene Products 166
Kennebec Journal 30
Kennedy, John F. 6
Kettering Foundation, The 27, 45, 49
Knauft, Edwin B. xxiii, 245-268, 270-271, 280
Knecht, Muriel 269
Knowles, Dr. Asa 25, 44
Kuzdzol, Barbara M. 170

-L-

Lady in Red 140, 245
Lally, J. Kevin 199-206
Lally, John K. Jr. 206
Larson, Roy 6
Leadership by default 83-84
Lebanon, NH 63, 65
   K-Ross Building Supply 63, 66
Lee, Edward M. xviii, 86, 91-107, 109, 110, 123, 130, 138, 139-141, 146, 152-154, 161, 162, 192, 247, 248, 251, 252, 259, 261, 265, 271, 273, 280
Lee & Pollard 94
Lee, Laura A. 205
Lee, William J. 202, 205, 206
Leo and Marie 177-181
Levenson, Sam xxviii, 3
Levi Strauss xxxv, 263
Levy, Inez "Sita" 44, 56
Life Magazine 28
Lilly Endowment, The xxiv, 27,
Lipscomb, James 49, 57, 58, 61 97, 107
Longsworth, Robert 43, 47
Lovejoy, Clarence E. 57
Lovejoy's College Guide 57
Lynn, John 58

-M-

Machias, ME 275
   Bluebird Motel 275
MacDonald, the Rev. Canon Kenneth 109
MacNamara, Mary 116
Macri, Greg J. Jr. 166, 265-266, 279
Maine Dollars for Scholars Project 117
Maine Public Service Co. 84-86
Maine, State of 33
   Hebron School 276
   Maine Turnpike and I-95 77-78
Manchester, NH xxxvi
   Amoskeag Mills 83
Mankato, MN 140,
   Carnegie Library 233
   Wick, Kagermeier and Skarr 233, 234
Mansfield, MA 95
Margolis, Fred 25, 161
Marin County (CA) Scholarship Project 167, 177
Martin-Marietta Corp. 53
Marvin Windows 233
Mayflower Hotel, Washington, DC 212

McCarthy, John 202
McGrath, Phyllis 196
McLaughlin, David T. xxxv, 125-128
Merriman, Bob 247
Minneapolis Foundation, the 120
Minnesota River, the xiii-xiv
Moon, Rexford G. Jr. 57
Mooney, Patricia A. 199-206
Mooney, Skip 129, 131, 132, 135
Moose Island, ME 274, 276
Moreen, Howard A. 164, 165, 168, 171, 264, 265, 280
Morehead State University 10-11
Morin, Frank E. 166, 167, 249, 256-257, 259, 261, 265, 267, 281
Morrison, Nate (Bristol town meeting) 13
Morse, Beatrice 56
Mudd, Roger 57, 60

-N-

Naegle Co., Minneapolis 234
Nashua Telegraph, The xxxii
National Airport, Washington, DC 256
National (Charities) Information Bureau 169, 246-248, 253
 Basic Standards in Philanthropy 247, 250
National Merit Scholarship program 99, 126, 192, 194
Nazi Germany 66
Nelsen, Dr. William C. xxvii-xxix, 218, 265
Nelson, Fred 219
New England Security Insurance Agency 162-163
Newfound Region, NH 13
New Hampshire Charitable Fund, Concord, NH 70,102, 104, 222
 NHCF Student Aid Program 71-75, 83, 98, 103, 105
New Hampshire College 73, 74, 98 100
New Hampshire Dollars for Scholars Project 117
New Hampshire Educator 16
New Hampshire Scholarship Locater Service 73-75, 98
New Hampshire Technical College at Manchester 87
Newsome, Paul 20
Newsome & Newsome 20
Newsweek 115, 116
New York Public Library 272
New York Telephone Co. 271
Nicollet County Bank 230, 236
Nilan, John 201
Nonprofit Management and Leadership xx
Norris, William B. 25, 43-62, 68, 82, 94, 95, 97, 162, 246, 280
Northeastern University 25, 44, 56
Notre Dame University 195
North Star Hotel, Minneapolis 175, 260
Norwest Foundation 233
NYNEX xxxv

-O-

O'Brien, Robert 7
Office Interiors of Minneapolis 233
Orme, William 192-197
Orr & Reno 21
Otter Tail Power Co. xix, 105, 233
Owatonna, MN 147

-P-

Parsons, Martha 14
Paulsen, Brian 233, 234
Permission by exception 62

Phelan, Colleen 144
Phelan, Joseph F. xxiii, xxxv, 9-16
Phelps, Edward 15
Plymouth State Teachers College 11
Portland Press Herald and Evening Express 23, 30
Precision Castparts Corp. xix
Presque Isle State College 29
Private Aid is a Private Matter 172
Profiles of Excellence: Admiring Success in the Nonprofit Sector 256
Purple tabs 258-259

-R-

Radman, Charles 25
Reader's Digest 7, 28, 53, 59, 115, 272
Rich, Lt. Peter B. 203
Reagan, Ronald 184, 229, 254
Roosevelt, A. Eleanor 6
Roosevelt Hotel, NYC 116
Rosenberg, Harry A. 48, 63-66, 95, 102, 162, 276
Rosenberg, Liesel 65, 66
Rotary Clubs
    Mansfield, MA 160
    Skowhegan, ME 35, 36, 37
    Wakefield, MA 201
    Westfield, MA 91
Rundell, Marilyn 263
Rust, Holly 133-135

-S-

St. Paul Club 117
St. Peter, MN xiii, 104, 138
    726 Lower Johnson Circle 188, 212, 262
    1505 Riverview Road xiv
    Economic Development Corp. 230, 232
    First National Bank, The 236
    Minnegasco Building 188, 216
    Nicollet County Bank 236
    School Board 221
    Swedish Kontur Imports 138
St. Thomas College, MN 125
Saturday Review of Literature, The 28, 59, 110, 115-118
Salem, NH 151
San Francisco Foundation 167, 177
Sauna Summit 226-227
Scholarship recipients as potential donors 74
Schroepfer, Clete 230
Scott, George C. 272
Scott Paper Co. Foundation 210
Scottsdale, AZ 141, 225
    Big Top Sale 142
    Clay's El Camino Ranch 142-143
    Gainey Ranch 144
    Scottsdale All-Arabian Show 142
Searle Pharmaceutical xxiv, 174
Seifert, Melissa 184, 185, 186
Seifert, Ralph H. 21, 80, 95, 98, 106, 107, 159-175, 184-190, 200, 214, 223-224, 227, 231, 232, 235-236, 237-238, 239, 253, 256, 257, 259, 261, 265, 273, 281
Seifert, Sandra 265
Seymour, Dr. Thaddeus 25, 58, 60
S&H Foundation 48
Shannon, Dr. James P. 124-125, 126-127
Shapiro, Edward M. 73, 131, 222, 231, 250
Sheraton West Side Hotel, NYC 55
Silver Dollars II 183-184

Simpson, Catherine 202, 204
Sinclair Oil Corp. 48
Skowhegan, ME 31, 33, 34, 36, 37
Sleeper, Gove W. 152-155, 183, 186, 189
Sleeper, Marcia 153, 154
Smart, Nelson xxxv, 35-38, 44
Smart's Funeral Home 35, 36, 38
Smith, Al xxxiii
   see also Hudson, NH
Smith, Hayden W. 261
Soviet grain market 235
Spaulding-Potter Charitable Trusts 21, 23, 24, 25, 27, 47, 49, 64, 70, 117
Spaulding, Gertrude 204
Spaulding, William R. 204, 205
Statement of Functional Expenses 253-254
Steele, David L. 95, 167, 221, 227
Stoddard, William 192-197
Struckhoff, Eugene C. 19-31, 33, 38, 44, 60, 70, 97, 121, 281
   Community Foundations 19
Suckling, Sir John 200
Sununu, John 152
Survival advice 58-59
Swenson, Beverly 263

-T-

Tadd, Al 241
Task Force on Private Sector Initiatives 254
Tax Reform Act of 1969 70, 255
   Alternative Minimum Tax 255
   Revenue Procedure 76-47 255-256
The Other 90% 59
Thibeault, Dr. Cornelius 203
Thomas, Clarence 218
Tiffany, Gordon 27
Time, Inc. 48, 271
Time Magazine 3, 28, 115

Tipton, John Beresford xxxv
Today Show, The 6
Tom Sawyer Theory of Management xxxi, xxxii, xxxiv, xxxvi, 272, 281
Toro Company, the xxxv, 103, 105, 123-128, 130, 131, 132, 140, 193
Toro Company Scholarship Program 125-128
Truschke, Ed 261
Tufts University 152

-U-

Unencumbered discretionary revenues 171
Uniroyal 53
Unitarian Universalist Church 21
   Unitarian Universalist Association 46
United Auto Workers 209
United Parcel Service 194
United States Equal Employment Opportunities Commission 174, 209, 212, 214, 217
United States Steel Foundation 73
University of Arizona 145, 146
University of Maine 29, 78
University of New Hampshire 9, 269
   Thompson School 15
Unrealized expenses 49, 61, 146

-V-

Valentine, Michael 59-60
Valkenburg, Alice 201
Valle's Steak House, Westbrook, ME 28

Vision 2000 xxv-xxvii
   community involvement xxvi
   family expectations xxvi
   student aspirations xxvi
Vorhaus, Michael 167

-W-

Wakefield Daily Item, The 200, 201-202, 203, 206
Wakefield, MA 199-207
   Academy of Our Lady of Nazareth 201
   Hartshorne House 206
   Wakefield High School 201
Walker, Daniel A. 25, 26, 31, 43, 44, 45-46, 49, 277
Walpole, NH 86
Wall Street Journal, The 209-210
Wallace, DeWitt 272
Warren, Alfred S. Jr. 210
Washington Sheraton Hotel 60
Waterbury, CT 93-94
Webster, Philip 161
Wedum Associates xxvii
Wedum Foundation xxvii-xxviii
Wedum, John A. xxvii xxviii
Wenzel, Chief of Police Merritt 199-200
Westfield, MA 95, 107
West Southport, ME 159, 265, 267
   Cozy Harbor 159, 265, 267
Weyerhaeuser Company Foundation 233
When I Grow Up, I Wanna Be... xvii
Whitman, Peter 210
Williams, David 13-14, 276
Williams, Mrs. Jimmie xxxv, 111-113
Williams, Roger 20, 21, 23, 44, 160, 161
   see also Carling Brewing Co.
Wilson, Penny 268

Woodbury, Richard 23, 28, 29, 30, 38
   see also *Portland Press Herald and Evening Express*

-X-

Xerox Corp. 261

-Y-

Yale University 25, 45, 277
   Program on Nonprofit Organizations 256

About the Author

Joseph F. Phelan has nearly thirty years experience in upper level nonprofit management. Twenty of those years were with Citizens' Scholarship Foundation of America. He ended his career with CSFA in 1986, following a six-year term as president. Phelan is also a former vice president of the University of New Hampshire (1986-1993) and is founding president of the University of New Hampshire Foundation (1989-1993). He is editor and principal contributing author of *College and University Foundations: Serving America's Public Higher Education*, a publication of the Association of Governing Boards of Universities and Colleges. He resides in Brookfield, NH, where he authors and counsels emerging nonprofit organizations and where he is currently working on a third book for the nonprofit sector.